the Kitchen Shortcut Bible

the
Kitchen
Shortcut
Bible

MORE THAN 200 RECIPES
to Make Real Food Real Fast

BRUCE WEINSTEIN and **MARK SCARBROUGH**

Photographs by Eric Medsker

LITTLE, BROWN AND COMPANY

NEW YORK BOSTON LONDON

Little, Brown and Company
Hachette Book Group
1290 Avenue of the Americas, New York, NY 10104
littlebrown.com

First Edition: June 2018

Little, Brown and Company is a division of Hachette Book Group,
Inc. The Little, Brown name and logo are trademarks of Hachette
Book Group, Inc.

The publisher is not responsible for websites (or their content) that
are not owned by the publisher.

The Hachette Speakers Bureau provides a wide range of authors for
speaking events. To find out more, go to hachettespeakersbureau.com
or call (866) 376-6591.

Interior design by Laura Palese

ISBN 978-0-316-50971-8
LCCN 2017964191

10 9 8 7 6 5 4 3 2 1

LSC-C

Printed in the United States of America

CONTENTS

INTRODUCTION

Let's just get this out of the way up front:

Work with sharp knives.

Chop two onions, not one, and freeze the rest.

Cook once but eat twice, repurposing leftovers.

Start with a clean kitchen and clean as you cook.

Work with a garbage bowl on the counter.

You might be able to recite those in your sleep. All of these rules are tried-and-true advice for quick cooking, repeated in hundreds of books and on zillions of websites.

They're not what this book is about. Instead, *The Kitchen Shortcut Bible* is about making the food you love—but preparing it faster, using common kitchen tools in ways you might not have imagined or working with standard ingredients that are long overdue for an updated approach. The book is also about rethinking recipes in unexpected ways: using the flavor punch of a jar of store-bought caponata for ratatouille, or the convenience of a package of wonton wrappers for crisp cookies, all while eating real food that's healthy and inexpensive. What's more, this cookbook is not about absurd gimmicks no one will ever use: making punch bowl ice rings in a Bundt pan or dicing hard-cooked eggs by passing them through a wire-mesh rack. Ever seen the mashed-up edges of that egg afterward? Ever tried to clean the rack? Blech.

In fact, this is a book of *recipes,* not hacks. Yes, there are plenty of tips and tricks throughout, some a little nerdy, some very cheffy. But it's important to realize from the get-go that these inspirational flashes and real-world solutions have been made subservient to the recipes themselves. There's no chapter called "More from Your Wok" or "Small Gadget Hacks." Rather, the recipes are arranged in chapters about the way they are in most cookbooks: breakfast, snacks, bigger meals, desserts. In the end, we believe that the best shortcuts deliver dishes, condiments, sauces, and the like, not just clever cooking ideas: a flavorful, quick applesauce with a potato ricer, or a complex sauce that magically tastes as if you let it simmer all day just by adding a few tablespoons of peanut butter, or rich and irresistible pudding from your microwave when you need a mug full of instant comfort.

After making a few of these recipes, we hope you'll adapt the techniques to make even more meals to fit your taste. Take our pasta colander suppers. You'll put most of the ingredients in a colander and boil the pasta in a saucepan, then pour the pasta and its hot water over those ingredients, blanching or softening them and turning the whole thing into a no-mess, one-pot dinner. The variations you can create from this technique are endless.

But don't jump out on your own at first. Some of these techniques are unconventional, so follow the recipe until you nail it down—*then* give it a twist. Such advice sounds schoolmarmish, but it's a good strategy when you're reinventing the layer cake (using just a food processor) or even preparing something as simple as bacon and eggs (using a single baking sheet).

Some recipes are one-offs. And some are presented in groups that show the many uses for a single kitchen tool, an unusual technique, or a too-often overlooked ingredient. Some recipes are designed to make weeknight fare (chicken cooked right out of the freezer) and some are admittedly fancier (a better way to roast a whole duck). Throughout, there are small, informal, narrative recipes tucked among the larger ones. All of our recipes show off a little Yankee ingenuity.

All this on-and-on about the recipes brings up a bigger question: What constitutes a shortcut? Well, sure, it should save time, that modern scarcity. If a new way through a classic recipe shaves off a few minutes, it counts—although this book is not just a book about cooking faster. We've also created shortcuts that simplify techniques to yield better results. *Better without more effort* isn't the usual way quick-cooking books judge their results; but again, *quick* isn't the only way to judge the value of a shortcut. If you veer off the crowded main road and take a back road through more beautiful countryside to arrive at the same place at the same time, you'll probably take that smaller road again and again. And you'll probably call it a shortcut, as in "that shortcut I take." Its value is not just in time saved.

In no recipe will you MacGyver a set of pliers or carburetor cleaning wires into a kitchen wand. And you'll never take apart a blender or break the hinge on a cherry pitter for a recipe. Instead, you'll use tools as they are, all of them common cooking implements, many the familiar graduation and wedding gift favorites that sit on a shelf year after year.

Much of the work for this book gets done in the *Test Kitchen Notes* that accompany most of the recipes (or that are found in the introductory material to some recipe sets). There are hundreds of ideas on how to speed things up. Many of these can be applied to recipes far beyond the one at hand.

Admittedly, a few of our shortcuts are whimsical *ta-da* moments. For example, we figured out how to make fat, chewy udon noodles with a meat grinder. Our technique doesn't really save you that much time (though it's much quicker than the traditional Japanese method). But the results are so incredible, we had to include the recipe. The same goes for our way of doing a standing rib roast. And paella. These are not traditional shortcut cooking recipes but rather a sort of new way to think through a tried-and-true dish for better results without additional effort (and in the case of the paella, with far less effort).

But most of our recipes deliver in all the most important categories: time saved, convenience added, and most importantly, flavor enhanced. You'll use instant potatoes for the fluffiest gnocchi and store-bought pizza dough for quick, delicious dumplings. You'll make no-cook sauces in advance and freeze them in plastic bags for a slow-cooker weeknight dinner with almost no work. Just add your protein of choice to the cooker and head off to your day!

And there's much more. Weeknight dinner solutions, all-day entrees finished in minutes, and plain delicious ways to make the dishes you love without standing over a hot stove. Like making individual dinner packets, freezing them, and cooking them straight from the freezer. Or using a slow cooker to turn tuna into the most absurdly delicious Sicilian preserved tuna without much work. Or making risotto in a microwave in mere minutes, without stirring.

So sure, follow the standard shortcut advice: Work with sharp knives, clean as you go, and set out a garbage bowl. But just get cooking. There's time to be saved. Mostly, there are better meals to be eaten

A Few Notes on Ingredients

Before you get started, there are a few ingredients used over and over that need a little explanation. All are pretty common; but with simple basics, the specifics matter.

Salt

You'll need both *table salt* and *kosher salt.* Table salt has a slightly milder (some would say "flatter") flavor, and it's best in most of these dishes. Kosher salt offers mineral undertones and a nice crunch. It's used to enhance flavors in some rubs or to garnish certain dishes.

Shredded Coconut

Shredded coconut is available either *sweetened* or *unsweetened.* Use whichever the recipe calls for (sometimes both). Unsweetened shredded coconut (often called "desiccated coconut") can be found in a powdery or a flaked version. Either will work here, although you should crush the flakes in your hands to measure them properly. Sweetened shredded coconut, familiar in (or on) some holiday cookies, is usually available in the baking aisle; unsweetened shredded coconut is most often available in the health-food or organic section (and at almost all health-food stores).

Rice Vinegar

Seasoned rice vinegar has sugar (and sometimes aromatics) in the mix; *unseasoned* is just that: no sugar (or aromatics, but usually salt). Seasoned rice vinegar is sometimes labeled as such; unseasoned, rarely so. Maddeningly, both are sometimes just labeled "rice vinegar." The recipes in this book only call for *unseasoned* rice vinegar, so read the ingredient panel to be sure there's no sugar in the brand you choose.

Rolled Oats

These steamed-then-flattened oat flakes are the traditional oats used to make oatmeal. Our recipes mostly call for rolled oats. Do not substitute steel-cut or quick-cooking (so-called "instant") oats unless they are specifically called for.

Parmigiano-Reggiano

That's the more formal name of the cheese commonly known as "Parmesan." The name is used here to encourage you to skip the canned stuff, buy a block chipped from a larger wheel, and grate it with a Microplane or the small holes of a box grater. Lightly pack the grated cheese into measuring cups for the right volume amount. As a general rule, 2 ounces of Parmigiano-Reggiano yields 1 cup of lightly packed, finely grated cheese.

Fat-Free Dairy

Throughout, ingredient lines in the recipes indicate whether low-fat or fat-free dairy will work by including those very terms in the ingredient lists. Both 1% and 2% milk count as low-fat. *Do not* use fat-free dairy (milk, yogurt, cream cheese) if the recipe does not specifically call for it. Many fat-free products (like sour cream) include stabilizers that can react badly over the heat and leave your dish (at best) unappetizing.

One Note About Microwave Ovens

They cook in a broad range of power, based on their wattage, anywhere from 700 watts up to 1250 and beyond. A fairly standard microwave oven in North America cooks at 950 watts. However, it's best to check the instruction manual for your model to know how your oven cooks when using our recipes. If you have a 1250-watt behemoth, you may want to cook at a slightly lower setting. And you'll definitely want to carefully watch the food inside.

And Finally...

Throughout this book, you'll find markers on the recipes to help you decide on the fly which is right for the moment—and which you might want to come back to at another time. Here's what you'll see:

FASTER. In general, these recipes shave minutes off *the total time* a more standard version of this recipe requires. Sometimes, we've bent the concept of "faster" to include a quicker prep time with the same cooking time the standard recipe would need.

EASIER. These recipes call for less work. But work itself is a broader notion than just time at the cutting board or the stove. "Easier" might also include fewer pots and pans, fewer tools and knives.

TASTIER. Not all shortcuts are about speed. Sometimes, a shortcut is about getting a better result with the same amount of effort you'd put into a more standard version of that recipe. For example, our recipe for a standing rib roast takes more time than most recipes but the effort is the same for unbelievable results.

VEGETARIAN. We've marked these recipes as call-outs to help make your selection easier. There's currently a raging online debate about whether eggs can be considered part of a vegetarian diet. We've gone old-school (in our 50s, we are by definition old-school) and assumed they indeed can be.

GLUTEN-FREE. Recipes with this tag are gluten-free, *provided* you use a few standard ingredients that have been certified gluten-free. For example, oats are gluten-free in their natural state but are often processed in facilities that also process wheat and therefore can contain trace amounts of its dust. Look for *certified gluten-free* rolled oats if wheat gluten is indeed a concern. These can be found in most large supermarkets—and certainly in all health-food stores as well as from online purveyors. And the same can be said for soy sauce and Worcestershire sauce. Neither needs to contain wheat (although many, even most, standard preparations do). There are gluten-free variations of both available in almost all supermarkets and certainly from a wide range of online sources. All that said, even if a recipe is marked "gluten-free," we'll go ahead and remind you which of these sorts of ingredients to watch out for, just to make doubly sure we're on the same page. And one more thing: Although most baking powder sold in the U.S. includes cornstarch or potato starch to absorb ambient moisture, some brands (particularly those from outside the U.S.) may use wheat to get the job done and must (again) be certified gluten-free to make sure you're creating the recipe to fit your dietary needs.

1

BREAKFAST

There may be no meal in greater need of shortcuts. After all, morning hours are precious, even on the weekends. These recipes, tips, and tricks—including lots of things to do with that waffle iron sitting in your cabinet—can jump-start those early hours and get you to your day faster.

You've undoubtedly heard the standard pleas in favor of breakfast. Some studies show that people who eat it weigh less. Others indicate those who partake have better blood sugar numbers. Or even better memory. Those people probably have cleaner houses and balanced checkbooks, too.

But forget all that and think about pleasure. Breakfast is a meal to savor, even when you're on the run, because the light will never look like this for the rest of the day, because the complications and irritations are mostly in the offing, and maybe because the newspaper won't read itself.

Sure, time for breakfast is a luxury in this ever-and-ever-more modern world where everything is fast, faster, *fastest*. To push breakfast into high gear, there are internet memes about shredding cold butter onto toast through a box grater. Or storing pancake batter in an old ketchup bottle. Or preparing oatmeal in a drip coffee maker.

Frankly, none of that appeals to us. If saving time is the sole point, nobody would ever eat breakfast at home. Just stop off at the grocery store, a bodega, or even a donut shop on your way to work.

These breakfast recipes aren't about magically adding minutes to your day. They're about getting some extra time to spend it right. To that end, what could be better than a warm bowl of toasty granola? Or absurdly fast yet amazingly creamy scrambled eggs? How about a helping of steel-cut oats you don't have to make when your eyes are barely open? Or even some pretty fine breakfast cookies that don't require you to turn on the oven? For just a moment, forget the vaunted breakfast promise of better health, cleaner houses, and balanced checkbooks. Here's to a few minutes of bliss before everything else starts in earnest.

TASTIER

VEGETARIAN

GLUTEN-FREE

The Creamiest, Lightest Scrambled Eggs in Under a Minute

Makes 2 servings

Basic scrambled eggs are easy and fast. But *really good,* super-creamy, custard-like scrambled eggs require 10, maybe 15 minutes of stirring over extremely low heat. The results are luxurious, even a revelation. But who has 15 minutes for two scrambled eggs? So we like this trick: Add a little cornstarch to beaten eggs. The thickener will bind natural moisture, rendering the eggs wonderfully creamy with little effort.

2 tablespoons whole, low-fat, or fat-free milk

1 tablespoon cornstarch

4 large eggs

3 tablespoons unsalted butter

Table salt and ground black pepper, to taste

1. Whisk the milk and cornstarch in a medium bowl until smooth. Crack the eggs into the bowl and whisk again until smooth.

2. Melt the butter in an 8- or 10-inch nonstick skillet set over medium-high heat. Once melted and just beginning to brown at the edges, swirl the pan to coat the surface and reduce the heat to medium.

3. Pour the egg mixture all around the skillet, not just in one spot. Cook, stirring constantly with a heat-safe silicone spatula, until the eggs form large curds, about 30 seconds. Keep cooking until the eggs are set to your taste—wet and creamy or dry and chewy.

4. Divide between two serving plates and season with salt and pepper to taste.

Test Kitchen Notes

- The results will be even more custard-like if the eggs are at room temperature. If possible, set them out on the counter for 20 minutes while you take your shower.

- You can't overdo the whisking in step 1. Whisk until there are no floating bits of unincorporated egg white.

Voilà! Poach eggs fast by pouring ⅔ cup water in a large microwave-safe ramekin and cracking a large egg into it. In a 950-watt microwave oven, cook on high for 35 to 50 seconds, until the egg is done to your desired firmness. Remove the egg from the water with a large, slotted spoon.

BETTER TOAST

Although it's a go-to shortcut breakfast, there are ways to make toast better—and to also save trips to the store.

First, use frozen, sliced bread. Don't thaw it, especially not in the microwave. Put a slice or two in your toaster. You'll need to experiment with the right settings for your model to hit your desired doneness, but you'll end up with a crunchier breakfast every time. And isn't that the point of toast?

After that, try these topping combos:

Tahini, blackberries, honey, and mint

Almond butter, hot red pepper sauce, and oregano

Cream cheese, halved cherry tomatoes, basil, and kosher salt

Mashed banana, walnut pieces, and grated nutmeg

Ricotta, walnut oil, table salt, and pepper

Mashed avocado, corn salsa or chow chow, and cilantro

Or slather it with some **Shortcut Pumpkin Butter:** In a medium saucepan, mix one 28-ounce can pumpkin (not pumpkin pie filling), ½ cup maple syrup, ½ cup unsweetened apple juice, 6 tablespoons dark brown sugar, and 1 teaspoon apple pie spice blend. Bring to a simmer over medium-low heat, then reduce the heat to very low and simmer slowly, stirring often, for about 20 minutes, until very thick and reduced to about 1½ cups. Pack the pumpkin butter into a glass or plastic container, seal, and store in the refrigerator for up to 2 months.

No-Hassle Bacon and Eggs for a Crowd

Makes 8 servings

Test Kitchen Notes

- There's no need to turn the bacon while it's baking. Both sides will crisp in the bacon's fat.

- The egg whites won't run out from under the pepper rings if the baking sheet is flat, not warped. (A new baking sheet costs less than 20 bucks.)

- The baking sheet must be hot when you add the eggs. If it's been out of the oven for a while after baking the bacon, slip it back in for a minute or two before proceeding.

- The recipe can be halved—or increased proportionally, depending on the size of the baking sheet.

- If desired, drain the bacon slices on a cutting board covered with paper towels.

- This recipe is gluten-free if you use certified gluten-free bacon. While the curing process does not routinely include gluten (some do use soy sauce), cross-contamination can be a factor in large processing facilities. Read labels carefully if this is a concern.

Ever tried to make fried eggs on the weekend? Ever stood at the stove for a really long time? Ever made your own breakfast when everyone else was already outside having fun? Here's the simple solution: a sheet-pan breakfast of fried eggs. We like ours with a splash of vinegar, a little culinary extravagance that brings out the naturally sweet notes in the yolks. Have lots of buttered toast on hand.

12 ounces thinly sliced bacon

2 large green or red bell peppers, preferably tall ones (rather than squat)

8 large eggs

2 teaspoons white wine vinegar

Ground black pepper, to taste

1. Position the rack in the center of the oven; heat the oven to 400°F.

2. Lay the strips of bacon on a large lipped baking sheet. Bake until brown and crisp, 10 to 12 minutes.

3. Meanwhile, slice off both the stem end and the bottom of each bell pepper. Use a paring knife to slice out the core and membranes inside each pepper tube. Evenly slice the cored peppers into eight ½-inch-thick rings (reserve the extras for salads or sandwiches).

4. Use kitchen tongs to transfer the cooked bacon to a serving platter. Set the pepper rings on the baking sheet in the bacon fat. Crack an egg into each ring.

5. Bake until the eggs are set to your desired degree, about 4 minutes for runny yolks, up to 6 minutes for harder set ones.

6. Remove the baking sheet from the oven, sprinkle the vinegar over the eggs (about ¼ teaspoon per egg), and sprinkle with pepper. Use a metal spatula to transfer the eggs in their rings to serving plates. Serve with the bacon.

 Voilà! You can skip the bell pepper rings here and use mason jar rings on the baking sheet. In fact, you can use those rings anytime you want to make perfectly round fried eggs: Just set them lipped side down on the baking sheet (or in a skillet), then crack the eggs directly into them. If you do use the bell pepper rings as the recipe states, they should be as evenly cut as possible. Set them on a cutting board to make sure they don't rock with uneven edges.

Fast, Warm, Comfy Granola

Makes 2 servings

Test Kitchen Notes

- For more flavor, try walnut, almond, or pecan oil.

- For even more flavor, use ½ cup rolled oats and ½ cup wheat, spelt, or barley flakes.

- You can double the recipe, but use a 12-inch nonstick skillet.

Homemade granola can take more than an hour: toasting the grains, adding the mix-ins, baking it all, cooling it. But you can make a small batch in a skillet in minutes. Better yet, stir all the *dry* ingredients together the night before, then cover the bowl and leave it on the counter until morning.

1 cup rolled oats (certified gluten-free if that is a concern)

¼ cup sliced almonds

2 tablespoons unsweetened shredded coconut

1 tablespoon maple syrup

1 tablespoon canola or vegetable oil

½ teaspoon ground cinnamon

¼ teaspoon table salt

Milk or yogurt for serving, optional

1. Stir the oats, almonds, coconut, maple syrup, oil, cinnamon, and salt in a medium bowl until the oats are evenly coated with the oil and spices.

2. Set a 10-inch nonstick skillet or large wok over medium heat for a minute or two.

3. Transfer the contents of the bowl to the skillet or wok. Cook, stirring often, until toasty and fragrant, 5 to 6 minutes. Serve warm on its own or topped with milk or yogurt if desired.

No-Peel Roasted Applesauce

Makes about 1 quart

What's the worst part of dealing with apples? Peeling, coring, and slicing them, of course. But once you roast them whole (a technique that also gives this applesauce an unbeatable depth of flavor), you can put them through a potato ricer and never stand over a cutting board. Due to the roasting and chilling time, this probably isn't weekday fare—unless you've planned ahead.

6 large baking apples, such as Rome or Braeburn, stemmed

2 tablespoons light brown sugar

½ teaspoon table salt

½ teaspoon ground cinnamon, optional

1. Position the rack in the center of the oven; heat the oven to 375°F.

2. Place the apples in a 9 x 13-inch baking dish. Roast until very soft, about 50 minutes. Cool in the baking dish on a wire rack for 30 minutes.

3. Place one apple in a potato ricer. Squeeze the pulp into a large bowl below. Scrape out the skins and seeds, then repeat with another apple and work through the batch.

4. Stir the brown sugar, salt, and cinnamon, if using, into the applesauce. Cover and refrigerate for at least 2 hours or up to 4 days.

Test Kitchen Notes

- Don't be aggressive with the ricer. The skins and pulp can rise up and overflow the sides.

- Sealed in 1-cup containers, the applesauce will keep in the freezer for up to 4 months.

No-Mess Zucchini Bread Pancakes

Makes twelve 4-inch pancakes

Test Kitchen Notes

- If you only have one baking sheet, do this recipe in batches: Position the rack in the center of the oven. When the first batch is done, just repeat pouring the 3-inch rounds of batter onto the pan. There's no need to grease the pan again or let it cool between batches.

- This recipe doesn't require a fancy, high-end, million-RPM blender, but it does require a sharp blade to handle the pieces of zucchini. If in doubt, consider replacing the one in your model. Almost all manufacturers sell replacement blades (or the whole housing with the blade under the canister) for a reasonable cost.

More! To make these pancakes the standard way, heat a nonstick skillet or griddle over medium heat for a minute or two, then add about a tablespoon of oil or butter and swirl it across the hot surface. Working with about 3 tablespoons of batter at a time, form your pancakes on the hot surface, making sure not to crowd the pan. Cook until bubbles open up near the edges of the pancake, less than 2 minutes. Flip the pancakes and continue cooking until brown, about 1 minute longer.

Zucchini pancakes are sure tasty. They're also a mess: The grated zucchini shreds must be squeezed to remove excess moisture. But our recipe factors in that moisture so you can make the batter right in a blender—no squeezing required. And with a couple of baking sheets, you can make a whole batch at once. One warning: The pancakes won't brown as deeply as if you made them in a frying pan, but you won't still be making pancakes when most everyone else is done with their breakfast.

1 small zucchini (about 8 ounces), cut into 1-inch pieces

2 tablespoons canola or vegetable oil, plus additional for greasing the baking sheets

½ cup whole, low-fat, or fat-free milk

1 large egg

¾ cup plus 2 tablespoons packed all-purpose flour

½ teaspoon baking powder

¼ teaspoon ground cinnamon

¼ teaspoon table salt

Unsalted butter and orange marmalade for serving, optional

1. Set two racks in the oven so they divide it into thirds; heat the oven to 400°F. Generously oil two large lipped baking sheets. Slip them into the oven while it heats.

2. Working in this order, put the zucchini, oil, milk, egg, flour, baking powder, cinnamon, and salt in a large blender.

3. Cover and pulse to make a thick but pourable batter, stopping the machine to scrape down the inside of the canister at least twice.

4. Carefully remove the (hot!) baking sheets from the oven. Pour the batter into 3-inch rounds across the surfaces, about 3 tablespoons of batter per pancake. Return the sheets to the oven and bake the pancakes, turning once, until set, 4 to 5 minutes in all. Serve warm with butter and marmalade, if desired.

WAFFLE-IRON MAGIC

How come a waffle iron gets treated like the good china, dragged out only for the holidays? It may well be the most underrated, underused tool in the kitchen, as if some mad chef fused the power of a professional broiler with the ease of a griddle.

These days, almost all waffle irons are labeled "Belgian." Once, this meant they made waffles with super-deep pockets to catch lots of jam and whipped cream. Today, it mostly means "round" (as opposed to June Cleaver's square waffles) and "small" (about a 7-inch diameter, or at least an iron that's just big enough for individual servings, not the giant models from the '50s and '60s that made landscapes of waffles).

The following recipes work best on an iron without super-deep pockets but with decided pockets nonetheless, maybe ¼ inch deep. All the recipes were tested on one of these 7-inch round irons, but you can jury-rig them for most other models, even square ones, by using only a portion of the iron, or making several stuffed sandwiches at once in various quadrants of the larger waffle iron, or even making one super-large waffle from a sheet of puff pastry.

No-Batter Super-Crunchy Waffles

Makes 8 waffles

Test Kitchen Notes

- A 7-inch iron fits one puff pastry quarter. You may be able to fit two quarters in larger machines.

- After flipping, cooking the pastry with the waffle iron open keeps the layers airy and extra-flaky.

- Don't grease the iron, unless there are burned bits from other breakfasts on the plates.

- Don't refreeze unused pastry. Make all the waffles, then freeze when cool. Heat in a toaster straight from the freezer.

Start with frozen puff pastry. Thaw it. Put it in the waffle iron. Done. No stirring, no mixing, no nothing. And don't just think about breakfast. Make these waffles later in the day, cut them into long strips, and serve the crunchy straws as appetizers that are ready for tapenade, garlic aioli, blue cheese dip, or Blender Hummus (page 74).

One 17.3-ounce box frozen puff pastry (2 sheets), thawed in the box overnight in the refrigerator

Butter, maple syrup, honey, date syrup, birch syrup, jam, and/or confectioners' sugar for serving

1. Unfold each sheet of puff pastry and cut into 4 quarters.

2. Heat a 6- to 8-inch round or a small square waffle iron. Place one square in the center of the iron, close the lid, and cook for one cycle, according to your taste.

3. Open the iron, flip the square so that it settles back into the pattern of the iron, and cook without closing the lid for 1 minute. Serve at once with whatever toppings you prefer.

More!   Standard supermarket brands of puff pastry are made with oil and come two sheets to a 17.3-ounce box. The recipes in this section were developed and tested with these brands.

Artisanal puff pastry brands, made with butter and available at high-end supermarkets, often offer one larger square sheet in a 14-ounce box. To make waffles or other fare in this section, cut this square into two rectangles and roll each to about 12 x 15 inches before dividing into quarters. These high-end brands are about triple the price and feature a more traditionally laminated dough with many flaky layers. However, they do not do quite as well in a waffle iron, resulting in less crunchy if still satisfying fare.

Crunchy and Fast Hash Browns

Makes 4 servings

In a skillet, hash browns splatter the kitchen with grease. In the oven, they never get crunchy enough. By using a waffle iron, you can cross a hash brown with a potato pancake for mess-free, crispier results. They even make a great dinner: Top them with smoked salmon and sour cream, set at the bottom of a bowl of beef or chicken stew, or use as a topping to a bowl of chili for a pseudo shepherd's pie.

1 large sweet potato, peeled and grated through the large holes of a box grater

1 large russet potato, peeled and grated through the large holes of a box grater

3 medium scallions, trimmed and thinly sliced

2 large eggs

¼ cup all-purpose flour

2 teaspoons baking powder

1 teaspoon table salt

½ teaspoon ground black pepper

Nonstick spray

1. In batches, squeeze the potatoes dry in your clean, dry hands. Place the shreds in a large bowl.

2. Stir in the scallions, eggs, flour, baking powder, salt, and pepper until everything is evenly coated in egg and flour.

3. Lightly coat the heating surfaces of a 6- to 8-inch round or a small square waffle iron with nonstick spray and heat it on high according to the manufacturer's instructions.

4. Scoop up ⅔ cup of the potato mixture and place in the waffle iron. Close and cook until crisp and golden brown, about 5 minutes, perhaps through several cycles. Transfer to a serving plate or platter and continue making more hash brown patties.

Test Kitchen Notes

- If you have a larger, square or rectangle waffle iron, make several of these at once.

- Cook the hash browns for fewer cycles for softer results. Not to our taste, but to each her or his own!

- There's baking powder in the mix. It helps maintain a little loft in the hash browns even under the weight of the waffle-iron lid.

Hot and Gooey Breakfast Grilled Cheese

Makes 2 sandwiches

These crisp sandwiches beat Hot Pockets by a country mile. They're a great on-the-go breakfast—as long as you take enough napkins to catch the drippy jam and don't wear a white shirt. Alter the jam and cheese to your taste.

Nonstick spray

¼ cup fig jam

4 slices oat bread

3½ ounces Cheddar cheese, thinly sliced

Test Kitchen Notes

- Use a cheese plane to make even, long strips of cheese.

- No cheese plane? Make thinner strips with a vegetable peeler.

- Don't be tempted to increase the amount of filling. More will make a mess.

- For an even quicker breakfast, assemble the sandwiches the night before. Seal on a plate under plastic wrap and store in the fridge.

1. Lightly coat the heating surfaces of a 6- to 8-inch round or a small square waffle iron with nonstick spray and heat it on high according to the manufacturer's instructions.

2. Meanwhile, spread 2 tablespoons jam on each of two slices of bread, leaving a ¼-inch border all around. Divide the cheese slices between the two pieces of bread, and top each with a second slice of bread.

3. Put one sandwich in the waffle iron, close, and cook for 1 minute. (Ignore the iron's presets.)

4. Open the iron, flip the sandwich, and rotate it 90 degrees, aligning it with the indentations. Close the iron and continue cooking until golden brown and crisp, about 1 minute longer.

5. Transfer the sandwich to a cutting board and repeat with the second sandwich. Cut them both in half diagonally and cool for a minute or two before serving, especially to kids.

Breakfast Ham and Cheese Croissandwiches

Makes 4 sandwiches

TASTIER

Sure, anybody can slap ham and cheese in a croissant. But our version, using croissant-like puff pastry, crosses the beloved sandwich with a gooey, melty grilled cheese, complete with lots of crisp edges. Consider this one just as good for lunch. Or dinner.

One 17.3-ounce box frozen puff pastry (2 sheets), thawed in the box overnight in the refrigerator

4 teaspoons Dijon mustard

8 thin slices provolone (about 4 ounces)

8 thin slices smoked ham (about 7 ounces)

1. Cut each sheet of puff pastry into quarters. Spread each quarter with 1 teaspoon mustard. Top each with a slice of cheese, a slice of ham, then another slice of cheese and another slice of ham. Then top with a plain quarter of puff pastry, tucking in any ham and cheese to leave a ¼-inch border all around. Pinch the edges to seal closed.

2. Heat a 6- to 8-inch round or a small square waffle iron on high according to the manufacturer's instructions.

3. Lay one stuffed sandwich in the iron. Close and cook for 2 minutes or until lightly browned. (Ignore the iron's presets.)

4. Open the iron, flip the sandwich, rotate it 90 degrees, and fit it back into the indentations. Cook for about 2 minutes longer with the iron open, until golden brown and crisp. Set aside a minute or two before serving.

Test Kitchen Notes

- Rotating the sandwich 90 degrees prevents it from cooking unevenly near the hinge of the waffle iron.

- To halve the recipe, thaw only one sheet of puff pastry. You can refreeze thawed, frozen puff pastry, although it may not rise quite as high after it's thawed a second time.

FASTER

VEGETARIAN

No-Roll, No-Fuss Cheese Blintzes

Makes 8 blintzes

Brunch got better! There's no need for crepes. Make crispier and crunchier blintzes with puff pastry in a waffle iron. For dessert, just add whipped cream.

⅓ cup whole-milk or low-fat ricotta

2 tablespoons regular or low-fat cream cheese, softened to room temperature

2 teaspoons granulated white sugar

½ teaspoon vanilla extract

⅛ teaspoon ground cinnamon

One 17.3-ounce box frozen puff pastry (2 sheets), thawed in the box overnight in the refrigerator

½ cup raspberry, blackberry, or strawberry jam, or orange marmalade

Confectioners' sugar for serving

1. Mix the ricotta, cream cheese, granulated sugar, vanilla, and cinnamon in a small bowl until thoroughly combined.

2. Unfold the puff pastry sheets; cut each into 4 quarters. Use a rolling pin to roll each quarter to a 6 x 6-inch square.

3. Spread 1 tablespoon of the cheese mixture on each square. Then fold each over to create a rectangle, sealing the edges well by pinching them together with your fingers.

4. Heat a 6- to 8-inch round or a small square waffle iron to high according to the manufacturer's instructions.

5. Place one stuffed rectangle in the center and close the lid. Cook for one cycle or until the bottom of the blintz is as brown as you like. Flip it over, fitting it back in the indentations. Cook without closing the lid for 1 minute to brown the other side. Transfer to a platter and continue making more blintzes.

6. Use a fork to stir the jam or marmalade in a small bowl until soft. Spoon about 1 tablespoon on top of each blintz. Dust with confectioners' sugar just before serving.

Test Kitchen Notes

- Do not use fat-free ricotta and cream cheese. They have too many stabilizers, which will break and make the blintzes soggy.

- Be sure to thoroughly seal the edges. If in doubt, moisten the edges before sealing.

- If you have a larger iron, go ahead and make several blintzes at a time.

Overnight, Yeast-Raised, No-Knead, Gingerbread

Makes 8 waffles

These are for the adults. They're not very sweet—but more savory, with the spicy kick of gingerbread. Here's our shortcut: Stir together a simple yeast batter the night before, then let it rise in the refrigerator overnight. No watching, no waiting, just a night's sleep. The next morning, break out the waffle iron to make individual gingerbreads. The results are stunning: light, flavorful, spiced bliss. A little melted butter on top and it's perfect.

1¾ cups whole, low-fat, or fat-free milk

½ cup (1 stick) unsalted butter

2 cups all-purpose flour

1 tablespoon dark brown sugar

1½ teaspoons instant yeast

1 teaspoon table salt

2 teaspoons ground dried ginger

½ teaspoon ground allspice

½ teaspoon ground cinnamon

½ teaspoon grated nutmeg

2 large eggs, at room temperature, lightly beaten

1 teaspoon vanilla extract

1. Place the milk and butter in a medium microwave-safe bowl or measuring cup. Microwave on high in 20-second increments, stirring after each. Once the butter is about three-quarters melted, remove the bowl or cup from the microwave and let sit on the countertop, stirring occasionally, until the mixture is between 105°F and 115°F.

2. As the mixture cools, whisk the flour, brown sugar, yeast, salt, ginger, allspice, cinnamon, and nutmeg in a large bowl until uniform.

3. Pour the cooled milk mixture over the dry ingredients. Stir just until the flour has been moistened, even if the batter is still grainy.

4. Stir in the eggs and vanilla just until uniform. Cover with plastic wrap and set in the refrigerator for at least 8 hours or up to 12 hours, until foamy, even spongy, and airy (it will not double in bulk).

5. Heat a 6- to 8-inch round or a small square waffle iron to high according to the manufacturer's instructions.

6. Give the batter a stir to remove some of the air. Add about ⅓ cup batter to the waffle iron. Cover and cook according to the manufacturer's instructions until set and brown. Serve warm.

Test Kitchen Notes

- Use a clean, instant-read meat thermometer to take the temperature of the milk mixture.

- Be careful not to overmix the batter. Stop the moment you see no more dry flour.

- To avoid further mixing the batter, the eggs must be already beaten when added.

- This recipe works best with a round 7-inch waffle iron, about the standard these days. If yours is larger (or smaller), you'll need to experiment with the right amount of batter for each piece of gingerbread.

 More! Instant yeast—granulated yeast, designed to dissolve instantly and not require proofing—is better here for the overnight rise. (Be careful not to confuse it with fast-rise or active dry yeast.) Look for small packets in the baking aisle of most supermarkets. Or look for larger, 1-pound packages at specialty and high-end food stores.

EASIER

VEGETARIAN

GLUTEN-FREE

Three No-Flip Omelets

Makes 1 to 2 servings

Test Kitchen Notes

- Each section of the ingredient list below makes a single waffle-iron omelet. Pick your favorite and have it all yourself, or split it if you like.

- Spray the iron quite well with nonstick spray so the omelet will easily release from it.

- For more flavor, instead of the nonstick spray, brush melted unsalted butter over the hot waffle-iron panels before adding the egg mixture.

- Double or triple this recipe at will, but whisk together the ingredients separately for each omelet.

Voilà! Don't have a slotted spoon to remove hard-boiled eggs from boiling water? Use a large whisk. Push it down gently over the egg, capturing the hot egg inside the cage. Run the egg under cool water while still in the whisk before removing.

Omelets are hard to flip—or worse, a devil to roll out of a small skillet and onto a plate the way chefs do. But with a waffle iron, you can make one in minutes, lose the flip problem, and end up with an omelet that is set on both sides without any fuss. In fact, the results here lie somewhere between an omelet and a frittata; but the overall feel and texture are more like an omelet—slightly fluffier and (if you can believe it) less flattened than a frittata can get in the oven. Once you get this technique down, you can vary it to your heart's content. Just don't add too much cheese to avoid a sticky mess.

Spinach and Parmesan Omelet

Nonstick spray

2 large eggs, at room temperature and well beaten

¼ cup baby spinach leaves

2 tablespoons finely grated Parmigiano-Reggiano (about ½ ounce)

½ teaspoon table salt

½ teaspoon ground black pepper

Spicy Pepper and Tomato Omelet

Nonstick spray

2 large eggs, at room temperature and well beaten

¼ cup drained sliced pimientos

2 tablespoons chopped sun-dried tomatoes

1 teaspoon capers, drained and minced

Up to ½ teaspoon red pepper flakes

Herb and Goat Cheese Omelet

Nonstick spray

2 large eggs, at room temperature and well beaten

3 tablespoons soft fresh goat cheese, crumbled (about 1½ ounces)

1 tablespoon minced fresh tarragon leaves

1 tablespoon minced fresh parsley leaves

1 tablespoon minced chives or the green part of a scallion

¼ teaspoon table salt

1. Generously coat the heating panels of a 6- to 8-inch round or a small square waffle iron with nonstick spray. Close and heat to high according to the manufacturer's instructions.

2. Whisk the remaining ingredients in a medium bowl or 1-quart measuring cup until the eggs are smooth and creamy.

3. Pour the egg mixture into the prepared iron. Cover and cook until set, 2 to 3 minutes. Serve immediately.

No-Laminate, No-Roll Chocolate Pockets

Makes 2 sandwiches

Like getting up at four a.m.? You'll have to if you want to make a proper *pain au chocolat,* that French breakfast favorite of dark chocolate in croissant dough. But don't worry—you can create a tasty chocolate sandwich in minutes with a waffle iron and potato bread. No, it won't have zillions of layers of flaky pastry. But it'll be a darn fine treat on a weekend morning with a hot latte on the side.

4 slices potato bread

2 tablespoons unsalted butter, at room temperature

4 ounces dark chocolate, preferably 70% cocoa solids, broken or chopped into small bits

1. Heat a 6- to 8-inch round or a small square waffle iron to high according to the manufacturer's instructions.

2. Meanwhile, smear each slice of bread with ½ tablespoon butter. Set two slices buttered side down (yes, *down*) on a cutting board. Divide the chocolate evenly on the unbuttered side of each slice, leaving a ¼-inch border. Top each with a second slice of bread, buttered side *up*.

3. Put one sandwich in the waffle iron, close, and cook for 1 minute. Open the iron, flip the sandwich over, and rotate 90 degrees, fitting it back into the indentations. Close the iron and continue cooking until the sandwich is golden crisp and the chocolate has melted, about 30 seconds.

4. Transfer the pocket sandwich to a cutting board and cook the second one as before. Cut them in half on the diagonal and cool at least 2 minutes before serving.

Test Kitchen Notes

- Potato bread is sweet by nature. Don't substitute semi-sweet chocolate, or it'll be overpowering.

- These stuffed pockets get superhot. Don't overstuff the bread.

- Cool well before serving.

NO-BAKE, NO-STICKY-FINGERS BREAKFAST COOKIES

No-bake cookies are a terrific on-the-go breakfast, sort of like granola bars with an even bigger flavor punch. But, frankly, no-bake cookies are a mess waiting to happen. Sure, they're soft and luxurious—which means they're murder on work clothes, with your sticky fingers ready to ruin your pants or skirt.

We've solved that by making them in muffin tins. Grab one or two paper-wrapped cookies and head out the door. Fold the paper down and use it to hold the cookie. Or fold it shut and store the cookie in your satchel for breakfast at your desk, once you've got coffee in hand.

As a bonus, the muffin tins are easy to store in the fridge. And the cookies won't break or bend during storage. Cover the tins with plastic wrap so the cookies won't dry out.

Of course, once the cookies are "set" by the chill, you can remove them from the tin and stack them in a sealable container to take up less space in the fridge. Leave them in their paper muffin cups to keep them from sticking together.

And one note: These do require a fairly large set of ingredients, some of which you'll only find at a very large supermarket or health-food store. However, these can become pantry staples since you'll want to make these breakfast cookies again and again.

No-Bake Vanilla-Coffee Protein Cookies

Makes 10 cookies

If you like protein bars, you'll be a fan of these soft cookies stocked with whey protein. They're soft and chewy, with the decided punch of coffee in the mix. Coffee beans are, in fact, edible once roasted. (Taste one sometime!) You can reduce the ground coffee by half for a less assertive flavor.

¾ cup sunflower butter

⅓ cup vanilla whey protein powder

2 tablespoons coconut or almond flour

2 tablespoons agave nectar

1 tablespoon dark brown sugar

1 tablespoon finely ground coffee, preferably an espresso grind

½ teaspoon vanilla extract

¼ teaspoon table salt, optional

2 tablespoons unsweetened cocoa powder

2 tablespoons confectioners' sugar

1. Line 10 cups of a standard muffin tin with paper liners.

2. Put the sunflower butter, protein powder, coconut flour, agave nectar, brown sugar, coffee, vanilla, and salt, if using, in a food processor. Cover and process until the mixture forms a coherent ball.

3. Uncover the food processor. Scrape down and remove the blade. Form the mixture into 10 balls, each about the size of a ping-pong ball.

4. Mix the cocoa powder and confectioners' sugar in a small bowl.

5. Roll each ball in the cocoa mixture, then drop into a prepared muffin cup. Press down to flatten into a cookie. Cover and store in the fridge for at least 1 hour or up to 1 week.

Test Kitchen Notes

- To make these dairy-free, substitute vanilla soy-based protein powder for the whey powder.

- The brown sugar adds a caramel-like flavor to the cookies; but if you're feeling extra health-conscious, you can skip it and use 3 tablespoons agave nectar— but also increase the amount of coconut or almond flour to 3 tablespoons.

- We wanted to keep these nut-free but you're welcome to substitute your favorite nut butter for the sunflower butter.

- Some whey powders may contain trace amounts of gluten from additives or flavorings. To make sure these breakfast cookies are gluten-free, be on the lookout to avoid food starches and glutamine—or check the manufacturer's websites for more information.

TASTIER

VEGETARIAN

No-Bake Dried Fruit, Nut, and Honey Cookies

Makes 10 cookies

Test Kitchen Notes

- Dried fruit should not be dry. It should be supple, even sticky, stocked with natural juices.

- For a bigger flavor burst, substitute walnut butter for the almond butter.

Voilà! No-bake cookies are great grab-and-go breakfasts, but you can even simplify the routine for your morning smoothie. Measure out the fruit and/or vegetables, place them in a freezer bag, and freeze. Leave out any yogurt or liquids. Dump the frozen contents of the bag into a blender, add the yogurt and/or liquid, and blend away.

Like Fig Newtons? Here's the taste without the bready exterior—and more heavily spiced, to boot. Ridiculously satisfying, these breakfast cookies would also be welcome any evening alongside an espresso shot or glass of brandy.

¾ **cup almond butter**

⅔ **cup graham cracker crumbs**

½ **cup walnut pieces**

4 large, pitted dates, preferably Medjool dates, halved

4 dried figs, preferably Turkish figs, stemmed and quartered

2 tablespoons honey

¼ **teaspoon vanilla extract**

¼ **teaspoon ground cinnamon**

¼ **teaspoon table salt, optional**

1. Line 10 cups of a standard muffin tin with paper liners.

2. Put the almond butter, ⅓ cup of the graham cracker crumbs, the walnuts, dates, figs, honey, vanilla, cinnamon, and salt, if using, in a food processor. Cover and process until a thick dough forms and comes together in clumps.

3. Spread the remaining ⅓ cup graham cracker crumbs on a plate. Open the food processor; scrape down and remove the blade.

4. Form the dough into 10 balls, each about the size of a ping-pong ball. Roll in the graham cracker crumbs and drop into the prepared muffin cups. Press down to flatten each ball into a cookie. Cover with plastic wrap and refrigerate for at least 1 hour or up to 1 week.

EASIER

VEGETARIAN

GLUTEN-FREE

No-Bake Carrot-Cake Cookies

Makes 10 cookies

Test Kitchen Notes

- Look for pre-shredded carrots in the produce section of most supermarkets.

- Feel free to swap out the pecans for whatever nut you prefer.

- To compensate for tree-nut allergies, substitute untoasted pumpkin seeds for the nuts.

- For an earthier if sweeter flavor, use ½ cup shredded carrots and ½ cup shredded parsnips.

- If you need to be 100 percent gluten-free, use certified gluten-free oats.

Voilà! For a fuller breakfast with these cookies, make hard-boiled eggs. But don't boil them—bake them. Put uncracked, large eggs in a mini muffin tin so the eggs don't roll around. Bake in a 325°F oven for 30 minutes. Afterward, use kitchen tongs to transfer the eggs to a large bowl of ice water. Chill for 5 to 10 minutes, then peel—or store, unpeeled, in the refrigerator for up to 3 days.

These are very soft no-bake cookies. They're also quite textural, too—that is, they're chunky and coarse, not smooth and creamy. If you really want to take them over the top, spread a little softened cream cheese on each.

1 cup shredded carrots (about 2 medium carrots)

1 cup rolled oats

¾ cup unsweetened shredded coconut

½ cup pecan pieces

½ cup golden raisins

3 tablespoons maple syrup

½ teaspoon ground cinnamon

¼ teaspoon ground dried ginger

¼ teaspoon grated nutmeg

¼ teaspoon table salt, optional

1. Line 10 cups of a standard muffin tin with paper liners.

2. Place the carrots, oats, ⅓ cup of the coconut, the pecans, raisins, maple syrup, cinnamon, ginger, nutmeg, and salt, if using, in a food processor. Cover and process until the mixture comes together as a dough.

3. Spread the remaining coconut (approximately ⅓ cup plus a rounded tablespoon) on a plate. Open the processor; scrape down and remove the blade.

4. Form the mixture into 10 balls, each about the size of a ping-pong ball. Roll in the coconut, then drop into the prepared muffin cups and flatten each into a cookie. Cover with plastic wrap and refrigerate for at least 1 hour or up to 4 days.

BREAKFAST PEEL POPS

Breakfast pops are a treat in the summer, whether you're heading out the door or just lazing out on the deck. However, there's no need to buy Popsicle molds. Use very small, so-called "snack-size," 1-cup resealable bags, then freeze to make a quick and easy version of Push Pops. (Well, more like peel pops, as you'll see.) To enjoy one, use kitchen shears to snip off one of the short ends of the pop. Peel down the plastic to reveal some of the treat, using the bag as a mess-free way to hold the cold pop (and to catch the drips). Keep peeling the plastic down—or pushing the pop up—as you enjoy.

Test Kitchen Notes

- Seal the bags carefully, pressing out any additional air.

- To freeze, lay them along the inside sides of an 8-inch square baking pan, so that the liquid rests on the bottom of the pan and the top of each bag folds over one of the pan's rims. Then secure the tops of the bags to the pan with Scotch tape. (The accompanying picture may give you a better idea how this process works.)

- Once hard, take the bags out of the baking dish and store flat in the freezer for up to 4 months.

Peanut Butter, Banana, and Blueberry Peel Pops

Makes 4 pops

Here's a smoothie in Popsicle form! Feel free to substitute any nut or seed butter for the peanut butter. If desired, add up to 2 tablespoons protein powder to the mixture in the blender.

1 cup regular or low-fat vanilla yogurt (do not use Greek yogurt)

1 small ripe banana, peeled and cut into chunks

2 tablespoons natural-style creamy peanut butter

2 tablespoons honey

½ cup fresh blueberries, roughly chopped

1. Put the yogurt, banana, peanut butter, and honey in a blender. Cover and blend until smooth. Stir in the blueberries.

2. Pour about ½ cup into each of 4 snack-size, 1-cup resealable plastic bags and seal. Roll lengthwise to form a tube of filling at one end (see photo on left). Freeze overnight (at least 12 hours), or for up to 2 months.

Voilà! Need ripe bananas for a dessert (or a smoothie)? Ripen them by baking them on a baking sheet in a 325°F oven until the skins are dark and the fruit is soft, about 6 minutes. Slit the peel lengthwise to scoop out the softened fruit.

EASIER

VEGETARIAN

GLUTEN-FREE

Creamy Strawberry Peel Pops

Makes 4 pops

A potato masher is the best tool for turning strawberries into a thick puree. Barring that, use a rigid pastry cutter—or even just two forks. In any event, make sure you don't have large bits of strawberry in the mix. Those end up too icy. One note: These peel pops are only gluten-free if you use certified gluten-free granola.

5 large strawberries, hulled

1¼ cups full-fat, low-fat, or fat-free plain Greek yogurt

3 tablespoons maple syrup

½ cup plain granola (without dried fruit or nuts)

½ teaspoon vanilla extract

1. Use a flatware fork or a potato masher to crush the strawberries into a mash in a medium bowl. Stir in the yogurt, maple syrup, granola, and vanilla until uniform.

2. Pour about ½ cup into each of 4 snack-size 1-cup resealable plastic bags and seal. Roll lengthwise to form a tube of filling at one end (see photo on page 40). Freeze overnight (at least 12 hours), or for up to 2 months.

Dairy-Free Avocado-Coconut Protein Peel Pops

Makes 4 pops

These have a tropical feel. The avocado adds richness without making the pops savory. The riper the avocado, the better—choose ones that are soft to the hand but not mushy. Check under the little nub at one end. The flesh should appear dark green, not light green or brown.

1 cup full-fat coconut milk

1 ripe avocado, peeled and pitted

3 tablespoons unflavored pure soy protein powder

2 tablespoons honey

2 tablespoons fresh lime juice

1. Blend the coconut milk, avocado, protein powder, honey, and lime juice in a covered blender until smooth.

2. Pour about ½ cup into each of 4 snack-size 1-cup resealable plastic bags and seal. Roll lengthwise to form a tube of filling at one and (see photo on page 40). Freeze overnight (at least 12 hours), or for up to 2 months.

MAKE-AHEAD
MORNING MIXES

Nothing beats having a make-ahead mix for pancakes or waffles on hand any morning you have a craving. Here are three of our favorites to stock your pantry.

Keep this in mind: These mixes include whole grains. They'll keep for a while but will go rancid in a couple of months (particularly the gluten-free mix). Store them in a tightly sealed container in a cool, dark pantry. Always smell them before you use them, just to be sure. They shouldn't have that acrid, slightly sour smell of grains gone bad.

If you're bleary-eyed in the morning, consider writing out the directions for a batch and keep it right in the container with the mix. Before coffee, any mistake is possible.

Whole-Grain Waffle Mix

Makes 8 batches, about 4 waffles per batch

These are the best bet for a Sunday morning—a little savory, a great vehicle for butter and syrup. Remember: The flashing lights or incessant beeps on a waffle iron are someone else's idea of how done your waffle is. The rule is usually this: Cook until no more steam escapes. If you like super-crunchy waffles, let the machine go through two complete cycles.

For the Mix

3½ cups all-purpose flour

2 cups whole-wheat or spelt flour

1⅓ cups yellow cornmeal

1 cup oat flour

¾ cup granulated white sugar

¾ cup malted milk powder

¼ cup baking powder

1½ tablespoons table salt

For Each Batch

1 cup plus 3 tablespoons Whole-Grain Waffle Mix

1 large egg

⅓ cup whole, low-fat, or fat-free milk

2 tablespoons unsalted butter, melted and cooled

1 teaspoon vanilla extract

Nonstick spray

To Make the Mix

1. Whisk the all-purpose flour, whole-wheat flour, cornmeal, oat flour, sugar, malted milk powder, baking powder, and salt in a large bowl. Pour into a large container, seal well, and store in a cool, dry, dark place for up to 2 months.

To Make a Batch

2. Stir the waffle mix with the egg, milk, butter, and vanilla in a medium bowl.

3. Lightly coat the inside of a 6- to 8-inch round or a small square waffle iron with nonstick spray. Heat on high according to the manufacturer's instructions, then pour a quarter of the batter into the iron.

4. Cover and cook according to the manufacturer's instructions and your desired degree of crunchiness.

Test Kitchen Notes

- A waffle batter should be a little thicker than a pancake batter, with a more pronounced, floury stickiness. It shouldn't immediately run to the sides of the iron.

- Whole grains store ambient humidity. Depending on their moisture content, you may need to add a little more milk to get the right consistency in the batter.

- Depending on how seasoned your iron is, you may have to spray it with nonstick spray after every waffle.

EASIER

VEGETARIAN

GLUTEN-FREE

Gluten-Free Pancake Mix

Makes 4 batches, about 16 pancakes per batch

Not only are these gluten-free, they're egg-free, too, thanks to the binding power of cornstarch. Store oat, white rice, and buckwheat flours in tightly sealed containers in the freezer to extend their freshness for up to 1 year. This mix, however, should be kept at room temperature since a cold grain mix can prevent the pancakes from rising in the skillet.

For the Mix

3 cups yellow cornmeal

2 cups oat flour

1½ cups white rice flour

1½ cups buckwheat flour

¾ cup granulated white sugar

¼ cup cornstarch

2 tablespoons baking powder

1 tablespoon baking soda

1 teaspoon table salt

For Each Batch

2¼ cups Gluten-Free Pancake Mix

1½ cups cultured buttermilk

¼ cup nut, canola, or vegetable oil, plus more for greasing the pan

1 teaspoon vanilla extract

To Make the Mix

1. Whisk the cornmeal, oat flour, white rice flour, buckwheat flour, sugar, cornstarch, baking powder, baking soda, and salt in a very large bowl. Pour into a large container, seal well, and store in a cool, dry, dark place for up to 2 months.

To Make a Batch of Pancakes

2. Mix the pancake mix with the buttermilk, oil, and vanilla until uniform.

3. Warm a large nonstick skillet or a large nonstick griddle over medium heat. Swirl a little oil in the skillet or spread on the griddle. Pour a scant ¼ cup of the batter onto the hot surface to create one pancake, then make more as desired without crowding. Cook until small bubbles open up across the surface, less than 2 minutes. Flip and continue cooking until lightly browned, about 1 minute. Make more pancakes as you can, regreasing the surface after ever other batch.

Test Kitchen Notes

- Make sure the oat flour is certified gluten-free.

- Baking powder made in the U.S. is almost always gluten-free; those from other countries may not be. Check the label or manufacturer's website.

- These grains can absorb varying amounts of ambient moisture, based on their age and the day's humidity. Play around with the final amount of buttermilk to get the right, thin, pancake-batter texture.

- For waffles, use 1⅓ cups buttermilk per batch.

Voilà! Don't throw out extra pancake or waffle batter. Cook it all up, then freeze the uneaten results. Drop the frozen pancakes or waffles into a toaster for a fast breakfast.

EASIER

VEGETARIAN

Malt and Cornmeal Pancake Mix

Makes 4 batches, about 16 pancakes per batch

Test Kitchen Notes

- For a lighter texture, use 3 cups cake flour and 3¾ cups all-purpose flour.

- To use this mix to make waffles, use 1 cup plus 2 tablespoons milk per batch.

- Our preference for these pancakes is to use a nut oil in the mix: pecan, walnut, even hazelnut. Store opened nut oils in the fridge for up to 3 months.

More! The grade markers for maple syrup have recently changed. Most producers now sell Grade A Golden Color with Delicate Taste (like the old Grade A or 1 Light Amber), Grade A Amber Color with Rich Taste (a sort of halfway point between the old Grade A Medium and Dark Amber), Grade A Dark Color with Robust Taste (a little darker than the old Grade B or Grade 2), and Grade A Very Dark Color with Strong Taste (the old "commercial grade" or Grade 3). Many people feel the best syrup for whole-grain or malt-flavored pancakes is Grade A Amber Color with Rich Taste. However, we like stronger flavors and will always go for Grade A Dark Color with Robust Taste.

Cornmeal is terrific in pancakes. It gives them a slightly nutty crunch, a better texture than the typical acreage of a merely soft waffle on a plate. The malted milk powder is another great addition, working its wheaty flavor into the batch. These need butter. Lots of butter.

For the Mix

6¾ cups all-purpose flour

1½ cups yellow cornmeal

¾ cup plus 2 tablespoons malted milk powder

¾ cup granulated white sugar

5 tablespoons baking powder

4 teaspoons table salt

For Each Batch

2¼ cups Malt and Cornmeal Pancake Mix

1¼ cups whole, low-fat, or fat-free milk

¼ cup nut, vegetable, or canola oil, plus more for the skillet or griddle

2 large eggs

1 teaspoon vanilla extract, optional

To Make the Mix

1. Whisk the flour, cornmeal, malted milk powder, sugar, baking powder, and salt in a very large bowl. Pour into a large container, seal well, and store in a cool, dry place for up to 3 months.

To Make a Batch of Pancakes

2. Whisk the mix with the milk, oil, eggs, and vanilla, if using, until smooth.

3. Warm a large nonstick skillet or large nonstick griddle over medium heat. Swirl a little oil in the skillet or spread on the griddle. Pour a scant ¼ cup of the batter onto the hot surface to create one pancake, then make more as desired without crowding. Cook until small bubbles open up across the surface, less than 2 minutes. Flip and continue cooking until lightly browned, about 1 minute. Make more pancakes as desired, regreasing the surface after every other batch.

Voilà! Cut unpeeled apples into ¼-inch-thick rings. Core the rings, then dip them in pancake batter and set on a hot, greased griddle to cook like pancakes until golden brown, turning once.

OVERNIGHT
HOT CEREALS

A slow cooker is the best tool to make a morning porridge. For one thing, you can stir the ingredients together the night before and don't have to worry about making breakfast before the coffee's kicked in. For another, slow cooking softens grains without drying them out.

However, various models of slow cookers work at different temperatures, even on low. If yours cooks hotter and you find dried bits of porridge at the edges, reduce the cooking time by an hour or increase the liquid used by 25 percent. The mixture can still stay on the keep-warm setting until you're out of bed.

All these porridges were made in a smaller, 4-quart slow cooker. If you want to use a 5- to 6-quart slow cooker, increase most of the ingredients by 50 percent, but increase any flavorings like dried spices or vanilla extract by only 25 percent.

No-Fuss Cantonese Congee

Makes 6 servings

Don't think of this as cream of rice cereal. For congee (rice porridge), the rice is overcooked until it almost dissolves, leaving behind only the suggestion of the chewy grains of rice. Congee is most often served as a savory breakfast in Chinatowns across the United States. Follow suit and serve our version with shredded rotisserie chicken meat, chopped peanuts, chopped cooked shrimp, and/or minced chives. Or go nuts and search out dried shrimp at Chinese markets. Only a few dried shrimp will provide a powerful pop of flavor in each bowlful.

8 cups water

1 cup raw long-grain white rice, such as basmati rice

2 tablespoons soy sauce (gluten-free if that is a concern)

2 tablespoons minced peeled fresh ginger

2 medium scallions, thinly sliced

½ teaspoon ground white pepper, optional

1. Mix all the ingredients in a 4-quart slow cooker.

2. Cover and cook on low for 10 hours, or until the mixture is a loose porridge. It can keep on the keep-warm setting for up to 4 hours longer. Serve warm.

Almond and Brown Sugar Steel-Cut Oatmeal

Makes 6 servings

A slow cooker takes the pain out of cooking steel-cut oats and turns this consummately healthy breakfast into a weekday morning treat. Use certified gluten-free steel-cut oats to guarantee that the porridge is gluten-free. While this porridge is fine on its own, you can also top it with a little warmed half-and-half or even cream. Hey, you're eating healthy oats, aren't you?

3 cups unsweetened apple juice

2 cups water

1 cup steel-cut oats

½ cup raisins

½ cup sliced almonds, optional

¼ cup packed brown sugar

½ teaspoon ground cinnamon

¼ teaspoon almond extract

¼ teaspoon table salt

1. Stir all the ingredients in a 4-quart slow cooker until the brown sugar dissolves.

2. Cover and cook on low for 6 hours. The oatmeal can stay on the keep-warm setting for up to 4 hours longer.

More! Got leftovers? Pack them into a solid layer in a small baking dish, then cover and refrigerate for up to 3 days. Cut the cold oatmeal into squares, then fry in melted butter in a nonstick skillet over medium-low heat until golden, turning once. Serve with maple syrup on the side.

Voilà! No slow cooker? Make oats in your rice cooker instead: Use 3 parts water to 1 part steel-cut oats, and add a pinch of table salt. Never fill the rice cooker above the halfway point since the oats foam. Cook the oats on the "porridge" setting, if your cooker has one. A rice cooker with so-called "fuzzy logic" will determine the amount of residual humidity in the batch to cook the oats perfectly each time, about 25 minutes. For other models, override the presets and cook the steel-cut oats at a low temperature for 20 minutes, then check the doneness and continue cooking for 5 or 10 minutes longer.

Savory, Cheesy Breakfast Polenta

Makes 6 servings

This savory porridge cries out for a fried or poached egg on top. Make sure you use regular polenta, not instant, which would turn too gummy during the long cooking. If you want a creamier polenta, reduce the water to 5 cups and add 1 cup heavy cream. By the way, the easiest way to dice a soft cheese like Brie is to chill it in the freezer for 30 minutes.

6 cups water

1½ cups regular (not instant) polenta

12 ounces chopped smoked ham or Canadian bacon

1 small leek, white part only, halved, thinly sliced, and washed to remove any grit

¼ cup golden raisins

2 teaspoons fresh thyme leaves

½ teaspoon table salt

½ teaspoon ground black pepper

4 ounces Brie, rind removed, the cheese diced

1. Mix the water, polenta, ham, leek, raisins, thyme, salt, and pepper in a 4-quart slow cooker.

2. Cover and cook on low for 6 hours. The polenta can stay on the keep-warm setting for up to 4 hours longer.

3. Stir in the Brie. Cover and set aside until melted, about 3 minutes. Stir well before serving.

Apple and Bulgur Porridge

Makes 6 servings

This one's got all the flavors of apple cake. Notice that the recipe calls for "regular" bulgur, not quick-cooking or instant. Because the slow cooker works so efficiently over such a long period of time, the more nutritious, standard bulgur will soften yet retain a great deal of its wheaty flavor.

3 large sweet apples, such as Gala, peeled, cored, and chopped

2½ cups water

2 cups whole or low-fat milk

1 cup regular bulgur

⅔ cup chopped pecans

⅓ cup packed light brown sugar

1 teaspoon vanilla extract

½ teaspoon ground cinnamon

¼ teaspoon table salt

Unsalted butter for serving, optional

Heavy cream for serving, optional

1. Stir the apples, water, milk, bulgur, pecans, sugar, vanilla, cinnamon, and salt in a 4-quart slow cooker until the brown sugar dissolves.

2. Cover and cook on low for 6 hours. The porridge can stay on the keep-warm setting for up to 2 hours longer.

3. Stir well and dish up into bowls. If desired, top each serving with a pat of butter and a drizzle of cream.

Dairy-Free Quinoa, Coconut, and Almond Porridge

EASIER

VEGETARIAN

GLUTEN-FREE

Makes 6 servings

Here's a high-protein breakfast, perfect for a busy day. Quinoa grains are naturally coated in a bitter compound (saponin), so it's best to rinse them before using, even if the packaging claims they've been rinsed. However, quinoa grains are tiny and will wash right through a standard colander. Either line one with paper towels and rinse repeatedly but very gently, or invest in a fine-mesh sieve to keep the grains from running down the drain.

2¾ cups almond milk

1¾ cups full-fat coconut milk

1½ cups white quinoa, rinsed

½ cup packed light brown sugar

½ cup sweetened shredded coconut

1 teaspoon almond extract

½ teaspoon table salt

1. Mix all the ingredients in a 4-quart slow cooker.

2. Cover and cook on low for 6 hours. The porridge can stay on the keep-warm setting for up to 4 hours longer.

2

SNACKS, LIGHT MEALS, AND INFUSED TEAS

The point of shortcut cooking is not just to make the main meals of the day. In this chapter, you'll find shortcuts for smaller fare like snacks and infused teas. These recipes run from nibbles and snacks for when friends drop by to simpler meals when you're short on time.

You know the rule: Things go faster if you prep before you cook. But it's not just about cutting and chopping ingredients. There's nothing worse than fishing for a garlic press in a messy drawer while the shrimp are already on the hot grill. Prepare for the whole job, not just parts of it.

And while we're at it, shortcut cooking is not just about prepping ingredients, reading the recipe through, and organizing your work space. No doubt about it: No matter how much the recipe or technique has been streamlined, it's still time-consuming. There are no instant meals. Even microwave-ready frozen dinners take time.

In the end, it's not how much time you have. It's about how you spend what you have. There's no point in cooking even snacks and nibbles if you're gritting your teeth, wondering why you're not doing something else.

It may sound like woo, but the best kitchen time-saver is a better attitude. In fact, the best answer to the fewer and fewer minutes we all have is to enjoy them, to relish them in the same way we would a little snack on a winter afternoon when it's too cold to do much of anything, or a refreshing drink on a summer evening when you just want to lounge on the deck.

We want those moments of simple pleasure, especially when we feel we're otherwise too busy. So let's commit to letting the hope of this low-grade pleasure color even the moments *before* we enjoy what we've made. Time can slow down in the kitchen, too, not just in a chair in front of the fire.

The mathematics of minutes and hours are relentless. We can't get more, no matter how hard we try. But we can savor the ones we have, even while we stand at a cutting board. Take a deep breath as you make one of these snacks or light meals and savor the light of the day—or maybe the gentle rain on the roof. Yes, modern life is all hurry. Even in the rush, you can embrace the passing moment as you prepare a little something to eat.

We promise to get you out of the kitchen quickly. But you do your part, too. You make time slow down as you create something to enjoy on your own or with those you love. We're doing this time-saving, shortcutting work together, the two of us writing this book and you using it. It'll actually take this team effort to make any shortcut worth even the small amount of time it requires.

GET ORGANIZED OUTSIDE
THE KITCHEN, TOO

To be a shortcut master, it's a good idea to apply a good level of organization, not just to your cooking, but to your shopping. Sure, it'd be great to spend 30 minutes on a Sunday afternoon checking out quinoa flour or the stock of fruit chutneys at a gourmet grocery. But mostly when you're shopping, your goal is to get home. Here are five tips to make the trip faster:

1. Organize your list. You know how your local supermarket is laid out. In fact, it's probably laid out like almost every other supermarket. Arrange your list, even on your smart phone, into the common categories: dairy, meat, vegetables, frozen foods, condiments, oils, baking items, cleaning products, etc.

2. Don't shop hungry. You'll slow down to stare at the muffins. You're also more likely to make dinner out of a bag of potato chips, rather than the things on your list.

3. Call ahead. The butcher or fish counters can have your order ready for you when you arrive. And phone ahead for unusual items. There's no need to waste time searching for curry paste if the store doesn't have it.

4. Shop alone. It's not just kids that slow you down. Consider spouses. Or boyfriends. Particularly boyfriends. And never make grocery shopping a social event. Plan time with your friends elsewhere.

5. If possible, avoid rush hour. The market's the most crowded on weekdays after work and on Saturday afternoons. Consider shopping after dinner, or right after breakfast, or even on a lunch break.

Four-Ingredient Stuffed Mushrooms

Makes 16 stuffed mushrooms

Making stuffed mushrooms, the retro favorite, is a lot of work: chopping, sautéing, cooling. But you can use just three ingredients to create a satisfying filling, especially if one of them is frozen creamed spinach. Look for it in the freezer case of most large supermarkets, often with the frozen winter squash purees. Packed into mushroom caps, the cheesy filling becomes a fleek snack or a light meal in minutes. Who's got the cocktails ready?

One 12-ounce package frozen creamed spinach, thawed

½ cup finely grated Parmigiano-Reggiano or Pecorino (about 1 ounce)

¼ cup Italian-seasoned dried breadcrumbs

16 large white button or cremini mushrooms, stems removed

1. Position the rack in the center of the oven; heat the oven to 350°F.

2. Mix the creamed spinach, cheese, and breadcrumbs in a small bowl until uniform.

3. Spoon about 1½ tablespoons of this mixture into each mushroom cap. Set them stuffed side up on a large lipped baking sheet.

4. Bake until the mushrooms are tender and the stuffing is lightly browned, about 20 minutes. Cool for at least 5 minutes or up to 30 minutes before serving.

Test Kitchen Notes

- Use either regular or whole-wheat seasoned breadcrumbs, but not panko.

- Look for mushrooms that are all the same size, 1½ to 2 inches across the caps.

- To save some time stemming mushrooms (and a lot of food waste), look through your grocery store's bins of loose mushrooms to find ones with their stems knocked off.

- Freeze any mushroom stems in a plastic bag to add to a pot of soup or stew.

FASTER

VEGETARIAN

Colander Wheat Berry Salad with Cauliflower and Raisins

Make 4 servings

Test Kitchen Notes

- Spring white wheat berries will offer a soft, luxurious texture; hard red wheat berries, more chew; and Kamut berries, a buttery, complex flavor.

- Keep the cauliflower florets from turning to a mush by putting them in the colander while they're still frozen.

- To be honest, this recipe works *best* with frozen cauliflower florets—which cook in no time under the hot water. If you use fresh florets, make sure they are chopped into fairly small pieces, at most 1 inch each.

Whole grains don't usually make it into a shortcut book because they take so long to cook. And true, this is not a technique to hasten their cooking. But this easy salad is a new way to think about cooking whole grains: Once they are tender, pour them and the hot cooking liquid over other ingredients in a colander to par-cook *them,* thereby making a salad with very little effort. This one keeps well in the fridge for several days, so you can make extra and eat on-the-go during the week.

1 cup raw wheat berries, preferably spring white wheat berries or Kamut berries

¼ cup green olive tapenade

3 tablespoons olive oil

1½ tablespoons white balsamic vinegar

½ teaspoon dried sage

¼ teaspoon ground cinnamon

¼ teaspoon table salt

¼ teaspoon ground black pepper

12 ounces fresh or frozen *small* cauliflower florets

½ cup golden raisins

¼ cup toasted shelled unsalted sunflower seeds

1. Bring a large saucepan of water to boil over high heat. Add the wheat berries, cover with the lid askew, reduce the heat to low, and simmer until tender, about 50 minutes.

2. Meanwhile, whisk the tapenade, olive oil, vinegar, sage, cinnamon, salt, and black pepper in a large bowl until uniform and a little creamy. Set aside.

3. Place the cauliflower florets in a large colander set in the sink. Drain the wheat berries slowly over the florets. Let stand for 1 minute if using frozen cauliflower or 2 minutes if using fresh; then rinse with cold water to stop the cooking. Drain well, shaking the colander several times.

4. Pour the wheat berry and cauliflower mixture over the tapenade mixture. Add the raisins and sunflower seeds. Toss well before serving.

Turkey Burgers That Never Dry Out

TASTIER

GLUTEN-FREE

Makes 4 patties

Face it: Turkey burgers can have the worst texture—some impossible mix of crumbly and gummy—mostly because the patties need to be cooked until close to well done for safety's sake. A lot of turkey burger recipes call for adding breadcrumbs soaked in milk or water—which gives the patties an unappealing, meat-loaf-like texture. Nix the bread and solve the problem with the simple trick of adding finely—and yes, very finely—chopped mushrooms to the meat. Unless you've got a great knife game, the best way to get the mushrooms prepped is to use a food processor. Pulse—don't process. And open the machine a couple of times to rearrange the larger mushroom bits so they can all hit the blade.

6 ounces white button mushrooms, cleaned (do not stem)

1 medium shallot, peeled and quartered

2 tablespoons olive oil, plus additional for the grate or grill pan

1 pound ground turkey breast meat

2 teaspoons Dijon mustard

1 teaspoon dried dill

½ teaspoon table salt

½ teaspoon ground black pepper

1. Put the mushrooms and shallot in a food processor; cover and pulse until finely chopped but not pureed.

2. Set a medium skillet over medium heat for a couple of minutes, then swirl in the oil. Add the finely chopped mushrooms and shallot; cook, stirring almost constantly, until the moisture comes out of the mushrooms and it evaporates to a glaze, 3 to 4 minutes.

3. Scrape the contents of the skillet into a large bowl and cool to room temperature, about 30 minutes.

4. Add the ground turkey, mustard, dill, salt, and pepper to the mushroom mixture. Stir well to combine until uniform, then divide into four equal portions and shape into ½-inch-thick patties.

5. Brush the grates clean and prepare a grill for direct, high-heat cooking; or heat a grill pan over medium-high heat for a couple of minutes. Brush the grates or the pan with olive oil. Add the turkey patties directly over the heat and cook, turning once, until an instant-read meat thermometer inserted into the thickest part of the patties registers 165°F, about 8 minutes.

Test Kitchen Notes

- Rinse mushrooms under lots of running water. They grow in unsavory circumstances. You don't need to be dainty with the, um, dirt by using some rinky-dink brush.

- The mushroom mixture will cool more quickly (in about 10 minutes) in step 3 if spread in a thin layer on a plate.

- Don't stint on the oil when brushing the grate or grill pan. Turkey burgers stick like mad. Use long-handled tongs to smear oil on a wadded up paper towel across the grate or grill pan.

- Want an easier solution all around? Oil the patties, not the grate.

 More! Turkey meat is usually labeled very accurately. If the package says "turkey breast," it's got skin and maybe bits of cartilage but it's white meat. If it says "turkey breast *meat*," it's missing the skin and other bits. And if it says "ground turkey," it's got everything, all the bits and pieces of the bird.

 Voilà! Don't like to touch raw turkey? Form the patties between two plastic lids: Scoop out a quarter of the mixture, place it on one lid, set another lid on top, and press gently to form a compact patty.

EASIER

VEGETARIAN

GLUTEN-FREE

Vegetable-Peeler Zucchini Noodles with Spicy Pine Nut Salsa

Makes 4 servings

Test Kitchen Notes

- The zucchini or yellow squash must be small—otherwise, the seeds become too prominent for this technique. Look for long, skinny yellow squash, rather than the ones with bulbous ends that tend to be full of seeds.

- For extra flavor, toast the pine nuts in a dry skillet over medium-low heat.

- The salsa has no salt in it because the noodles are already salted. Add a little if you're making the salsa on its own to use as a dip or even to slather on steaks off the grill.

- There's no need to peel either zucchini or yellow squash before turning them into noodles. A few strips will have an edible coating along one side. However, if you insist on pitch-perfect aesthetics, by all means peel off that skin before making the noodles.

No spiralizer required! A vegetable peeler can make long, thin "noodles" from zucchini or fresh yellow squash. Press firmly but not hard to create thin, pliable strips. And work around the squash on all sides, down to the seedy core—which you then discard to move on to the next squash.

2 medium zucchini (about 12 ounces each) or 4 small yellow summer squash (about 6 ounces each)

½ teaspoon kosher salt

¾ cup packed fresh parsley leaves

¾ cup olive oil

¼ cup pine nuts

¼ cup fresh lemon juice (about 2 medium lemons)

¼ cup loosely packed fresh cilantro leaves

2 tablespoons packed fresh oregano leaves

1 tablespoon minced garlic

Up to 1 teaspoon red pepper flakes

1. Run a vegetable peeler down the zucchini or down and around the squash, using moderate pressure to create a flexible but not paper-thin strip. Continue to peel more strips, rotating the vegetable a bit for each slice and working until you've used up the vegetable down to its seedy core before moving on to the next one. Place all the strips in a bowl and toss with the salt. Set aside for 10 minutes.

2. In the order listed, place the parsley, olive oil, pine nuts, lemon juice, cilantro, oregano, garlic, and red pepper flakes in a food processor. Cover and process into a chunky sauce, stopping the machine once to scrape down the inside of the bowl.

3. Blot the squash noodles dry and return them to the bowl. Pour the sauce over them and toss well to coat. Serve at once.

No-Chop French Onion Soup

Makes 6 servings

Test Kitchen Notes

- Frozen chopped onions release more moisture as they begin to cook—which is why you have to start them over high heat.

- That's also why you have to squeeze the second batch dry: So you don't water down the soup.

The worst part of making classic French onion soup is chopping all the onions! Here's the good news: You can indeed use frozen chopped onions. But you have to modify the standard technique, using some of them up front for flavor and then more toward the end for texture. In fact, consider this the rule for frozen chopped onions in all stews, soups, and braises: most up front, the rest toward the end. True, you don't save much off the standard stovetop timing here. (Physics is physics. Caramelizing will always take time.) But the results are as good as the real thing, made easier by modern convenience.

6 tablespoons (¾ stick) unsalted butter

2 pounds frozen chopped onions (do not thaw)

3 tablespoons brandy

7 cups no-salt-added beef broth

2 teaspoons minced fresh sage leaves, optional

2 teaspoons fresh thyme leaves

½ teaspoon table salt

½ teaspoon ground black pepper

6 thick French bread slices, lightly toasted

2 cups shredded Gruyère (about 8 ounces)

1. Melt the butter in a Dutch oven set over high heat. Measure out ¾ cup frozen chopped onions and set aside at room temperature. Pour the remaining frozen onions into the Dutch oven and cook in the butter, stirring frequently as they reduce, until the onions thaw and any additional liquid boils away, about 10 minutes.

2. Reduce the heat to *very* low, cover, and cook, stirring frequently at first but then less so as the heat calms down, for 30 minutes.

3. Uncover the pot and continue cooking, stirring often, until the onions are a deep golden brown, about 1 hour.

4. Increase the heat to medium. Stir in the brandy and scrape up any browned bits in the pot as it comes to a boil. Add the broth, sage (if using), thyme, salt, and pepper.

5. Working over the sink, squeeze the remaining chopped onions dry in small handfuls to get rid of excess moisture, then stir them into the pot. Reduce the heat again to very low. Cover and simmer slowly for 1 hour.

6. Position the oven rack about 6 inches from the broiler element; heat the broiler. Divide the soup into six broiler-safe serving bowls, perhaps set on a large lipped baking sheet. Float a piece of bread in each bowl, then top the bread with about ⅓ cup cheese. Broil (watch carefully!) until the cheese melts and bubbles, about 2 minutes.

Crisp, No-Chop, Waffle-Iron Cauliflower Patties

FASTER

VEGETARIAN

Makes 10 patties

Don't put away that waffle iron from breakfast! Here's the easiest way to make cauliflower patties. You don't need to get out the food processor because riced cauliflower is available in almost all supermarkets (in the produce section's refrigerator case).

4 large eggs

12 ounces riced cauliflower (about 3 cups)

2 cups Italian-seasoned panko breadcrumbs

1 cup finely grated Parmigiano-Reggiano (about 2 ounces)

Nonstick spray

1. Whisk the eggs in a large bowl until very smooth. Use a wooden spoon to stir in the cauliflower, breadcrumbs, and cheese to form a thick batter.

2. Lightly spray the heating panels of a 6- to 8-inch round or a small square waffle iron. Heat to high according to the manufacturer's instructions.

3. Add a heaping ½ cup of the batter, close the iron, press gently, and heat until golden brown and set, about 2 cycles in most irons. Transfer to a serving platter and continue making more patties.

Test Kitchen Notes

- If you have only plain panko, season them by mixing 2 cups with 1 teaspoon dried parsley, ½ teaspoon onion powder, ½ teaspoon dried oregano, ½ teaspoon table salt, ¼ teaspoon garlic powder, and ¼ teaspoon sugar.

- The batter is thick, even more so than that for oatmeal cookies. Even the weight of the iron's top won't smooth it out. Mound some batter in the center of the waffle iron, then close and press down gently on the handle for the most even thickness across the patty.

- For a full meal, top the patties with a chopped salad and a creamy dressing.

- Want to go further? Put a patty on top of a bowl of chili—or at the bottom of a bowl of beef or chicken stew.

- For a quick snack, make them half-size (or break them into quarters) and serve instead of crackers with chutney or another dip.

- Got leftovers? Freeze them, and reheat straight from the freezer in a toaster.

More! To make the patties without a waffle iron, lightly coat a large nonstick skillet with nonstick spray, then set it over medium heat for a minute or two. Make a couple patties with a rounded ½ cup batter for each. (A ½-cup ice cream scoop works best.) Set them in the skillet, then press to about ½ inch thick with a metal spatula. Cook, flipping halfway through, until golden brown and set, about 5 minutes.

Box-Grater Gazpacho

Makes 10 servings

Test Kitchen Notes

- To core tomatoes, cut them in half through the core, then use a paring knife to remove the hard, pale white or beige section at the top and the tough bits right underneath it.

- Long, seedless cucumbers usually come wrapped in plastic because they're not waxed to preserve them.

- Running celery over a box grater can be hard, since the "strings" loosen and ball up. If you're finding it challenging, strip the stalks of these strings before you start.

Voilà! Here's another summery, no-cook soup for a light meal in the evening: Puree 2 cups store-bought cantaloupe cubes with ½ cup mango nectar. Pour the mixture into a large bowl and stir in 1 minced small shallot, 6 shredded basil leaves, 3 dashes hot pepper sauce, and ¼ teaspoon table salt. Chill for at least 2 hours. Top each serving with store-bought cooked lump crabmeat or cocktail shrimp.

Yep, the food processor's a great tool. Yep, it's a mess to clean up. And when it comes to gazpacho, it juices the vegetables other than the tomatoes (like the cucumber and celery), rendering this classic cold soup too much like vegetable soup, not a cold tomato soup with chunks of vegetables in the mix. Using a box grater cuts down on the cleanup and keeps the vegetables crunchier. It also lets the tomatoes maintain a certain toothsome texture, even in the soup. We add tomato juice to compensate—and the result is pure heaven. Work right over the serving bowl, grating the vegetables into it.

4 pounds red ripe tomatoes (about 6 large), cored

1 large seedless (or English) cucumber

2 medium celery stalks

1 small yellow onion, peeled

Up to 2 medium garlic cloves, peeled

Two 4½-ounce cans chopped mild green chiles (about 1 cup)

2 cups tomato juice, preferably salt-free

¼ cup sherry vinegar

2 tablespoons fresh lemon juice

1 teaspoon table salt

Up to 1 teaspoon freshly ground black pepper

Several dashes hot sauce, such as Tabasco sauce, to taste

Olive oil for serving

1. Grate the tomatoes, cucumber, celery, and onion through the large holes of a box grater into a large bowl. Grate the garlic through the small holes of that box grater into the same bowl.

2. Stir in the chiles, tomato juice, vinegar, lemon juice, salt, pepper, and hot sauce. Cover and refrigerate for at least 4 hours or up to 3 days.

3. Ladle into bowls or mugs. Drizzle a little olive oil over each before serving.

Better Guacamole

Makes 4 to 6 servings

This recipe's all about texture. Mashing avocados with a fork leaves the bits too chunky. Whirring them in a food processor turns them into baby food. The best tool for guacamole is an old-school potato masher, which will render the dip into a nice mix of chunky and smooth.

4 medium-size ripe Hass avocados, halved, pitted, and peeled

12 cherry tomatoes, quartered, or grape tomatoes, halved

1 small shallot, minced

3 tablespoons fresh lemon juice

1 tablespoon minced fresh oregano leaves, optional

½ teaspoon ground cumin, optional

½ teaspoon table salt

Several dashes hot red pepper sauce, to taste

1. Place the avocados in a large bowl. Use a potato masher to make them as chunky or creamy as you like.

2. Stir in the tomatoes, shallot, lemon juice, oregano (if using), cumin (if using), salt, and hot sauce. Serve immediately.

More! An avocado pit put on the dip does *not* keep guacamole from turning brown. Oxidization happens whenever the flesh of the avocado is exposed to air. If you're not going to serve the guacamole right away, lightly press plastic wrap against its surface and store in the fridge for at most a couple of hours. But remember: Guac tastes best at room temperature.

Test Kitchen Notes

- Unless you live in an avocado orchard, buy relatively firm avocados a few days before you need them, then leave them on the counter to soften. Placing them in a sealed paper bag with a banana will speed up the process by a day or so.

- If you're really in a hurry, wrap each unpeeled avocado individually and tightly in aluminum foil. Set in a 175°F oven for 10 minutes. That should do the trick.

- Refrigeration stops avocados from softening. If yours become perfect before you need them, store on a refrigerator shelf, not in the crisper.

Blender Salsa Verde

Makes 3 cups

Test Kitchen Notes

- For a fresher tasting, raw salsa, skip broiling the tomatillos.

- To seed a jalapeño, cut off its stem, then slice it in half lengthwise. Use a very small paring knife or a serrated grapefruit spoon to gently remove the seeds and their white membranes.

- While it's standard to wash your hands after handling hot chiles, capsaicin (the chemical that produces the spicy burn) is not water soluble. It's fat soluble. If you didn't wear rubber gloves as you worked with the chiles, rub your hands thoroughly with a little oil, then wash them with lots of warm, soapy water.

- Cilantro can be sandy. Rinse the leaves well, then blot dry with paper towels.

While we were in the groove of rethinking tools to create better classic sauces and dips, we found that a blender makes the best salsa. That's because it does indeed extract the juice from vegetables without chopping them into a puree. And it saves you time at the cutting board! This salsa will be wetter than a sauce or a dip, so it will nicely coat a tortilla chip or Spanish omelet. But it will still have the crunchy texture of veggies and herbs. It's also got a little tequila in the mix, perhaps a surprise ingredient. That little bit of alcohol will bring the flavors of the natural sugars in the vegetables more to the fore, softening some of their rough edges. Of course, you can substitute water for a spikier (and booze-free) flavor.

4 medium tomatillos, husked, rinsed, and quartered

3 tablespoons tequila (or water)

1 tablespoon apple cider vinegar

1 small jalapeño chile, stemmed, seeded, and quartered

¼ cup loosely packed fresh cilantro leaves

¼ cup frozen chopped onion, thawed and squeezed dry

1 teaspoon granulated white sugar

½ teaspoon table salt

1. Position the oven rack 6 inches from the broiler element; heat the broiler.

2. Lay the tomatillos on a lipped baking sheet. Broil, tossing once or twice, until blistered and evenly blackened, about 3 minutes.

3. Scrape the tomatillos and any juice on the baking sheet into a large blender. Let cool for 5 to 10 minutes.

4. In this order, add the tequila, vinegar, chile, cilantro, onion, sugar, and salt to the blender. Cover and blend until the mixture becomes a chunky salsa. If your blender has a pulse function, use it to avoid over-blending. Serve at once or store in a sealed container in the fridge for a couple of days.

Not-Deep-Fried-but-Much-Better-than-Baked Crab Egg Rolls

EASIER

Makes 12 egg rolls

If you don't have the equipment or the inclination to deep-fry homemade egg rolls, established wisdom says you must brush them with oil and bake them. But this technique is a less-than-satisfying alternative. It inevitably creates rolls with soggy bottoms because the baking sheet prevents the wrappers from crisping. And the point of an egg roll is the crunch, right? Here's a hybrid technique that involves pan-frying them so you 1) don't have to waste a quart of oil and 2) can skip the mess of deep-frying—but you still get the same shattering crunch. In other words, it's a true modern shortcut.

2 tablespoons hoisin sauce

2 tablespoons unseasoned rice vinegar

12 ounces bean sprouts

8 ounces pasteurized crabmeat, picked over for shells and cartilage

Twelve 8-inch egg roll wrappers

At least 2 tablespoons peanut oil or vegetable oil, more depending on the size of your pan

1. Stir the hoisin sauce and vinegar in a medium bowl until smooth. Add the bean sprouts and crabmeat. Toss gently until evenly coated.

2. Place one egg roll wrapper on a clean, dry work surface so that one corner of the wrapper is oriented toward you. Put a heaping 3 tablespoons of the crab mixture in the middle of the wrapper. Fold the point nearest you up and over the filling. Fold the two "side" corners over the filling. Moisten the top corner with a little water, fold it toward you, making sure it leaves no gaps in the wrapper, and gently press down to seal it in place. Place the stuffed roll on a baking sheet seam side down.

3. Repeat step 2 for the remaining wrappers.

4. Heat 2 tablespoons oil in a large nonstick skillet set over medium heat. Add as many stuffed rolls (seam side down) as you can without crowding, at least ½ inch between each egg roll. Cook, turning at least once, until golden brown on all sides, about 6 minutes. If your pan requires you to work in batches, add an additional 2 tablespoons oil for the next batch.

Test Kitchen Notes

- Egg roll wrappers are most often found in the produce section's refrigerator case.

- Do not use wonton wrappers, spring roll wraps, or rice paper wrappers.

- The stuffed egg rolls can be frozen on a lipped baking sheet, then stored in a plastic bag in the freezer for up to 4 months. Cook them straight from frozen, increasing your cooking time to 8 to 9 minutes per batch.

A ROAD MAP FOR A COMPOSED SALAD

There are two ways to make a salad. The most common way is to put everything in a bowl, add the dressing, and toss it all together. Unfortunately, the dressing is usually unevenly distributed and the whole thing looks a bit like a mangled mess.

Better, then, to arrange and layer everything on individual plates to make a *composed salad,* then drizzle the dressing on top—an eye-catching presentation, all the various ingredients displayed on the plate. Here's how to do it:

1. Start with 2 cups shredded or torn lettuce per person. Use bagged mixes or combine two lettuces: Bibb and Romaine, iceberg and endive, red leaf and baby oak leaf, spinach and radicchio. Think about pairing similar tastes: bold with bold, mild with mild. Or consider textural contrasts: crunchy Romaine or Belgian endive with softer mesclun mixes. Arrange on the plates.

2. Lay 3 to 4 ounces protein per person over the greens. You can use skinless meat from a rotisserie chicken (or roast turkey from the deli counter); peeled, deveined, and cooked shrimp; grilled, baked, or boiled salmon from the prepared food counter; canned or grilled tuna; crabmeat; or diced ham.

3. Add about 1 cup veggies and/or fruit per person—like small broccoli florets, shredded zucchini, shredded carrots, drained canned (packed in water) quartered artichoke hearts, thin bell pepper strips, snow peas, sugar snap peas, thinly sliced red onion, thinly sliced celery, sliced peaches, sliced nectarines, whole berries, sliced apples, sliced pears, and/or even sliced dried apricots.

4. For crunch, add 2 tablespoons chopped toasted nuts per person. The choice is yours: shelled pistachios, cashews, pecans, or walnuts. Just be sure to use *unsalted* nuts.

5. If you'd like, add 1 to 2 ounces shredded, shaved, or crumbled cheese per person—we like blue cheese, Cheddar, Gouda, Asiago, or fresh goat cheese, among others. In general, choose hard or semi-soft cheeses, rather than soft cheeses like Reblochon (with fresh goat cheese being the standout exception).

6. Finally, drizzle about 3 tablespoons of your favorite bottled salad dressing over each salad. Or go with 1½ tablespoons olive oil and 1½ tablespoons balsamic vinegar. If you're having an informal dinner with friends, prepare the composed salads through step 5, cover loosely with plastic wrap, and store in the fridge until you're ready to add the dressing just before serving.

7. Grind lots of black pepper over each plate, sprinkle on some crunchy kosher salt, and you're ready to enjoy a tasty, easy meal.

Blender Hummus

Makes about 2½ cups

Store-bought hummus is super-creamy and smooth, part of its enduring popularity as a tasty snack. The homemade stuff, however, often has a grainy texture, since a food processor cannot grind the fibrous chickpeas as smoothly as they should be. But a blender is the perfect solution. Because of its narrow, almost conical shape, it will force the chickpeas onto the blades by their own weight and thereby make hummus as smooth as the store-bought varieties. A turbo blender (like a Blendtec or a Vitamix) does an even better job, but such fancy equipment's not necessary. However, depending on your blender's power and torque, you may need to add a little water to your hummus as it mixes to keep the ingredients moving in that familiar whirlpool over the blades.

Test Kitchen Notes

- Each section of the ingredient list below makes one 2½-cup batch. Take your pick!

- If your hummus isn't blending evenly, turn off the machine to rearrange and tamp down the ingredients until the mixture loosens up enough to blend more easily.

- If you have a turbo blender, let the machine run a couple of minutes for super-smooth hummus that will also be slightly warm for serving.

- Store the hummus, covered, for several days in the refrigerator. Better yet, store a batch in the covered blender canister.

Lemon Hummus

One 14½-ounce can chickpeas

¼ cup liquid from the can of chickpeas

3 tablespoons fresh lemon juice

¼ cup olive oil

2 tablespoons tahini

½ teaspoon ground cumin

½ teaspoon table salt

Artichoke Hummus

One 14½-ounce can chickpeas

One 6½-ounce jar marinated artichoke hearts (do not drain)

2 tablespoons olive oil

2 tablespoons tahini

½ teaspoon freshly ground black pepper

Spinach Hummus

One 14½-ounce can chickpeas

¼ cup liquid from the can of chickpeas

¼ cup packed baby spinach leaves (about 1 ounce)

3 tablespoons white balsamic vinegar

2 tablespoons tahini

1 medium garlic clove, peeled

1 teaspoon table salt

½ teaspoon freshly ground black pepper

RECIPE CONTINUES ➡➡

Voilà! Clean a blender without slicing your fingers on the blade by using 1 cup hot water and 1 teaspoon dishwashing liquid. Cover and run on high for 1 minute, then rinse thoroughly.

Sun-Dried Tomato Hummus

One 14½-ounce can chickpeas

½ cup liquid from the can of chickpeas

½ cup store-bought marinated sun-dried tomatoes with their liquid (about 4 ounces with the liquid)

2 tablespoons tahini

1 tablespoon balsamic vinegar

1 medium garlic clove, peeled

⅛ teaspoon table salt

Olive Hummus

One 14½-ounce can chickpeas

½ cup liquid from the can of chickpeas

¼ cup pitted green olives (a little less than 2 ounces)

¼ cup olive oil

2 tablespoons tahini

2 tablespoons fresh lemon juice

2 teaspoons za'atar, optional

1 small garlic clove, peeled

1. Drain and rinse the chickpeas, reserving as much of the liquid from the can as the batch requires.

2. Place all the ingredients in a large blender in the order listed. Cover and pulse, scraping down the inside of the canister occasionally between pulses. Continue pulsing until smooth. The mixture will become quite thick. If it's too thick, add water in 1-tablespoon increments to thin it out.

BETTER LIVING
WITH A
GARLIC PRESS

You've probably got one in a drawer. You probably haven't used it in a while. That's too bad. Unless you have a very good knife game, mincing the garlic can lead to uneven bits, some of which can burn and turn astringent over the heat before the larger ones soften. Because a garlic press juices the garlic, it also yields a milder, sweeter flavor overall. What's more, a garlic press is for way more than garlic! You can put pickled jalapeño rings, cocktail onions, even fresh ginger through the press to produce unrivaled rubs, marinades, spreads, and sauces without all the chopping. So get out that press. You're going to need it.

TASTIER

VEGETARIAN

GLUTEN-FREE

Roasted Garlic and Pickled Onion Cheese Spread

Makes 4 to 6 servings

Test Kitchen Notes

- Make the preparation easier by buying roasted garlic from the salad bar at your supermarket. Since those cloves sit around in oil or condense through natural evaporation over time, their garlic flavor can be much more assertive. Reduce the amount to 4 *large* cloves (rather than a whole small head as directed).

- Pickled onions are often found in supermarkets with the relishes and sauces—and sometimes in "bulk" in the salad bar of larger markets.

- For a more complex flavor, substitute so-called "tipsy onions" for the pickled onions. A bar staple, these small cocktail onions have been soaked in dry vermouth.

- Low-fat cream cheese may contain gluten additives. Check the ingredients or the manufacturer's websites if this is a concern.

Here's how to make a homemade version of Boursin, the popular, flavored cheese spread made with soft Gournay cheese. Our recipe calls for a combination of cream cheese and butter, easier-to-find alternatives that turn out spectacularly well with all the additional flavorings. A garlic press will help crush the pickled onions to just the right consistency for a smooth spread. Discard any tough or fibrous bits left behind in the press. Serve the spread with rye crisp crackers or bagel chips, or dollop it into baked potatoes instead of butter and sour cream.

1 small garlic head

6 tiny pickled onions, drained

8 ounces regular or low-fat cream cheese

½ cup (1 stick) unsalted butter, softened to room temperature

2 tablespoons minced chives or fresh parsley leaves

1 teaspoon table salt

½ teaspoon ground black pepper

1. Position the rack in the center of the oven; heat the oven to 375°F.

2. Slice the top quarter off the garlic head to expose the cloves. Wrap the cut head in aluminum foil and bake until soft and tender, about 45 minutes. Open the foil and cool at room temperature for at least 15 minutes or up to 2 hours.

3. Use a small fork or a toothpick to get the garlic cloves out of their papery wrappers. Squeeze them, a few at a time, through a garlic press and into a medium bowl.

4. Squeeze the pickled onions, one at a time, through the garlic press and into the bowl. Discard any solids left in the press.

5. Stir the cheese, butter, chives, salt, and pepper into the garlic and onion mixture until creamy and smooth.

6. Pack the mixture into a small crock or a larger ramekin. Serve at once or cover and refrigerate for up to 4 days. Set the spread out at room temperature for at least 30 minutes to soften before serving.

Ginger-Marinated Chicken Tenders

EASIER

GLUTEN-FREE

Makes 6 servings as snacks or 3 as a light meal

By putting ginger through the press, you can make a concentrated ginger juice, terrific on chicken tenders. Mince the fresh ginger before pressing it so that you can press out as much juice as possible.

¼ cup peanut oil

¼ cup unseasoned rice vinegar

1½ tablespoons granulated white sugar

2 tablespoons minced peeled fresh ginger

1 pound chicken tenders

Nonstick spray

Vegetable oil for the grate or grill pan

1. Whisk the oil, vinegar, and sugar in a medium bowl until the sugar dissolves.

2. Put half the ginger into a garlic press and squeeze the juice into the oil mixture. Discard the solids in the press and squeeze the rest of the ginger into the bowl. Stir well, add the chicken tenders, and toss to coat. Set aside at room temperature for 15 minutes or refrigerate for up to 1 hour.

3. Brush the grate clean, brush it with nonstick spray, and prepare the grill for direct, high-heat cooking; or brush a nonstick grill pan with oil and set it over medium-high heat for a couple of minutes.

4. Add the tenders and grill, turning once, until cooked through, 5 to 6 minutes. Serve at once.

Test Kitchen Notes

- The marinade is also a tasty dressing. Toss it with shredded rotisserie chicken meat and bagged slaw mix for an easy salad.

- For more flavor, look for Asian brands of peanut oil, which are often barely refined, sometimes with bits of peanut floating right in the oil.

- For more peanut flavor, serve the skewers with a peanut dipping sauce (page 244).

Voilà! Use a small serving spoon to remove the peel from fresh ginger by turning the spoon upside down and digging gently along the surface of the skin to remove the papery bits. If the ginger is very fresh—say, with just the hint of a watery peel, the sort usually found at Asian supermarkets—there's no need to peel it at all.

More! To make pork tenders using this technique, start with a 1-pound pork tenderloin. Slice it widthwise into three even segments. Stand these up and cut each lengthwise into quarters. Marinate the pork for 15 minutes at room temperature or up to 1 hour in the fridge. When ready to grill, slide a few cubes onto each of a handful of bamboo skewers, leaving space between each cube. Grill for about 7 minutes, turning a couple of times.

A Better Caesar Salad

EASIER

VEGETARIAN

Makes 4 to 6 servings

Not only is putting anchovies through the garlic press easier (and less messy) than mincing them on a cutting board; it's also a better way to get the anchovies into a smooth paste. Why not just use premade anchovy paste? With the press, you can use better quality, juicy anchovies, packed in oil instead of water. They're also less salty than anchovy paste.

About 3 cups bread torn into about 1-inch chunks (crusts included), preferably from a country boule

Up to ½ cup plus 3 tablespoons olive oil

1 medium garlic clove, peeled

1 to 2 jarred or tinned anchovy fillets

1 large egg yolk

2 tablespoons white balsamic vinegar

2 teaspoons Dijon mustard

2 teaspoons Worcestershire sauce

1 teaspoon finely grated lemon zest

½ teaspoon table salt

½ teaspoon ground black pepper, plus additional for garnishing if desired

¼ cup finely grated Parmigiano-Reggiano (about ½ ounce)

3 Romaine hearts, leaves separated and chopped

1. Position the rack in the center of the oven; heat the oven to 375°F.

2. Toss the bread chunks and 2 tablespoons olive oil on a large lipped baking sheet. Bake, tossing occasionally, until golden brown and crisp, about 15 minutes.

3. Cool on the baking sheet for at least 15 minutes, or up to 3 hours, tossing occasionally to keep the bottoms from getting soggy.

4. Press the garlic and then the anchovies through a garlic press into a large serving bowl. Whisk in the egg yolk, vinegar, mustard, Worcestershire sauce, lemon zest, salt, and pepper until fairly creamy. Drizzle in a little olive oil, maybe 1 tablespoon, and whisk it until uniform. Then continue drizzling in up to ½ cup more oil, whisking all the while, to form a thick dressing. Taste it for sourness. If it's too acidic, add a little more olive oil until it tastes smooth and rich. Stir in the cheese.

5. Add the lettuce and toss well but gently. Serve at once, sprinkling the croutons over each plateful. Garnish with more black pepper, if desired.

Test Kitchen Notes

- Tearing some of the bread (instead of slicing all of it) for homemade croutons creates more nooks and crannies to hold the dressing.

- To choose quality anchovies, look for plump, whole fillets packed in oil. By the way, anchovies packed in jars are easier to store in the fridge than those packed in flat tins.

- There's a lot of internet craziness about never cutting lettuce with a knife. Seriously? Cutting or tearing—either way you're still damaging the lettuce cells. It's called cooking. Use a knife and stay off strange websites.

TASTIER

GLUTEN-FREE

Sweet and Spicy Shrimp Skewers

Makes 6 servings as snacks or 3 as a light meal

Test Kitchen Notes

- Look for jarred "tamed" jalapeño rings if heat is your concern.

- There's no need to soak bamboo skewers for quick grilling—under 10 minutes. They may singe on the ends but won't burn excessively or catch fire.

- Lay the skewers so that the shrimp, not the skewers' wooden ends, are closest to the flame or heat source.

Voilà! Lentils would be a great side dish for these skewers or tenders. (They're also a great snack mixed into hummus, tossed into soups, or served on their own with your favorite salad dressing.) Since brown lentils stand up best to storage, they're the best choice to keep on hand. To cook brown lentils, put them in a medium saucepan, add lots of water until they're submerged by at least 2 inches, and bring to a boil over high heat. Reduce the heat and cook until the lentils are tender, about 15 minutes. Drain, cool, and store in a plastic bag in the fridge for up to a week. Cooked brown lentils, chopped apple, and a creamy dressing make a perfect snack or light salad.

Here's a terrific marinade for shrimp, made by putting garlic, pickled onions, and pickled jalapeños through the garlic press. In fact, you can skip the shrimp and use the marinade for chicken thighs, beef strip steaks, or even boneless center-cut pork chops, all without skewering them for tasty fare from the grill. However, we offer a great technique for keeping the shrimp long and straight, each on its own skewer. Use it not only in this recipe but anytime you want grilled shrimp for wraps or burritos, or just as proper dipping vehicles.

4 small pickled cocktail onions

2 tablespoons pickled jalapeño rings

1 medium garlic clove, peeled

2 tablespoons ginger jam, orange marmalade, or honey mustard

1 pound medium shrimp (about 30 per pound), peeled and deveined

Vegetable or canola oil for the grill grate

1. One by one, put the cocktail onions, jalapeño rings, and garlic through a garlic press, catching anything that comes through the holes or over the side of the press in a bowl below. Stir in the jam. Add the shrimp and toss well until evenly coated. Refrigerate for at least 1 hour or up to 2 hours, stirring once or twice.

2. Brush the grill grate clean, and heat your grill to high heat. Meanwhile, starting with the fatter end of one shrimp, spear it lengthwise end-to-end onto a bamboo skewer, thereby straightening out the shrimp. Repeat to skewer all the shrimp.

3. Brush the grate with oil. Set the skewers directly over the heat and grill, turning halfway through, until the shrimp are pink and firm, about 6 minutes. Cool a couple of minutes before serving.

BETTER
VEGGIE BURGERS

Veggie burgers are often dry and crumbly—and require too much chopping for such shoddy results. With beans in the mix, they're much easier. These, in fact, are even luxurious, thanks to the addition of rolled oats, which bind the patties without turning them cakey. As a bonus, all these burgers are gluten-free if you use certified gluten-free oats.

Test Kitchen Notes

- Don't fear the fat in the skillet. More will make the burgers crunchier. But be judicious: You don't want to deep-fry the burgers, as they'll turn soggy minutes away from the skillet. Add more oil slowly as necessary to get a golden crust.

- Not all canned beans are created equal. Some are wetter and softer. If the processed batter is too soft to form patties, add 2 tablespoons potato starch or cornstarch, cover, and process until smooth. Then place the food processor bowl in the fridge for a couple of hours to let the mixture firm up.

- Remember to scrape down and remove the blade of the food processor before you plunge your hands into the bowl.

- Prepare the burgers ahead (including cooking them) and freeze on a baking sheet until hard. Transfer to large plastic bag, seal, and store in the freezer for several months. Reheat them right from the freezer by placing on a baking sheet in a 350°F oven for 15 minutes or so.

TASTIER

VEGETARIAN

GLUTEN-FREE

Chili Black Bean Burgers

Makes 6 burgers

Make a double batch of the "batter" for these tasty vegetarian patties and keep the remainder covered in the fridge for several days: more patties (almost) at the ready to cook up for quick lunches or dinners. Serve in toasted kaiser rolls with coleslaw for extra crunch.

2 tablespoons olive oil, plus more as necessary

½ cup finely chopped yellow onion

One 15-ounce can black beans, drained and rinsed

½ cup pecan pieces

½ cup rolled oats (certified gluten-free if that is a concern)

1 large egg

Up to 2 teaspoons bottled red hot sauce, such as Frank's Red Hot or Texas Pete

½ teaspoon ground cumin

½ teaspoon dried oregano

½ teaspoon table salt

½ teaspoon ground black pepper

1. Heat 1 tablespoon of the oil in a large nonstick skillet over medium heat. Add the onion and cook, stirring often, for 3 minutes or until softened. Transfer to the bowl of a food processor fitted with the chopping blade. Set the skillet aside to use to cook the burgers; do not wash it.

2. Add the beans, pecans, oats, egg, hot sauce, cumin, oregano, salt, and pepper to the bowl of the food processor. Process, scraping down the inside of the bowl occasionally, until the mixture forms a coarse paste. Scrape down the sides and remove the blade.

3. Heat the remaining 1 tablespoon oil in the same skillet over medium heat. With clean, wet hands, form the black bean mixture into 6 patties. Slip each into the skillet, working with only as many as will fit the pan without crowding, and cook for 7 minutes, turning halfway through, until set and crispy on the top and bottom. If the skillet is exceptionally dry, add a tablespoon of oil for each additional batch.

Voilà! Press an apple slicer through the center of a peeled onion. The resulting onion sections will be much easier to chop.

Falafel Burgers

Makes 6 burgers

Why deep-fry falafel balls when you can make tasty patties in almost no time? Traditionally, falafel is made with parsley, but we skipped it here—it turns the burgers a lurid green. Consider mincing fresh parsley leaves, mixing them with vinegar and a little salt, and serving as a condiment for bunless, "open-faced" burgers. Or serve in pita pockets with chopped tomatoes and a squeeze of lemon juice. In either case, add some sour cream or plain yogurt if desired.

2 tablespoons olive oil, plus more as necessary

½ cup finely chopped yellow onion

Up to 2 teaspoons minced garlic

One 15-ounce can chickpeas, drained and rinsed

½ cup roasted unsalted cashews

½ cup rolled oats (certified gluten-free if that is a concern)

1 large egg

½ teaspoon ground cardamom

½ teaspoon ground cumin

¼ teaspoon ground cinnamon

½ teaspoon table salt

¼ teaspoon ground black pepper

1. Heat 1 tablespoon of the oil in a large nonstick skillet over medium heat. Add the onion and garlic; cook, stirring often, until softened, about 3 minutes. Transfer to the bowl of a food processor fitted with the chopping blade. Set the skillet aside for cooking the patties; do not wash it.

2. Add the chickpeas, cashews, oats, egg, cardamom, cumin, cinnamon, salt, and pepper to the bowl of the food processor. Process, scraping down the inside of the bowl occasionally, until the mixture forms a coarse paste. Scrape down the sides and remove the blade.

3. Heat the remaining 1 tablespoon oil in the same skillet over medium heat. With clean, wet hands, form the chickpea mixture into 6 patties. Slip each into the skillet, working with only as many as will fit the pan without crowding, and cook for 7 minutes, turning halfway through, until set and crispy on the top and bottom. If the skillet is exceptionally dry, add a tablespoon of oil for each additional batch.

White Bean and Almond Burgers

Makes 6 burgers

These are a little sweet and exceptionally creamy—which is why we prefer them fried in butter, rather than a more neutral oil. Try them in potato rolls with a flavorful condiment like caponata or tapenade—or even bunless with coleslaw on top. You can also serve in toasted brioche buns with sliced cucumbers and lots of creamy mayonnaise. Or put them in hamburger buns with a little mayonnaise and lots of kimchi. They'd also be welcome on top of a composed salad (see page 72). If you're working in batches to cook the patties, use 1 tablespoon butter for frying each batch.

3 tablespoons unsalted butter, or more as necessary

½ cup finely chopped shallots

One 15-ounce can white beans, such as great northern or navy, drained and rinsed

½ cup sliced almonds

½ cup rolled oats (certified gluten-free if that is a concern)

1 large egg

1 tablespoon minced fresh tarragon leaves

2 teaspoons Dijon mustard

¼ teaspoon table salt

½ teaspoon ground black pepper

1. Melt 2 tablespoons of the butter in a large nonstick skillet over medium heat. Add the shallots and cook, stirring often, until softened, about 3 minutes. Transfer to the bowl of a food processor fitted with the chopping blade. Set the skillet aside for cooking the patties; do not wash it.

2. Add the beans, almonds, oats, egg, tarragon, mustard, salt, and pepper to the bowl of the processor. Process, scraping down the inside of the bowl occasionally, until the mixture forms a coarse paste. Scrape down the sides and remove the blade.

3. Heat 1 tablespoon butter in the skillet over medium heat. With clean, wet hands, form the bean mixture into 6 patties. Slip each into the skillet, working with only as many as will fit the pan without crowding, and cook for 7 minutes, turning halfway through, until set and crispy on the top and bottom. If the skillet is exceptionally dry, add a little more butter for each additional batch.

A ROAD MAP FOR PESTO

Pesto is a no-cook herb sauce, usually made with fresh basil. But it can actually be made with any number of herbs. Here's the way you can create your own signature version, based on what's in the produce section, at your farmers' market, or even in your garden. You'll end up with about 1 cup. Toss with still-warm cooked and drained pasta, smear on burgers as a condiment, drizzle on tomato slices, or spoon on baked potatoes.

1. For a mixed-herb pesto, start with 1¼ cups of a primary fresh herb. Choose from basil, parsley, and cilantro. Then add ¼ cup of a secondary, complementary fresh herb, like dill, oregano, sage, rosemary, mint, tarragon, chervil, or marjoram. Good combinations are basil and oregano, basil and tarragon, parsley and dill, and cilantro and sage. (In a pinch, you can also use just 1½ cups of the primary herb, omitting the secondary herb entirely.) Use only the leaves of the herbs and not the woody stems. To measure, pack the leaves tightly into a measuring cup. Place the herbs in the bowl of a large food processor fitted with the chopping blade.

2. Add ¼ cup finely grated hard, aged cheese. Try Parmigiano-Reggiano, aged Asiago, or Pecorino. A crumbly, dry, aged goat cheese or a super-aged Gouda will also work.

3. Add 3 tablespoons chopped unsalted nuts or seeds, such as almonds, walnuts, pecans, shelled pistachios, or pine nuts. If you've got extra time, toast the nuts or seeds in a dry skillet over medium-low heat to give them more flavor—but cool them before adding to the food processor.

4. Snap the lid onto the food processor and give the mixture a few pulses. Add 3 tablespoons olive oil or a nut oil from the same nut you added to the mix—or perhaps 1½ tablespoons oil plus 1½ tablespoons water for a lower-fat alternative. Continue processing until coarsely textured and thick, scraping down the inside of the bowl once or twice to make sure everything is chopped to the same consistency.

5. Finally, add 1 teaspoon table salt and ½ teaspoon ground black pepper. If you like, also add up to 2 tablespoons of an additional flavoring agent: drained and rinsed capers, drained jarred pimientos or roasted red peppers, pliable soft sun-dried tomatoes, lemon zest, and/or minced garlic. Process just until well combined. The pesto should still be grainy although without any bits of nuts or other ingredients in the mix.

6. Store in a sealed container in the refrigerator. To prevent browning, press a piece of parchment paper directly onto the exposed surface of the pesto before putting the lid on the container.

BETTER
INFUSED TEAS

Flavorful infused teas can be made with a French press coffee maker. The press can hold boiling water, necessary for extracting many of the flavors. And the plunger not only helps strain out these bits but actually extracts more flavor from them as you press down. Remember: The better the black tea, the better the tea drink.

Test Kitchen Notes

- Wash the press well if you've used it for coffee. Disassemble the components and soak them in soapy water—or use warm water and baking soda if you fear any sudsy aftertaste. Rinse well with copious amounts of fresh water.

- Most importantly, dry your press well with paper towels after washing to remove more of the coffee oils.

- Then clean the press well after you make an infused tea—unless you want your coffee to taste like whatever you infused your tea with! Or skip some of this obsessiveness by buying a second French press to use for these infusions.

- Beware: Some manufacturers refer to a 32-ounce French press as an "8 cup" model (because they make eight small cups of coffee, rather than hold the volume amount of 8 cups).

Iced Tea Quencher with Ginger and Pineapple

EASIER

VEGETARIAN

GLUTEN-FREE

Makes five 8-ounce servings

Here's a tropical iced tea that's great on a hot weekend afternoon. Or maybe with a Hawaiian pizza. Most supermarket produce sections have cored and peeled pineapple spears in the refrigerator case. Chop them into small bits for the best flavor. For a tropical cocktail, stir 1 cup gold rum and ½ cup superfine white sugar (or granulated white sugar) into the pitcher of tea until the sugar dissolves.

4 bags plain black tea

½ cup chopped peeled fresh pineapple

One 2-inch-long ginger knob, peeled and chopped

Boiling water

1. Place the tea bags, pineapple, and ginger in a 32- to 34-ounce French press. Fill with boiling water. Set the lid and plunger in place without pressing down. Steep at room temperature for 1 hour.

2. Press the plunger down and pour the tea into a large pitcher. Add 2 cups cold water, stir well, and serve over ice.

Voilà! Tzatziki is a Greek yogurt-cucumber sauce, but it can become a light meal to go with one of these iced quenchers in the summer—or anytime, really—when you add more veggies and even some berries to the mix. Blueberries add a tart/sweet pop, a decided bit of complexity in the creamy concoction. For each serving, mix ½ cup diced peeled seeded cucumber, ⅓ cup shredded carrots, ⅓ cup blueberries, 2 tablespoons chopped red onion, 2 tablespoons fat-free plain Greek yogurt, 1 teaspoon honey, ½ teaspoon dried dill, ¼ teaspoon minced garlic, and ¼ teaspoon ground black pepper in a large bowl. Spoon it into a whole-wheat pita pocket.

Spiced Turmeric Tea

Makes four 6-ounce servings

Hot turmeric tea is popular these days for its health benefits. Here's a sweetened chilled or room-temp version with lots of fragrant spices—a great afternoon quencher. Fresh turmeric shows up even in our rural New England supermarkets—it looks sort of like a carrot version of ginger. Using the fresh variety is important here. Wrap any unused pieces of turmeric in paper towels, seal in a plastic bag, and store in your fridge for up to 2 weeks.

1 small orange or tangerine, quartered and seeded

Three 2-inch pieces fresh turmeric root, peeled and roughly chopped

One 4-inch cinnamon stick, broken into a few large pieces

3 tablespoons honey

2 teaspoons black peppercorns, optional

¼ teaspoon table salt

Boiling water

Thinly sliced orange rounds, for serving

1. Place everything in a 32- to 34-ounce French press. Fill with boiling water, stirring until the honey dissolves. Set the plunger and lid in place without pressing down; steep at room temperature for 15 minutes.

2. Press the plunger down, pushing a bit to extract more juice from the orange. If desired, place an orange round in each glass or cup before pouring in the infusion. Serve at room temperature or over ice in tall glasses.

Summer Lemonade with Lemongrass and Blackberries

Makes four 6-ounce servings

This infusion has a light, fresh flavor, best on a summer afternoon. Scrub the lemons with a potato brush or any clean scrub brush to get rid of any preservative wax on their peels. To bruise lemongrass, place the stalks on a cutting board and strike them with the thicker back of the blade of a chef's knife (not the cutting side of the blade).

3 medium lemons

⅓ cup fresh blackberries

¼ cup granulated white sugar

One 4-inch lemongrass stalk, white and pale green parts only, bruised and roughly chopped

Boiling water

1. Squeeze the juice from 2 of the lemons into a 32- to 34-ounce French press. Cut the remaining lemon into eighths, remove the seeds, and add the wedges to the press, along with the blackberries, sugar, and lemongrass.

2. Fill with boiling water; stir until the sugar dissolves. Set the plunger and lid in place without pressing down. Steep at room temperature for 1 to 1½ hours.

3. Press the plunger down. Pour the infused lemonade over ice in tall glasses.

Proper Chai

Makes five 8-ounce servings

Here's a hot, spicy drink that's best on a fall weekend. Don't use fat-free milk here—the drink needs a little dairy fat to enrich its texture.

4 bags plain black tea

3 tablespoons granulated white sugar

Two 4-inch cinnamon sticks, broken into large pieces

One 1-inch ginger knob, peeled and chopped

8 white or green cardamom pods, crushed in a garlic press or with the side of a chef's knife against a cutting board

2 star anise pods

⅛ teaspoon table salt, optional

Boiling water

2 cups whole or low-fat milk

1. Place the tea, sugar, cinnamon sticks, ginger, cardamom pods, star anise, and salt, if using, in a 32- to 34-ounce French press. Fill with boiling water, stirring until the sugar dissolves. Set the plunger and lid in place without pressing down. Steep for 1 hour.

2. Heat the milk in a small saucepan over medium-low heat until bubbles fizz around the edge of the milk.

3. Press the plunger of the press down, then pour the infusion into the milk and stir well. Serve hot.

Voilà! It's easy to run out of milk. Consider buying a few cartons of shelf-stable, no-refrigeration milk to use in a pinch. They're often available in the supermarket's drink aisle. Just make sure you keep those expiration dates in mind.

3

PASTA, PIZZA, AND DUMPLINGS

Pasta is a go-to weeknight dinner because it's hearty, satisfying, and often within reach after work or a busy day. But it can be made even better and faster if we help you reimagine a few basic techniques and change the way you approach a few key ingredients.

But first, a word about equipment. Pasta requires larger cookware than you might think. No, you don't want to use a Dutch oven unless it's specifically called for. But break out the large saucepan and the big colander, if only to give the pasta plenty of space to cook, to help the sauce reduce, and to make sure nothing tasty gets accidentally sloshed down the drain. As you'll see, some of these recipes *require* a very large colander. A new one is around ten bucks.

The recipes in this chapter show some of the largest range in the book: from a kid-friendly carbonara that you can make in minutes to a simple (if not everyday) way to make fat, tasty udon noodles to enliven a pot of chicken soup. There are dinner-party-worthy gnocchi in a third of the time and one-pot weeknight pasta suppers that save you cleanup later on. The recipes show off the nature of a true shortcut: a bit of simplifying in the service of, well, betterifying.

Not a one of these recipes calls for fresh pasta. They're all made with dried—which should be a pantry staple for quick cooks. However, not all dried pasta is created equal. Look for sturdy, thick noodles for a better texture after cooking. The old saw is not true for all things but it's almost always true for dried pasta: You get what you pay for. Some of these recipes have gluten-free substitutions. Use gluten-free noodles that require cooking, not just soaking.

But before you rush off to the recipes, here's one small, counterintuitive tip about cooking not just pasta but almost everything more efficiently: Be open to change. Don't plan out your meals too far in advance. Quick-cooking books aplenty praise the virtues of the monthly meal planner. "On the first weekend of the month, sit down to write out everything you'll eat for the next 30 days."

Sure, it sounds good to set dinner menus far in advance. But it's pretty stifling, too. What if you hear a friend mention a great, new idea for vegetables or read about a newfangled weeknight casserole? Or what if next Thursday comes and you don't want the salmon dinner you've scheduled? Or better, if someone walks in and offers to take you to dinner?

Give yourself the freedom to plan ahead *and* to fly by the seat of your pants. A recipe you don't want to cook becomes by nature a slower one. And a little grace in the kitchen (and in life) goes a long way toward making everything better.

Marinara Sauce in Minutes

Makes about 3½ cups

Test Kitchen Notes

- Frozen chopped onions, available in the frozen vegetable section of your supermarket, are a good time-saver and work well in this simple marinara because we use them to add sweetness, not texture.

- Because of their excess moisture, start those frozen onions on high to reduce them quickly.

- No-salt-added canned tomatoes are best. Add salt to the final dish, even if you just spoon marinara over cooked pasta, rather than starting with overly salty canned tomatoes.

Voilà! A wooden spoon placed over a pot of boiling pasta can keep it from boiling over. The spoon pops many of the bubbles as they rise up. It's not fail-safe but it'll work enough that you can get to the stove before a mess happens. And less cleanup is more time saved!

Honestly, this marinara sauce will take you about 5 minutes longer than opening a jar and heating it on the stove—mostly because of canned crushed tomatoes, almost a reduced sauce on their own. And the results are far superior, with a lovely and balanced sweet/tart flavor. If you want to double or even triple the recipe, the sauce will take longer to mellow and become flavorful, perhaps up to three times the stated timings. Freeze 1-cup portions in sealed containers for a stash of marinara and better meals in the months ahead.

2 tablespoons olive oil

1 cup frozen chopped onions (do not thaw)

One 28-ounce can plain crushed tomatoes

2 teaspoons minced garlic

2 teaspoons dried oregano

1 teaspoon dried basil

½ teaspoon granulated white sugar

½ teaspoon table salt

Up to ¼ teaspoon red pepper flakes, optional

1. Warm the olive oil in a large saucepan over high heat. Add the onions and cook, stirring almost constantly, until they give off their liquid and it mostly evaporates, about 3 minutes.

2. Reduce the heat to low. Stir in the tomatoes, garlic, oregano, basil, sugar, salt, and red pepper flakes, if using.

3. Stir well and bring to a low simmer. Simmer, uncovered but stirring fairly often, for 5 minutes, or until the sauce has reduced by a quarter to a third of its original volume. It should taste thick and rich. Use at once or store in a covered container in the fridge for up to 4 days.

Microwave Pasta Carbonara

Makes 2 servings

The mere notion that you can make a creamy carbonara pasta dish in minutes—using dried pasta that cooks right in the sauce—is in and of itself pretty amazing. But the fact that kids (okay, sure, and you) will love it is an even better notion! This technique will only work in a glass loaf pan. The higher sides help contain the inevitable foam as the pasta cooks and also retain more heat for quicker cooking. (And if you don't know that the microwave's no place for a metal pan, just trust us on this one.)

1 cup dried small elbow macaroni (about 4 ounces)

1 cup whole or low-fat milk (do not use fat-free)

1 large egg yolk

½ teaspoon ground dried mustard

½ teaspoon dried thyme

¼ teaspoon table salt

¼ teaspoon ground black pepper

3 ounces Canadian bacon, diced

¾ cup shredded Parmigiano-Reggiano (about 1½ ounces)

1. Place the macaroni in a 9 x 5-inch microwave-safe glass loaf pan. Add enough water just to cover the pasta.

2. In a 950-watt microwave oven, cook on high for 5 minutes, stopping the microwave for a few seconds if the pasta begins to foam over the dish, then continuing to cook as directed. The pasta should be almost tender and the water almost gone. Carefully drain out any excess (but very hot!) water.

3. Whisk the milk, egg yolk, mustard, thyme, salt, and pepper in a small bowl until uniform. Pour over the macaroni; add the Canadian bacon and cheese. Stir well.

4. Microwave on high for 4 minutes, pausing the microwave twice as the pasta cooks to stir thoroughly, until the pasta is almost tender, with some chew left. Set aside at room temperature for 5 minutes, stirring occasionally, before serving.

Test Kitchen Notes

- You must use small elbow macaroni to get the timing right.

- Shred the Parmigiano-Reggiano with the large holes of a box grater, rather than grating it into powdery dust. If you've got kids who don't stand on ceremony, you can substitute ¾ cup shredded Cheddar or Jack cheese.

- This recipe is calibrated for a 950-watt microwave. If using a 1200-watt oven, shave about a minute off the cook times in both steps 2 and 4—and watch for overflow from super-heating.

- If the pasta begins to foam over the top of the pan in step 2, stop the microwave, wait a few seconds, and start again.

- To double the recipe, use a second loaf pan and microwave separately.

Voilà! Did you know you can freeze enough PB&J sandwiches to last your kids a whole month? Put the peanut butter (or almond butter, walnut butter, or sunflower seed butter) on both sides of the bread with the jelly in the middle. The coated bread won't get soggy as it thaws in their lunch box or after school.

Instant Gnocchi

Makes 4 servings

Test Kitchen Notes

- For the instant potatoes, let the tap run until the water steams. It has to be hot enough to melt the potato flakes.

- Look for the dough to have the consistency of Play-Doh—that is, it shouldn't be elastic but should come apart in clumps.

Here's how to skip the 2 hours it takes to bake and cool russet potatoes just to make gnocchi: Use potato flakes, sometimes called "instant mashed potatoes." These are just potatoes that have been cooked, mashed, and dehydrated. And they're not just an incredible shortcut. They actually make better gnocchi: light, airy little dumplings, unbelievable with melted butter and nutmeg (as here) or with marinara sauce (page 98) or even a creamy cheese sauce (see **More!**).

1½ cups hot tap water

1 cup dehydrated potato flakes

2 large eggs, at room temperature

1 teaspoon table salt

2 cups all-purpose flour or more as needed, plus more for dusting

½ cup (1 stick) unsalted butter

Grated nutmeg and ground black pepper, for garnish

1. Mix the hot water and potato flakes in a large bowl. Stir with a wooden spoon until smooth, then continue stirring until the mixture thickens. Cool for 5 minutes.

2. Meanwhile, bring a large pot of water to a boil over high heat.

3. Once the potato mixture is cool (but not fully back to room temperature), add the eggs and salt. Stir until uniform. Add 2 cups flour. Stir with a wooden spoon until a soft, pliable dough forms, adding more flour as needed to prevent the mixture from being sticky.

4. Divide the mixture into 6 equal pieces. Lightly dust a clean, dry work surface with flour. Roll one piece of dough under your palms into a 1-inch-diameter cylinder. Cut this cylinder into 1-inch pieces, then roll each gently against the back of a fork's tines to make little grooves in each. (Those grooves help catch and hold the sauce, but if you're really pressed for time, you can skip making the grooves and go with more pillow-like gnocchi.) Repeat with the remaining pieces of dough.

5. Once the water is boiling, reduce the heat so the water is at a bare simmer, not a rolling boil. Drop all the gnocchi in the pot. Cook until the gnocchi float, about 4 minutes from the time they hit the water. Drain in a colander set in the sink.

6. Melt the butter in a very large skillet over medium heat. Continue cooking until the butter just begins to brown at the edges, a couple of minutes. Add the gnocchi and toss gently for about half a minute to heat them through. Some of them may get a little crusty. Divide among serving plates and top with grated nutmeg and lots of ground black pepper.

 More! To bake the gnocchi with a Parmesan cream sauce, start by heating the oven to 350°F. Meanwhile, melt 3 tablespoons unsalted butter in a large, oven-safe skillet. Whisk in 3 tablespoons all-purpose flour to make a blond paste. Slowly whisk in 2 cups whole or low-fat milk (do not use fat-free) and 1 cup chicken broth; continue whisking until bubbling and slightly thickened. Whisk in ¾ cup finely grated Parmigiano-Reggiano (about 1½ ounces) and ½ teaspoon table salt. Add the cooked gnocchi and toss well. Arrange the cooked and drained gnocchi in a single layer in the pan and bake, uncovered, until lightly browned and bubbling, 15 to 20 minutes.

White Clam and Spinach Pizza

Makes one 12-inch pie

Test Kitchen Notes

- If your creamed spinach is still frozen, microwave it until thawed.

- Some frozen creamed spinach is essentially chopped spinach with little balls of frozen sauce scattered throughout. Make sure these balls are evenly spaced across the pizza before baking.

- If you can't find fresh pizza dough in the refrigerator case at your supermarket, buy a 1-pound ball of dough from your local pizza shop.

- To substitute a prebaked pizza crust, bake the pizza for only 10 minutes. The cheese may not fully melt, but you can finish the pizza under the broiler.

- For a fancier pie, use a vegetable peeler to shave slices of Parmigiano-Reggiano over the top, rather than just sprinkling the pie with grated cheese.

Frozen creamed spinach is a 1950s throwback that still finds its way into the freezer case of most supermarkets. It's a terrific tool for making the sauce for this pizza, a more substantial version of the white pizzas made famous in New Haven, Connecticut.

All-purpose or semolina flour, for dusting

1 pound pizza dough

One 12-ounce package frozen creamed spinach, thawed

6½ ounces chopped cooked shucked clams (canned or thawed frozen)

1 cup finely grated Parmigiano-Reggiano, Pecorino, or other hard aged cheese (about 2 ounces)

1 teaspoon minced garlic

1 teaspoon dried oregano

½ teaspoon red pepper flakes

1. Position the rack in the center of the oven and heat the oven to 475°F.

2. Dust a clean, dry work surface with flour. Press and stretch the pizza dough into a 12-inch round. Transfer the dough, floured side down, to a large baking sheet.

3. Spread the creamed spinach over the pie, leaving a ½-inch border at the edge. Top with the clams, cheese, garlic, oregano, and red pepper flakes.

4. Bake until the crust is puffed and browned at the edges, about 17 minutes. Cool on the sheet for 10 minutes before transferring to a cutting board and slicing into wedges.

Voilà! If you're grating fresh Parmigiano-Reggiano, put on some music and grate more than you need. Pour the remainder into a sealable plastic freezer bag, squeeze out the excess air, seal, and store in the fridge for up to 2 weeks.

Creamy, Cheesy Stuffed Shells

Makes 3 servings

No doubt, this casserole is still a bit of work. That "easier" tag is a little misleading. What's easier here is the filling. It's got a secret ingredient that makes it spectacular. No doubt, creamed spinach is rich; but you'll make it elegant with lemon zest and fennel seeds.

One 12-ounce package frozen creamed spinach, thawed

¾ cup grated mozzarella (about 3 ounces)

1 large egg yolk

1 teaspoon finely grated lemon zest

1 teaspoon fennel seeds, crushed

12 large dried pasta shells (4 ounces), cooked and drained according to the package instructions

1½ cups plain marinara sauce, store-bought or homemade (page 98)

1 cup finely grated Parmigiano-Reggiano, Pecorino, or other hard, aged cheese (about 2 ounces)

1. Position the rack in the center of the oven and heat the oven to 350°F.

2. Mix the creamed spinach, mozzarella, egg yolk, lemon zest, and fennel seeds in a medium bowl. Stuff about 2 tablespoons of the mixture into each shell.

3. Spread half the sauce in the bottom of a 9-inch square baking dish or a 10-inch round pie plate. Place the shells on top. Spoon the remaining sauce over the shells and sprinkle with the Parmigiano-Reggiano.

4. Bake until the cheese has melted and the sauce is bubbling, about 20 minutes. Cool for 5 minutes before serving.

Voilà! Save time making stuffed shells by using egg roll wrappers rather than dried pasta shells. The egg roll wrappers don't need boiling in advance! Place the filling of your choice inside a wrapper, roll it closed, and set it in the baking dish. Cover with plenty of sauce and bake as directed.

Test Kitchen Notes

- Use a 2-tablespoon cookie or ice cream scoop to fill each shell.

- Semi-soft cheeses like mozzarella (or Jack or Colby) can be more easily grated if they're placed in the freezer for 30 minutes or so.

- To double the recipe, use a 9 x 13-inch baking dish. If the stuffed shells are in one layer in the dish, the timing should remain the same—although they may require an extra few minutes if the shells are packed very tightly together.

- For a fancier dish, substitute crumbled soft goat cheese for the mozzarella.

- For an even easier dish, skip boiling the dried pasta shells and use egg roll wrappers. See the **Voilà!** for a little more information on this trick.

- To make ahead, assemble the casserole in a freezer-to-oven baking dish. Follow the recipe but don't bake the casserole. It'll keep, covered, in the freezer for up to 4 months. Bake it straight from the freezer, covered for 20 minutes and then uncovered for about 20 minutes longer.

One-Skillet Loaded Mac and Cheese

Makes 4 servings

Test Kitchen Notes

- There's no added salt since the mustard and cheese are salty.

- The skillet you use must have a lid. The pasta cooks properly only when covered in the oven.

- Make it even easier by using the precut carrot matchsticks found in the produce section.

- Or just use 3 cups thawed frozen chopped vegetables.

- You can skip step 5 if you don't want a browned top.

More! If you want a crunchy topping, stir together 1 cup plain panko breadcrumbs, 2 tablespoons cooled melted unsalted butter, and the remaining quarter of shredded cheese used in step 4 in a small bowl. Sprinkle evenly over the baked casserole, cover, and bake for 5 minutes, as directed. Then broil until golden brown and crunchy, 1 to 2 minutes.

Don't boil water for pasta! You don't need to in this satisfying version of the classic. By adjusting the liquid ratios of traditional mac and cheese, you can get the raw pasta to cook right in the sauce (and the starch from the pasta makes the sauce thick and luxurious). You're done before you know it with no additional pots or colanders to clean up. Admittedly, this recipe is not just mac and cheese. It's got lots of vegetables (almost an equivalent amount of the pasta), enough to count as a full meal. Plus, it's a good way to get picky kids to look forward to eating their veggies.

4 tablespoons (½ stick) unsalted butter

¼ cup all-purpose flour

3 cups whole or low-fat milk (do not use fat-free)

1 cup vegetable broth

1 tablespoon Dijon mustard

1 teaspoon dried thyme

½ teaspoon dried sage, optional

½ teaspoon ground black pepper

8 ounces dried ziti pasta

2½ cups loosely packed shredded Cheddar cheese (about 10 ounces)

3 cups chopped fresh broccoli florets and/or shredded carrots

1. Position the rack in the center of the oven; heat the oven to 350°F.

2. Melt the butter in a 12-inch oven-safe skillet over medium-low heat. Add the flour and whisk until it forms a smooth, pale, blond paste. Do not brown. Increase the heat to medium. Whisking all the while, add the milk in a slow, steady stream. Continue whisking until the mixture has thickened and is bubbling, about 1 minute. Whisk in the broth, mustard, thyme, sage if using, and pepper. Stir in the pasta until evenly and thoroughly coated.

3. Cover the skillet, transfer to the oven, and bake, stirring once, until the pasta is tender, about 18 minutes.

4. Add three-quarters of the cheese and all the vegetables to the casserole; stir until uniform. Sprinkle the remaining cheese on top. Cover and bake until the cheese melts, about 5 minutes.

5. Remove the skillet from the oven and use pot holders to position the rack 4 to 6 inches from the broiler element. Heat the element, then slip the skillet onto the rack and broil until the top is lightly browned, 1 to 2 minutes. Cool for at least 5 minutes before serving.

Slow-Cooker Lasagna with Sausage and Arugula

Makes 6 servings

By using a slow cooker to make lasagna, you don't have to boil dried lasagna noodles—and you don't have to resort to no-boil noodles which can end up gummy and unappetizing. The trick here is to break the dried pasta to fit the shape of your slow cooker (whether round or oval), making even layers of pasta as you build the lasagna.

2 tablespoons olive oil

1½ pounds bulk sweet Italian sausage (that is, the meat without any casings)

3 cups packed baby arugula leaves, chopped

½ teaspoon table salt

3 tablespoons unsalted butter

3 tablespoons all-purpose flour

3 cups whole, low-fat, or fat-free milk

1½ cups finely grated Parmigiano-Reggiano (about 3 ounces)

2 large egg yolks, well beaten in a small bowl

Up to ½ teaspoon grated nutmeg

4 cups (1 quart) plain marinara sauce, store-bought or homemade (page 98)

1 pound uncooked dried lasagna noodles

1. Heat the oil in a large skillet set over medium heat. Add the sausage and brown well, stirring occasionally, about 5 minutes.

2. Drain the grease. Add the arugula and salt to the skillet and stir over the heat until wilted, just a few seconds. Set aside.

3. In a large saucepan, melt the butter over medium-low heat, then whisk in the flour until the mixture forms a thick paste. Cook, whisking constantly, for no more than 30 seconds, just to get rid of the raw flour taste. Do not allow the mixture to brown. Whisk in the milk in a slow, steady stream and continue cooking, whisking almost constantly, until the mixture bubbles and thickens, 3 to 4 minutes.

4. Remove from the heat and whisk in 1 cup of the Parmigiano-Reggiano along with the egg yolks and nutmeg. Continue whisking until smooth, then set aside.

Test Kitchen Notes

- If your slow cooker has a nonstick finish, use only nonstick-safe utensils.

- This lasagna is made without ricotta (or—heaven forfend!—cottage cheese). You'll make a thickened Parmesan sauce to add more moisture to the slow cooker as the lasagna cooks.

- You can make a gluten-free version of this lasagna by substituting uncooked dried gluten-free lasagna noodles (ones that require cooking, not just soaking). Some of these from Italian makers are quite toothsome and even stand up better than more standard wheat lasagna noodles. To make a gluten-free cheese sauce, melt the butter as directed, then omit the flour and whisk 3 tablespoons potato starch into the milk in a large bowl until smooth before adding this mixture to the pan. Whisk *constantly* over low heat until thickened (potato starch has a tendency to fall out of suspension and burn on the bottom of the pot). And one more thing: Make sure the sausage is gluten-free, without any wheat as a binder.

RECIPE CONTINUES ▶▶

- For an electric multi-pot (a pressure-cooker and slow-cooker hybrid), which is often taller than most slow cookers, adjust the layering to create one more pasta/marinara/meat/cheese sauce layer.

- Admittedly, the first piece of this lasagna will be scooped out, not cut. In fact, this casserole is probably more scooped than cut.

5. Spoon a thin layer of marinara sauce into the bottom of a 5- to 6-quart slow cooker. Cover the sauce with about a third of the noodles, breaking them to fit and patching them together in one layer. Spoon a third of the remaining marinara sauce over the noodles, sprinkle a third of the meat over the sauce, and top with a third of the cheese sauce.

6. Make two more layers of noodles, marinara, meat, and cheese. Sprinkle the remaining ½ cup Parmigiano-Reggiano evenly over the top.

7. Cover and cook on low for 4 hours. The lasagna can be kept on the machine's keep-warm setting for up to 2 hours.

Meat-Grinder Udon

Makes 2 main-course or 4 light-meal servings (can be doubled)

Fresh udon is a thing of beauty: thick, chewy noodles that take to soups and stews like nothing else. Unfortunately, fresh udon is also quite rare in North America, mostly because it's very fragile and doesn't transport well. Here's a shortcut way to make udon using a meat grinder. (Even the gizmo on a stand mixer will work.) Serve in udon broth (see **More!**) or tossed with Spicy and Crunchy Peanut-Sesame Sauce (page 244). Or drop them into a pot of chicken or beef soup for an unbelievable treat. Or use them as a bed for your favorite beef, pork, or chicken braise.

2½ cups all-purpose flour, plus more for the noodles

2 teaspoons table salt

⅔ to ¾ cup cool water

1. Mix the flour and salt in a large bowl, then add ⅔ cup water and stir until a rough dough forms, adding more water in small increments just to get the dough to cohere without being sticky.

2. Dust a clean, dry work surface with flour. Knead the dough until smooth and supple, about 10 minutes. Set aside, covered with a clean kitchen towel, to rest for 1 hour.

3. Assemble a meat grinder with the fine die grind plate in place but without the blade behind it.

4. Turn the machine on high and drop small balls of the dough into the feed tube, pushing them down with the auger. Keep adding more balls until the noodles start to extrude and reach about 10 inches. Stop the machine and use kitchen shears to cut the noodles free.

5. Pull apart any noodles that are stuck together. Toss them with a little flour, make a small nest of them, and set this nest on a large baking sheet. Then soldier on, making more noodles from small balls of the dough. Covered with a clean, dry kitchen towel, the noodles can remain at room temperature for up to 1 hour.

6. To cook the noodles, bring a large pot of water to a boil over high heat. Add the noodles and cook for 5 minutes before testing for doneness. The noodles should have a definite chew but without any raw, sticky feel. If necessary, cook for 1 or 2 minutes longer, then drain in a colander set in the sink.

Test Kitchen Notes

- These noodles are not like egg-based Italian fresh pasta. They're plainer but with an incredible texture.

- Kneading the dough is tough. Get ready to give your fingers a workout. Japanese home cooks sometimes seal the dough in a plastic bag, then knead it with their feet while they're knitting or reading.

 More! To make the classic udon broth, combine 3 cups store-bought dashi (a seaweed and fish broth), ½ cup soy sauce, and ½ cup mirin in a saucepan. Bring to a simmer, then pour over the cooked noodles in bowls. Garnish with thinly sliced scallions.

MISE YOUR KITCHEN

People who cook fast know the importance of *mise-en-place,* a French term that means "set in place," often shortened in English to just *mise* ("meez"), as in the cheffy question, "Have you done your *mise*?" In other words, have you chopped, diced, or otherwise prepared your ingredients, gotten out the necessary equipment, and laid it all within easy reach, so that completing the dish is little more than tossing things into the skillet or pan?

The notion of a proper *mise* holds for your home kitchen as well. Learn to set things in place to make your environment efficient. If you're running hither and yon to find your spices or dig out a saucepan from a pile of plastic containers, you're wasting time and energy. To that end:

1. Have a spice drawer. If you can afford the space, lay the bottles of dried herbs and spices in a drawer near your work area. It's easier to see them all serried up, rather than having to dig through bottles on a shelf.

2. Declutter your counters. You need room to work, so open up precious countertop real estate. Do you need decorative frippery in the kitchen? Put away that big fruit bowl until it's actually filled with fruit.

3. Declutter your drawers. Don't dig for measuring spoons; organize those drawers! Especially your knife drawer. You can get a nasty cut digging through it. In fact, knives should never be stored free-floating in a drawer. Buy a holder that's specifically made for drawers. We do not recommend a magnetic, wall-mount knife holder, especially in a home kitchen overrun with children.

4. Center your storage on your stove. Arrange your kitchen so that the things you use at the stove are near it. Move your pots, pans, whisks, and wooden spoons to the cabinets and drawers nearby so you have them at ready access. You don't need the flatware near your burners!

5. Stack sealable containers and baking dishes in the cabinets. If they're jammed willy-nilly on the shelf, they can fall out of the cabinet when you open the doors. A little investment in neatness really pays off.

6. Hang your pots and pans. If you want to free up cabinet space, a hanging rack is a great way to keep your cookware within reach. As a bonus, you won't stack nonstick skillets or pans on top of each other, a good way to nick them and ruin the coating.

7. Don't forget to mise the refrigerator. Put the things you use often near the front of the shelves. The milk should be in front of the fish sauce—unless you're making a ton of Thai dishes! That said, don't store milk in the fridge door where it will be subject to greater temperature fluctuations.

COLANDER
PASTA SUPPERS

Why would you waste the hot water used to cook pasta? By pouring it over vegetables (or even shrimp) in a colander, you can cook right in the sink without much effort at all! But a couple of warnings: You'll need a large, 5-quart colander. And you'll need to make sure you don't finely chop or mince anything that could fall through the colander's holes. The Thai noodle recipe uses gluten-free rice noodles. Feel free to substitute gluten-free ziti or linguine in the first two recipes as well. However, be sure to use dried gluten-free noodles that must be cooked on the stove (not just softened in a bowl); read the package instructions before buying.

Colander Ziti with Ham, Asparagus, and Parmesan Cream Sauce

FASTER

GLUTEN-FREE

Makes 4 servings

This luxurious pasta dish provides a quick meal for a weeknight—and a cream sauce without another pan to clean. The only trick is to use thin asparagus spears with no thick, fibrous ends. As long as you work in the stated timings, the egg yolks will cook to a safe temperature without curdling. However, if you're concerned or are cooking for someone with a compromised immune system, look for pasteurized, in-the-shell eggs at larger supermarkets.

6 ounces very thin asparagus stalks, trimmed and cut into 1-inch pieces (about 1½ cups)

7 ounces diced smoked ham (about 1 cup)

¾ cup heavy cream

4 large egg yolks, at room temperature

¾ cup finely grated Parmigiano-Reggiano (about 1½ ounces)

1½ tablespoons chopped fresh tarragon leaves

½ teaspoon ground black pepper

¼ teaspoon table salt

12 ounces dried ziti (gluten-free if that is a concern)

1. Bring a large saucepan or pot of water to a boil over high heat.

2. Meanwhile, put the asparagus and ham in a colander set in the sink.

3. Whisk the cream, yolks, cheese, tarragon, pepper, and salt in a large, heat-safe serving bowl until creamy and smooth.

4. Pour the ziti into the boiling water. Cook according to the package directions just until tender to the bite but with some chew, 6 to 9 minutes depending on the brand.

5. Slowly drain the pasta and its cooking water over the asparagus and ham in the colander. Set aside for 1 minute.

6. Whisk the cream mixture one more time. Dump the hot mixture from the colander on top of the sauce and toss well, stirring until the cheese melts and the pasta is evenly coated. Serve at once.

Test Kitchen Notes

- If you can only find thick spears of asparagus, buy about 8 ounces and shave them down with a vegetable peeler before cutting them into sections.

- By putting the spears in the colander, not in the pot with cooking pasta, you keep the vegetable crunchy, not mushy.

Voilà! In general, the water for cooking pasta should be quite salty, more so than just a pinch of salt for a pan of, say, vegetables. Pasta cooking water should taste about like sea water (about 1 tablespoon table salt per quart of water). *That said,* in these colander pasta suppers, *don't* salt the water to this extent since it's a cooking medium for other things beyond the pasta. In fact, we let the sauce carry the salt in this modified pasta technique.

FASTER

GLUTEN-FREE

Thai-Inspired Basil Colander Noodles

Makes 4 servings

Test Kitchen Notes

- For less heat, halve the chiles and remove the seeds and their membranes before slicing. Work with rubber gloves if you're sensitive to a chile's heat.

- Look for oyster sauce, a sticky-sweet Asian condiment, near the soy sauce in larger supermarkets. Its thickeners often contain gluten. If that is a concern, look for gluten-free oyster sauce from online suppliers.

- Fresh rice noodles are too soft for this dish. Use dried rice noodles for better texture. These can be tricky to track down. Look for them in health-food stores and very large, gourmet supermarkets.

Voilà! Don't add oil to the water as pasta cooks. The oil makes the noodles so slick that the sauce has a hard time sticking to them.

Here's a stir-fry without a wok! Cook the chicken in the pot, then add the pasta. (We can't put the chicken in a colander and expect it to cook through as in other versions of this technique.) When you drain the noodles, the hot water will then soften the shallots (getting rid of their raw-onion flavor) and soften the bite of the chiles.

2 or 3 medium fresh jalapeño chiles or 1 or 2 fresh long green Anaheim chiles, stemmed and thinly sliced into rings

2 medium shallots, thinly sliced into very thin rings

½ cup chicken broth

⅓ cup roasted unsalted peanuts

½ cup packed basil leaves, roughly chopped

6 tablespoons oyster sauce

2 tablespoons fish sauce

1 tablespoon hot red pepper sauce, such as Sriracha

1 tablespoon granulated white sugar

1 pound boneless skinless chicken breasts, thinly sliced as if for stir-fry

12 ounces uncooked dried wide rice noodles

1. Bring a large saucepan or pot of water to a boil over high heat.

2. Meanwhile, put the chiles and shallots in a large colander set in the sink.

3. Put the broth, peanuts, basil, oyster sauce, fish sauce, pepper sauce, and sugar in a large, heat-safe serving bowl.

4. Drop the chicken into the boiling water. Cook for 5 minutes at a high boil.

5. Add the noodles and cook just until they're tender, about 2 minutes, stirring a few times.

6. Slowly drain the chicken, noodles, and their cooking water over the chiles and shallots. Let it alone for 1 minute.

7. Pour the still-hot ingredients in the colander into the serving bowl. Toss well until the noodles are coated in the sauce and everything is evenly distributed throughout. Serve at once.

FASTER

GLUTEN-FREE

Colander Linguine with Spicy Buttery Shrimp, Lemon, and Peppers

Makes 4 servings

Test Kitchen Notes

- You must use small shrimp so they cook quickly when soused with the boiling water. Do not use tiny "salad" shrimp.

- If you can only find medium shrimp (about 30 per pound), butterfly each one by slicing open (without splitting it in half) from tip to tail.

- Pour the hot water (and pasta) slowly into the colander so that you get the maximum amount of heat against the shrimp.

While this recipe gives you a great weeknight meal, consider it a template for a host of buttery shrimp and pasta main courses. Feel free to swap out the oregano for your favorite herb and perhaps replace the bell pepper strips with broccoli florets, thin yellow squash rounds, and/or thawed frozen artichoke heart quarters.

1 pound small shrimp (40 to 50), peeled and deveined

2 medium red bell peppers, cored, seeded, and thinly sliced into strips

⅔ cup chicken broth

6 tablespoons (¾ stick) unsalted butter, cut into small bits

¼ cup white vermouth or dry white wine

Grated zest of 1 medium lemon (about 2 teaspoons)

1 teaspoon minced garlic

1 teaspoon dried oregano

Up to ½ teaspoon red pepper flakes

¼ teaspoon table salt

12 ounces linguine (gluten-free if that is a concern)

1. Bring a large saucepan or pot of water to a boil over high heat.

2. Meanwhile, put the shrimp and bell pepper strips in a large colander set in the sink.

3. Combine the broth, butter, vermouth, lemon zest, garlic, oregano, red pepper flakes, and salt in a large, heat-safe serving bowl.

4. Pour the linguine into the boiling water and cook according to the package directions until tender but still slightly chewy, 6 to 8 minutes depending on the brand.

5. Slowly pour the pasta and its cooking liquid into the colander to drain. Rearrange the pasta as necessary to cover the shrimp. Set aside for 2 minutes or until the shrimp are pink and firm.

6. Pour the still-hot pasta mixture into the bowl with the broth mixture. Toss well until the butter melts and coats the pasta evenly. Serve at once.

ONE-POT STOVETOP PASTA SUPPERS

Here's the math: It takes 10 to 12 minutes to bring a pot of water to a boil, then another 5 to 8 minutes to cook dried pasta. In just about the same amount of time, you can create an entire pasta meal by cooking dried pasta in the liquid used to create a sauce in a skillet or a saucepan—without waiting for a pot to boil.

Yes, you must adjust liquid amounts accordingly. But cooking the pasta in the sauce gives it much more flavor than cooking it in water alone. What's more, the dish is completed all in one pot, not two (or three). Just watch the stirring guidelines in each of these recipes: no stirring, then much more, and finally all the time—all to keep the pasta from sticking. All that stirring also dislodges some of the pasta's starch into the sauce, further thickening it.

One-Pot Chorizo Mac and Chickpeas

Makes 6 servings

Chorizo comes in two forms: dried, a Spanish specialty; and "fresh" (that is, raw), sometimes called "Mexican chorizo," the sort called for here. Look for it in the butcher case of larger supermarkets. It's a highly spiced sausage, a hot pop against all the cheese and pasta in this main-course version of mac and cheese.

2 tablespoons olive oil

1 small yellow onion, chopped

1 medium green bell pepper, cored, seeded, and chopped

2 medium celery stalks, chopped

1 pound fresh chorizo sausage, any casings removed

One 28-ounce can diced tomatoes, preferably no-salt-added

2 cups chicken broth

One 15-ounce can chickpeas, drained and rinsed

2 tablespoons mild paprika

1 tablespoon dried oregano

1 teaspoon fennel seeds

7 ounces dried ziti (or gluten-free dried penne if gluten is a concern)

2 cups finely grated pepper Jack cheese (about 8 ounces)

1. Warm the olive oil in a Dutch oven set over medium heat. Add the onion, bell pepper, and celery. Cook, stirring often, until softened, about 4 minutes.

2. Crumble in the chorizo and brown well, stirring often, about 4 minutes.

3. Stir in the diced tomatoes, broth, chickpeas, paprika, oregano, and fennel seeds until uniform.

4. Stir in the pasta. Bring to a full simmer, then cover and reduce the heat to low. Simmer slowly for 5 minutes. Then continue simmering, covered but stirring often, for 10 minutes. Finally, simmer uncovered, stirring almost constantly to prevent sticking, until the pasta is tender, about 5 minutes longer.

5. Remove from the heat and sprinkle the cheese on top. Cover and set aside for 5 minutes to blend the flavors and absorb any remaining liquid.

Test Kitchen Notes

- Larger supermarkets may carry loose chorizo sausage meat—so you won't have to bother to take it out of its casings.

- Canned fire-roasted tomatoes will add more flavor than regular diced tomatoes.

- If using gluten-free pasta, substitute penne, often thicker than gluten-free ziti and better able to stand up to this technique.

- You need lots of space to cook the pasta. Do not use a large saucepan rather than the Dutch oven.

One-Pot Orzo with Artichokes and Tomatoes

Makes 6 servings

Test Kitchen Notes

- A heat-safe silicone or wooden spatula is a better tool than a wooden spoon to keep the dish from sticking at the end of its cooking.

- Use only frozen artichoke heart *quarters,* not the larger artichoke hearts. Or substitute one 14-ounce can or jar of artichoke hearts packed in water for the frozen ones; drain and cut each into quarters.

- For the best flavor, buy a block of feta packed in salt water, rather than pre-crumbled feta. Crumble it into bits about the size of the orzo.

Voilà! Save the liquid from any feta or fresh mozzarella container to add to your pasta sauce for extra flavor.

Think of this as a pasta version of a Greek-inspired risotto. Tiny orzo pasta is cooked in a sauce loaded with veggies and spices, then tossed with plenty of cheese. For a larger meal, consider using this orzo dish as the base for swordfish or shrimp kebabs.

2 tablespoons olive oil

1 small yellow onion, chopped

1 medium yellow bell pepper, stemmed, cored, and chopped

2 teaspoons minced garlic

1 pound fresh plum tomatoes, chopped

2 teaspoons dried oregano

2 teaspoons dried dill

½ teaspoon ground cinnamon

½ teaspoon table salt

4 cups (1 quart) vegetable broth

12 ounces dried orzo

9 ounces frozen artichoke heart quarters, thawed

1½ cups crumbled feta (about 8 ounces)

1. Warm the olive oil in a Dutch oven set over medium heat. Add the onion, bell pepper, and garlic; cook, stirring often, until the onion turns translucent, about 3 minutes.

2. Stir in the tomatoes, oregano, dill, cinnamon, and salt. Cook, stirring occasionally, until the tomatoes begin to soften and collapse, about 4 minutes.

3. Stir in the broth, orzo, and artichoke quarters. Bring to a full simmer, then cover and reduce the heat to low. Simmer slowly for 5 minutes. Then continue simmering, covered but stirring often, for 5 minutes. Finally, simmer uncovered, stirring almost constantly to prevent sticking, until the pasta is tender, about 5 minutes longer.

4. Remove from the heat, crumble the feta on top, and stir well. Cover and set aside for 5 minutes to blend the flavors and absorb any remaining liquid.

One-Pot Creamy Mushroom Pasta Supper

Makes 4 servings

Because of the milk and cream in the sauce, it's even more important to watch for sticking as you stir the pasta here, particularly toward the end as some of the starch from the pasta starts to thicken the sauce. In fact, this recipe calls for whole-wheat pasta to cut down on some of that attendant starchiness that would make the dish too gummy.

2 tablespoons unsalted butter

1 small yellow onion, chopped

8 ounces cremini mushrooms, thinly sliced

2 tablespoons all-purpose flour

2 cups vegetable broth

1½ cups whole or low-fat milk

½ cup heavy cream

1 teaspoon dried thyme

1 teaspoon dried sage

½ teaspoon table salt

½ teaspoon ground black pepper

10 ounces dried whole-wheat ziti (or dried gluten-free penne if gluten is a concern)

1 cup finely grated Parmigiano-Reggiano or aged Pecorino (about 2 ounces)

1. Melt the butter in a Dutch oven set over medium heat. Add the onion and cook, stirring occasionally, until softened, about 3 minutes.

2. Add the mushrooms and continue cooking, stirring often, until the mushrooms release their liquid and the pan dries out again, about 4 minutes.

3. Stir in the flour until the mushrooms and onions are well and evenly coated. Pour in the broth in a slow stream, stirring constantly. Stir in the milk, cream, thyme, sage, salt, and pepper.

4. The minute the sauce is steaming hot and just beginning to bubble, stir in the ziti. Bring to a full simmer, then cover and reduce the heat to low. Simmer slowly, stirring often, for 5 minutes. Then continue simmering, covered but stirring more often, for 10 minutes. Finally, simmer uncovered, stirring almost constantly to prevent sticking, until the pasta is tender, about 5 minutes longer.

5. Remove from the heat and stir in the cheese. Cover and set aside for 5 minutes to blend the flavors and absorb any remaining liquid.

Test Kitchen Notes

- Cremini—sometimes called "baby bella" mushrooms—have lots of flavor but will turn the sauce a little dark. Substitute white button mushrooms for pickier eaters.

- In step 2, make sure the moisture from the mushrooms evaporates so the pasta doesn't end up too soupy.

EASY DUMPLINGS
FOR STEWS
AND BRAISES

Store-bought pizza dough is a secret weapon for way more than pizza! Rather than stirring a dough together, make toothsome, satisfying dumplings by setting lumps of that dough right on top of a stew. For these recipes, use only fresh pizza dough, not canned (and of course not the prebaked crusts you find at the supermarket).

You can buy raw fresh dough in the refrigerator case of many large supermarkets (often in the dairy or shredded cheese section) and at many pizza parlors (although not necessarily at the big chains).

And here's a bonus. These recipes can be *much* faster if you use the pressure-cooker alternative, found in the **More!** section immediately after each recipe.

Dump-and-Simmer Chicken Stew with No-Work Dumplings

EASIER

Makes 4 hearty servings

Not only are we using pizza dough to make easy dumplings, we're also making a super-flavorful chicken dinner by stewing chicken thighs with vegetables. You'll create a crazy delicious supper—and save lots of work on the dumplings. (The pressure-cooker version below saves even more time.)

2 to 2½ pounds bone-in skin-on chicken thighs

1 large yellow onion, roughly chopped

3 medium carrots, peeled and chopped

2 medium celery stalks, chopped

One 14-ounce can chicken broth

1 teaspoon minced garlic

½ teaspoon kosher salt, plus more as needed

1 bay leaf

Water as needed

Up to 2 tablespoons chopped fresh parsley leaves

½ pound fresh pizza dough

Ground black pepper, to taste

1. Place the chicken, onion, carrots, celery, broth, garlic, salt, and bay leaf in a Dutch oven. Add enough water so the ingredients are covered by 2 inches.

2. Bring to a boil over high heat, stirring occasionally. Cover, reduce the heat to low, and simmer until the chicken is very tender, about 1 hour.

3. Turn off the heat and transfer the chicken thighs to a cutting board. Cool for 10 minutes or so, just until you can handle them.

4. Pull the skin off the thighs and discard. Debone and chop the meat. Stir the meat back into the stew, add the parsley, and bring it back to a low simmer over medium-high heat.

5. Break the pizza dough into 8 balls; drop these on top of the stew. Cover, reduce the heat to low, and simmer slowly until the dumplings are puffed and cooked through, 15 to 20 minutes. Discard the bay leaf. Season with salt and pepper to taste.

Test Kitchen Notes

- For more flavor, toss a chicken back or even a chicken neck into the pot. Just remember to pull it out before serving.

- If desired, stir in up to ½ cup heavy cream with the chopped, deboned meat in step 4.

- A Dutch oven will work but a wide, high-sided pot, like a large sauté pan or an enamel-coated, cast-iron casserole (sometimes called a "French casserole") will work even better because there'll be more space for the dumplings to spread without fusing.

 More! To make the stew in a pressure cooker, complete step 1 in a stovetop or electric pressure cooker. Lock the lid onto the pot and bring it to high pressure. Cook at high pressure for 15 minutes in a stovetop pot (15 psi) or for 23 minutes in an electric pot (9 to 11 psi). Use the quick-release method to bring the pressure back to normal. Complete step 3 as written. Then complete step 4 with the stovetop pot set over medium heat or the electric pot turned to its simmer function. Do not lock the lid onto the pot or engage the pressure valve when you cover the pot in step 5.

EASIER

No-Bean Chili with No-Work Cheesy Dumplings

Makes 4 hearty servings

Test Kitchen Notes

- Use 2 pounds lean ground beef if you can't find *lean* ground pork.

- Substitute unsalted butter for the neutral-flavored oil for a richer chili. Or go all out and use walnut oil for a decidedly elegant flavor at the bottom of the homey stew.

Here's a hearty, satisfying, wintry meal. Yes, it takes some time to simmer the chili but the effort's worth it because the dumplings are so soft and light. Note that these dumplings are steamed, not baked. They won't brown very much, but stay a pale beige color. If this bothers you, sprinkle them with mild paprika before steaming to give them some color. Top the chili with pickle relish, pickled sliced jalapeño chiles, sliced radishes, and/or diced avocado.

2 tablespoons canola or vegetable oil

1 medium yellow onion, chopped

1 medium green bell pepper or 2 medium Anaheim peppers, stemmed, cored, and chopped

1 pound lean ground beef

1 pound lean ground pork

¼ cup chile powder

1 tablespoon ground cumin

2 teaspoons dried thyme

2 teaspoons minced garlic

½ teaspoon table salt

Up to ½ teaspoon ground cloves

One 28-ounce can crushed tomatoes, preferably no-salt-added

2 cups no-salt-added chicken broth

½ pound fresh pizza dough

1 cup finely shredded Cheddar (about 4 ounces)

1. Heat the oil in a Dutch oven set over medium heat. Add the onion and pepper(s); cook, stirring often, until the onion turns translucent and softens a bit, about 4 minutes.

2. Crumble in the ground beef and pork. Cook, stirring often to break up the chunks, until lightly browned throughout, about 4 minutes.

3. Stir in the chile powder, cumin, thyme, garlic, salt, and cloves. Cook, stirring, until aromatic, less than 1 minute. Pour in the tomatoes and broth; bring to a full simmer.

RECIPE CONTINUES ➡️

4. Cover, reduce the heat to low, and simmer slowly for 1 hour, stirring occasionally.

5. Meanwhile, roll the dough out into a very rough 6- to 8-inch square. Sprinkle the cheese over the dough, then knead in the cheese, turning the dough onto itself, folding and refolding it, all while pulling and twisting to get the cheese distributed throughout. Divide the dough into 8 portions; roll each into a ball, place on a plate, cover with plastic wrap, and refrigerate until the chili is done simmering.

6. Drop the dough balls on top of the chili. Cover and continue simmering slowly until the dumplings are puffed and cooked through, 15 to 20 minutes. Let stand for a couple of minutes off the heat before serving.

 More! To make the chili in a pressure cooker, complete the recipe through step 3 in a stovetop pressure cooker set over medium heat or an electric pressure cooker turned to its browning or sauté function. Once the tomatoes and broth are in the pot, lock on the lid and bring it to high pressure. Cook at high pressure for 12 minutes in the stovetop cooker (15 psi) or for 18 minutes in the electric cooker (9 to 11 psi). As the chili cooks, complete step 5. Use the quick-release method to bring the pot's pressure back to normal. Unlock and remove the lid, then complete step 6 with the stovetop pot set over medium-low heat or the electric pot turned to its simmer function. When covering the pot in step 6, do not lock it in place or engage the pressure valve.

Creamy Pork and Cabbage Stew with Caraway Dumplings

EASIER

Makes 4 hearty servings

Pork shoulder makes this quite a rich dish. For a somewhat leaner dish, use boneless leg meat, sometimes called "fresh ham" (that is, not cured or smoked). But don't even consider substituting cut-up boneless center-cut pork chops or pork loin because they'll end up dry and tough. Instead, just go for it.

2 tablespoons unsalted butter

2 pounds boneless skinless pork shoulder, trimmed and cut into 2-inch pieces

1 medium yellow onion, sliced into thin half-moons

1 tablespoon all-purpose flour

1 cup unsweetened apple cider

1 cup chicken broth

½ cup heavy cream

1 tablespoon Dijon mustard

1 teaspoon dried sage

1 teaspoon dried thyme

½ teaspoon table salt

½ teaspoon ground black pepper

3 cups shredded cored green cabbage

1½ teaspoons caraway seeds

½ pound fresh pizza dough

1. Melt 1 tablespoon of the butter in a high-sided sauté pan or skillet set over medium heat. Add half the meat and brown it well, turning occasionally, about 4 minutes. Transfer to a bowl. Add the remaining 1 tablespoon butter and the rest of the meat and brown it well, then transfer to the bowl.

2. Add the onion to the pan and cook, stirring occasionally, until lightly browned, about 5 minutes. Sprinkle the flour over the top and stir to coat. Cook a few seconds, then pour in the cider and stock, stirring until the flour dissolves. Bring the mixture to a simmer, stirring constantly.

3. Stir in the cream, mustard, sage, thyme, salt, and pepper until smooth. Stir the meat and any juices into the pan.

4. Cover, reduce the heat to low, and simmer slowly, stirring occasionally, until the meat is very tender, about 2 hours.

5. Stir in the cabbage and cook for 10 minutes. Meanwhile, knead the caraway seeds into the pizza dough, turning it onto itself, folding and refolding it, all while pulling and twisting it to get the seeds distributed uniformly throughout. Divide the prepared dough into 8 even balls.

6. Drop the dough balls into the stew, cover, and simmer slowly until the dumplings are puffed up and cooked through, about 15 minutes longer.

Test Kitchen Notes

- For an even easier prep, substitute 3 cups bagged slaw mix for the shredded cored cabbage.

- To slice an onion into thin half-moons, vertically slice it in half (through the stem), then set these halves cut side down on a cutting board. Now make thin slices across the onion.

 More! To make this stew in a pressure cooker, complete the recipe through step 3 in a stovetop pressure cooker over medium heat or an electric pressure cooker on the browning or sauté function. Once the meat is back in the mix, lock the lid on the pot and bring it to high pressure. Cook at high pressure for 25 minutes in a stovetop pot (15 psi) or for 40 minutes in an electric pot (9 to 11 psi). Use the quick-release method to bring the pot's pressure back to normal, then complete steps 5 and 6, either by setting the stovetop pot over medium-low heat or by turning the electric pot to its simmer function. When covering the pot in step 6, do not lock it in place or engage the pressure valve.

EASY FRIED DUMPLINGS AND STUFFED ROLLS

Fresh bread makes the easiest dumplings and stuffed rolls. But it's got to be *fresh* bread. If it's stale, it won't roll into the thin, pasta-like sheets that are necessary to make these delicious appetizers and finger foods.

What's more, plain "whipped" bread (think Wonder Bread) won't work because it's too soft and light to hold up to any fillings. And don't look to the bakery section of the store. Those breads are too coarse and too chewy. You're looking for the standard, North American sandwich bread, brands like Pepperidge Farm, found in the bread aisle of most supermarkets.

Store any unused bread slices in the freezer until you want to make another round of these. All the dumplings and rolls can be assembled up to 4 hours in advance; place them on a large plate, cover tightly with plastic wrap, and refrigerate until you're ready to fry them.

Spicy Herbed Goat Cheese Hand Pies

Makes 12 hand pies

These are sweet and savory little pies, each one a big bite of flavor. Take care: They can be quite hot inside, so cool them for a few minutes before serving. Potato bread has more sugar than, say, rye bread, and browns very quickly, much faster than some other breads. Keep your eye on these as they fry. Turn them often but allow them to get quite brown for the best crunch. If you don't like goat cheese, use a 50/50 combo of farmer's cheese and regular cream cheese.

12 ounces soft goat cheese, cool but not cold

1 teaspoon fresh thyme leaves

1 teaspoon red pepper flakes

12 potato bread slices (about 1¼ ounces per slice)

About 2 cups canola oil

6 tablespoons honey

1. Mix the cheese, thyme, and red pepper flakes in a small bowl until uniform.

2. Cut the crusts off the bread slices. On a clean, dry work surface, use a rolling pin to roll each one to a flattened square, less than ¼ inch thick, but not really larger than the original slice, just more compressed.

3. Put a small bowl of water near your work space. Place about 1½ tablespoons of the cheese mixture in the middle of one piece of flattened bread. Dip a clean finger in the water and moisten the four edges of the bread. Fold the bread square crosswise in half, thus surrounding the filling. Press the edges firmly together to seal. Set aside and make 11 more small hand pies.

4. Pour enough oil into a 10-inch round high-sided skillet or sauté pan to make a depth of about 1 inch. Clip a deep-frying thermometer to the inside of the pan, set it over medium heat, and bring the oil up to 350°F.

5. Fry the hand pies two or three at a time, turning once, until golden and crisp, about 1 minute per batch. Transfer to a wire rack to drain and continue until all the rolls have been fried. To serve, cool for a few minutes, then drizzle the honey over the rolls, about ½ tablespoon for each.

Reuben Rolls with Spicy-Hot Russian Dip

Makes 12 rolls

TASTIER

Spice up your next party with these easy, newfangled eggrolls, a sort of deli fusion: the filling for a Reuben sandwich in a crisp, light shell.

½ cup finely chopped deli corned beef (about 2½ ounces)

6 tablespoons roughly chopped drained sauerkraut

¼ cup shredded Swiss cheese (about 1 ounce)

¾ cup regular or low-fat mayonnaise

3 tablespoons pickle relish or mild chow chow

2 tablespoons ketchup

Up to 1 tablespoon minced drained pickled jalapeño rings

12 fresh rye bread slices, preferably seeded rye (about 1¼ ounces per slice)

About 2 cups canola oil

1. Combine the corned beef, sauerkraut, and cheese in a large bowl. Set the filling aside.

2. Mix the mayonnaise, relish, ketchup, and minced jalapeño in a small serving bowl until uniform. Set the dip aside as well.

3. Cut the crusts off the bread slices. On a clean, dry work surface, use a rolling pin to roll each one to a flattened square, less than ¼ inch thick, but not larger than the original slice, just very compressed.

4. Put a small bowl of water near your work space. Place about 1½ tablespoons of the corned beef filling in the middle of one piece of flattened bread. Using clean fingers, dip them in the water and moisten the four edges of the bread. Fold the bread square crosswise in half, thus surrounding the filling. Press the edges firmly together to seal. Set aside and make 11 more filled rolls.

5. Pour enough oil into a 10-inch round high-sided skillet or sauté pan to make a depth of about 1 inch. Clip a deep-frying thermometer to the inside of the pan, set it over medium heat, and bring the oil up to 350°F.

6. Fry two or three of the rolls at a time, turning once, until golden and crisp, about 2 minutes per batch. Transfer to a wire rack and continue frying more. Serve with the dip on the side.

Fried Potato Dumplings with Spiced Cranberry Sauce

Makes 12 dumplings

These are sort of like samosas—but certainly easier to make. They can be a terrific dinner with a chopped salad on the side—or great snacks for an afternoon on the deck. Remember: Use supermarket, bread-aisle rye bread, not the fancy stuff from the bakery. If you don't want to make the cranberry sauce, serve with store-bought cranberry chutney or cranberry relish.

2 cups fresh or frozen cranberries (about 7 ounces)

⅓ cup water

¼ cup granulated white sugar

¼ cup honey

2 tablespoons apple cider vinegar

½ teaspoon ground cinnamon

½ teaspoon ground dried ginger

¼ teaspoon ground cloves

¼ teaspoon table salt

2 medium Yukon Gold potatoes (about 9 ounces total), peeled and diced

1 tablespoon unsalted butter

1 tablespoon plain yogurt

2 teaspoons yellow curry powder

12 fresh rye bread slices, preferably seeded rye (about 1¼ ounces per slice)

About 2 cups peanut or canola oil

1. Stir the cranberries, water, sugar, honey, vinegar, cinnamon, dried ginger, cloves, and salt in a large saucepan set over medium heat until the sugar dissolves. Bring to a simmer, then reduce the heat to low and simmer slowly until the berries are soft and the sauce has thickened a bit, about 20 minutes. Set the sauce aside to cool for at least 30 minutes or up to 3 hours.

2. Fill a large saucepan with water, add the potatoes, and bring it to a boil over high heat. Boil until the potatoes are tender and easily pierced with a fork, about 15 minutes.

3. Drain the potatoes in a colander set in the sink. Pour them into a medium bowl and add the butter, yogurt, and curry powder. Use a potato masher or a pastry cutter to mash thoroughly, until no lumps remain. Cool the potato filling for 10 minutes.

4. Meanwhile, cut the crusts off the bread slices. On a clean, dry work surface, use a rolling pin to roll each one to a flattened square, less than ¼ inch thick but not really larger than the original slice, just much more compressed.

5. Put a small bowl of water near your work space. Place about 1½ tablespoons of the potato filling in the middle of one piece of bread. Using clean fingers, dip them in the water and moisten the four edges of the bread. Fold the bread square crosswise in half, enclosing the filling. Press the edges firmly together to seal. Set aside and make 11 more filled dumplings.

6. Pour enough oil into a 10-inch high-sided skillet or sauté pan to make a depth of about 1 inch. Clip a deep-frying thermometer to the inside of the pan, set it over medium heat, and bring the oil up to 350°F.

7. Fry the stuffed dumplings two or three at a time, turning once, until golden and crisp, about 2 minutes per batch. Transfer to a wire rack to drain and continue until all the dumplings have been fried. Serve with the cranberry sauce spooned on top or on the side.

FASTER

Ham and Caraway Mini Pasties

Makes 12 pasties

Well, they're mini only in comparison to some of the giant ones that come out of some pasty shops. These are also much lighter, if absurdly easy. Serve with grainy mustard or honey mustard.

1 tablespoon unsalted butter

1 small yellow onion, finely chopped

½ cup finely chopped smoked deli ham (about 1¾ ounces)

2 tablespoons raisins, finely chopped

1 teaspoon caraway seeds

1 teaspoon dried dill

12 fresh rye bread slices, preferably a seeded rye (about 1¼ ounces per slice)

About 2 cups canola oil

1. Melt the butter in a small skillet set over medium heat. Add the onion and cook, stirring often, until softened but not yet begun to brown, about 3 minutes. Scrape the contents of the skillet into a medium bowl. Stir in the ham, raisins, caraway seeds, and dill. Cool the filling for 10 minutes.

2. Cut the crusts off the bread slices. On a clean, dry work surface, use a rolling pin to roll each one to a flattened square, less than ¼ inch thick, but about the same size as the original slice, just more compressed.

3. Put a small bowl of water near your work space. Place about 1½ tablespoons of the ham filling in the middle of one piece of flattened bread. Dip a clean finger in the water and moisten the four edges of the bread. Fold the bread square crosswise in half, thus surrounding the filling. Press the edges firmly together to seal. Set aside and make 11 more pasties.

4. Pour enough oil into a 10-inch high-sided skillet or sauté pan to make a depth of about 1 inch. Clip a deep-frying thermometer to the inside of the pan, set it over medium heat, and bring the oil up to 350°F.

5. Fry the pasties two or three at a time, turning once, until golden and crisp, about 2 minutes per batch. Transfer to a wire rack to drain and continue until all of the pasties have been fried.

Crisp Fig and Caponata Mini Dumplings

Makes 16 mini dumplings (can be doubled)

These dumplings are much smaller than those in the previous recipes, bite-size but stocked with lots of flavor, thanks to store-bought caponata, an eggplant spread. Examine the jars in your market. Some have copious amounts of oil and not many vegetables. Choose one with lots of vegetables—or drain off the excess oil to keep these dumplings crisp and light. For a quick dip, press a garlic clove into 1 to 2 cups sour cream and stir until uniform.

½ cup store-bought eggplant caponata (about 3½ ounces)

2 dried black mission or white Turkish figs, stemmed and minced

8 potato bread slices (about 1¼ ounces per slice)

2 cups canola oil

1. Mix the caponata and figs in a small bowl until uniform.

2. Cut the crusts off the bread slices; cut each slice into quarters. On a clean, dry work surface, use a rolling pin to roll each one to a flattened square, less than ¼ inch thick, about the same size as the original quarter, but more compressed.

3. Put a small bowl of water near your work space. Place about 1½ teaspoons of the caponata filling in the middle of one square of flattened bread. Dip a clean finger in the water and moisten the edges of the bread. Set another small square on top and press the edges together to seal in the filling. Set aside and make 15 more mini dumplings.

4. Pour enough oil into a 10-inch high-sided skillet or sauté pan to make a depth of about 1 inch. Clip a deep-frying thermometer to the inside of the pan, set it over medium heat, and bring the oil up to 350°F.

5. Fry two or three of the dumplings at a time, turning once, until golden and crisp, about 1½ minutes per batch. Transfer to a wire rack and continue frying more. Serve hot.

TASTIER

VEGETARIAN

Mushroom Mini Ravioli

Makes 16 mini ravioli (can be doubled)

Have marinara sauce (page 98) at the ready for these small, crunchy ravioli. Or toss them into a composed salad for a better take on croutons. If you've got a medium shallot with two lobes, use only one of them.

8 ounces white button or cremini mushrooms

1 small shallot, peeled and cut into several pieces

1 tablespoon unsalted butter

1 teaspoon dried thyme

1 teaspoon dried sage

½ teaspoon table salt

2 tablespoons finely grated Parmigiano-Reggiano

8 fresh challah or egg bread slices (about 1½ ounces per slice)

About 2 cups canola oil

1. Put the mushrooms and shallot in a food processor, cover, and pulse until finely ground but not a paste. If necessary, open the machine once and scrape down the sides to grind the mushrooms more evenly.

2. Melt the butter in a medium skillet set over medium heat. Add the mushroom mixture and cook, stirring quite often, until the mushrooms release their moisture and it evaporates, about 5 minutes. Stir in the thyme, sage, salt, and cheese. Cool the filling for 20 minutes.

3. Cut the crusts off the bread slices; cut each slice into quarters. On a clean, dry work surface, use a rolling pin to roll each one to a flattened square, less than ¼ inch thick, but about the same size as the original quarter, just more compressed.

4. Put a small bowl of water near your work space. Place about 1½ teaspoons of the filling in the middle of one square of flattened bread. Dip a clean finger in the water and moisten the edges of the bread. Set another small square on top and press the edges together to seal in the filling. Set aside and make 15 more ravioli.

5. Pour enough oil into a 10-inch high-sided skillet or sauté pan to make a depth of about 1 inch. Clip a deep-frying thermometer to the inside of the pan, set it over medium heat, and bring the oil up to 350°F.

6. Fry the ravioli two or three at a time, turning once, until golden and crisp, about 1½ minutes per batch. Transfer to a wire rack and continue until all the ravioli have been fried.

Voilà! If you don't have a rolling pin, an empty (clean!) wine bottle works just as well.

4

MAKE-AHEAD
MEALS

Here's a chapter of meals you can make far in advance and cook, for the most part, right out of the freezer. Yes, it takes some planning, maybe a little Saturday afternoon prep. But it'll be worth it when you throw something frozen-and-soon-to-be-dinner onto a baking sheet, into a skillet, or even into a slow cooker—and your cooking is done.

What this wide range of dishes all have in common is that they can be made weeks, maybe even months, in advance. A number of these recipes use the freezer: freezer meat loaves, make-ahead freezer-to-oven packets, and even some braising sauces that need no cooking before going into the slow cooker (that you can freeze flat, then toss—with some protein—right into the cooker or the pot for a hearty supper without much fuss).

There are also a few recipes that might be outside the norm (or at least the everyday): like using that slow cooker to confit tuna or chicken, or making no-knead yeast bread dough to freeze months in advance.

You know that old saying: *You've got to spend time to save time.* We've always hated it, mostly because it's such a joyless sentiment. It sounds like drudgery, the sort of thing said along with a wagging, bony finger and a *tsk tsk.*

Rather than spending time, how about *investing* it? Or better yet, because nobody knows how investments turn out these days, how about just enjoying it? Take a minute to savor your work. You've reached a stage in your life where you can in fact spend a few minutes for meals ahead. Step back and relish where you are. Pay attention to the moments you have.

Sure, making these recipes is a matter of carving out a little time to prepare them. You may even begrudge the time on Saturday afternoon. But try not to. Try to find the joy in the time you have, the moments you've got to do a small kitchen task. You certainly won't begrudge that time spent when you walk in on Wednesday evening, dead tired, and pull something out of the freezer to toss in the oven.

TWO EASY IDEAS TO
SPEED UP YOUR COOKING

Here are a couple of ways you can really up your game in the kitchen and get a meal on the table faster.

1. Beef up your equipment with small, simple purchases. Everybody knows about the benefits of a well-stocked pantry. But you can also stock up on the tools in your drawers and cabinets to make meal prep go much faster.

For starters, buy additional sets of measuring cups and spoons. Rather than washing them as you work, toss that 1-teaspoon measuring spoon in the sink to wait for cleanup when you've finished, then pick up another to get on to the next step of the recipe.

For a little more money, invest in two or three large mixing bowls, rather than a multi-size set. You can usually make a little something in a big bowl, but you can never make a lot of something in a small bowl. Sometimes, you can't even make a little something in those little bowls. Wow, it can be a mess on the counter when you try to stir together a small tuna salad in a small bowl.

Finally, get a pair of dishwasher-safe kitchen shears. There's nothing like them for snipping the fat off chicken thighs or pork chops, for mincing herbs, for dicing fruit, or even for cutting up a cooked chicken on a cutting board.

2. Shop the salad bar at your supermarket. No, not so you'll make your dinner there. (Okay, maybe sometimes.) But instead, so you'll pick up pre-chopped celery, diced onion, maybe thinly sliced onion rings, sliced zucchini, and more. Think of the salad bar as the professional prep station for your kitchen.

Yes, many supermarkets now offer prepped vegetables in bags in the produce section. Often, you don't need that much sliced celery or chopped bell pepper. You can buy much smaller amounts at the salad bar.

Sure, you will spend more. No doubt about it. But you won't crowd up your fridge with waggly bits of unused vegetables that are inevitably bound for the garbage in a week, or maybe just a few days.

One warning: Watch out for marinades, sauces, and spice blends on those items at the salad bar. They can create flavor confusion in your dish. Look for the pure, straightforward ingredients, the kind you'd chop or prep yourself at home.

Freezer-to-Oven Meat Loaves

Makes 2 meat loaves, 4 to 6 servings each

Test Kitchen Notes

- Don't squeeze the moisture out of the breadcrumbs, as you might in a traditional meat loaf recipe.

- In step 2, kneading the ground beef mixture together with clean, dry hands works best to get an consistency.

- Lean ground beef gives a better overall texture.

- Here's an even easier idea: Buy two disposable 9 x 13-inch baking pans, form the two loaves as directed, then set in the two pans. Cover with plastic wrap, freeze, and later bake in that pan straight from the freezer.

Voilà! A standard, shiny, metal baking sheet cooks savory foods faster and more efficiently than dark or insulated ones. While insulated sheets may keep some cookies from burning, they're not the best for roasting or baking main-course fare.

Admittedly, these are meat *lumps,* not *loaves,* because they're baked on a lipped baking sheet rather than in a loaf pan. They can't very well bake in loaf pans because they've got more liquid in them than standard meat loaf. That extra moisture helps them stay tender through the freezing/thawing/baking cycle they have to endure. The moisture does indeed bake off, leaving a crisp top and toothsome inside. Forgoing a loaf pan also lets your meat loaves brown across a larger surface area while baking.

1 cup whole or low-fat milk

1 cup plain panko breadcrumbs

3½ pounds lean ground beef, at least 90 percent lean

2 large eggs, beaten in a small bowl

¼ cup reduced-sodium tomato paste

2 tablespoons Worcestershire sauce

2 tablespoons Dijon mustard

1 tablespoon dried sage

1 tablespoon dried thyme

1 teaspoon garlic powder

1 teaspoon onion powder

1 teaspoon table salt

1 teaspoon ground black pepper

1. Stir together the milk and breadcrumbs in a large bowl; set aside for 10 minutes.

2. Stir the ground beef, eggs, tomato paste, Worcestershire sauce, mustard, sage, thyme, garlic powder, onion powder, salt, and pepper into the breadcrumb mixture until uniform.

3. Divide the mixture in half and form each into a rounded loaf, like a football cut in half lengthwise but without the pointed ends. Set the loaves on a large baking sheet and freeze. Once frozen, tightly wrap the loaves individually in plastic wrap and store in the freezer for up to 4 months.

4. To bake, position the rack in the center of the oven; heat the oven to 325°F.

5. Unwrap a frozen meat loaf and set it on a large lipped baking sheet. Bake until an instant-read meat thermometer inserted into the thickest part of the loaf registers 165°F, about 1 hour and 45 minutes. Cool for a few minutes on the baking sheet before serving.

Lentil and Porcini Pasta Sauce

Makes 4 to 6 servings over pasta

EASIER

VEGETARIAN

GLUTEN-FREE

Here's an earthy pasta sauce that you can throw together and keep in the freezer until you add it straight to the pasta pot. (Keep a quart of vegetable broth in the pantry so you're ready to make the sauce anytime.) It's sort of a veganized Bolognese, thick and hearty, best over wide noodles like mafaldine or even hollow ones like bucatini. If you don't mind the dairy, shave strips of Parmigiano-Reggiano over each bowlful. The lentils need to break down and thicken the sauce (but they don't need to melt), so this is not a quick weeknight dish. But the convenience of a bag of easy pasta sauce in the freezer can turn a Saturday night with friends into something special.

One 28-ounce can crushed tomatoes, preferably fire-roasted

2 cups dry brown lentils

1 medium yellow onion, chopped

2 tablespoons olive oil

2 tablespoons tomato paste

2 tablespoons soy sauce (gluten-free if that's a concern)

1 tablespoon minced garlic

¼ ounce dried porcini mushrooms, crumbled

1 tablespoon dried marjoram

Up to 1½ teaspoons mild smoked paprika

½ teaspoon ground turmeric, optional

½ teaspoon ground black pepper

4 cups (1 quart) vegetable broth

1. Stir the tomatoes, lentils, onion, olive oil, tomato paste, soy sauce, garlic, dried mushrooms, marjoram, smoked paprika, turmeric (if using), and black pepper in a large bowl until the tomato paste dissolves. Pour into a 1-gallon plastic bag, seal, and freeze flat. Store in the freezer for up to 4 months.

2. To cook the sauce, remove the frozen block from the bag and place in a Dutch oven, chipping it to fit in one layer at the bottom of the pan. Add the broth. Melt the sauce over medium heat, stirring often.

3. Reduce the heat to low, cover, and simmer slowly until the lentils are super-soft and the sauce has thickened, 1½ to 2 hours.

 More! To make the sauce in a slow cooker, chip the frozen block to fit in a 5- to 6-quart slow cooker. Pour in the broth, cover, and cook on low for 7 hours or until the lentils are soft.

Test Kitchen Notes

- For an easier prep, use 1 cup frozen chopped onion. Do not thaw.

- The soy sauce adds a savory, umami richness. It's also why there's no salt in the recipe.

- Use a pair of kitchen shears to easily cut the dried mushrooms into tiny bits.

- Feel free to substitute dried sage or dried oregano (or a combination of them) for the dried marjoram.

- While this sauce is gluten-free (if you use the appropriate soy sauce), it should of course be put over gluten-free noodles, if this is a concern.

Voilà! While dried herbs and spices are a pantry staple, they don't last forever. Most dried leafy herbs need to be replaced once a year. Dried spices like cinnamon can last a couple of years but then begin to lose their punch. (And they do so even sooner in humid climates.) Always store dried herbs and spices in a cool, dark place to extend their lives as long as possible.

Streamlined Homemade Pastrami

Makes 6 to 8 servings

By starting with a store-bought corned beef from your supermarket's deli case, you can add liquid smoke and create a darn fine pastrami with little fuss. It'll keep, tightly covered, for about a week in the fridge—or wrap it when cooled and freeze it for several months. Look for sales on packaged corned beef just before and certainly right after March 17, Saint Patrick's Day. Stock up and make several pastramis that you can keep in the freezer.

One 3- to 4-pound low-sodium corned beef, drained

1 tablespoon cracked yellow mustard seeds

1 tablespoon cracked coriander seeds

1 tablespoon cracked fennel seeds

1 tablespoon ground black pepper

One 4-ounce bottle liquid smoke

About 3 cups water

1. Rinse the corned beef and pat dry with paper towels.

2. Combine the mustard seeds, coriander seeds, fennel seeds, and black pepper in a small bowl. Rub this mixture over both sides of the corned beef.

3. Set a steamer rack or basket in a large Dutch oven or a soup pot. Place the coated corned beef on the rack or in the basket. Pour the liquid smoke into the pot, to the side of the meat so it doesn't dislodge any spices. Add the water in the same way, just enough so that it stops about ¼ inch below the bottom of the steamer rack or basket.

4. Cover and bring to a boil over high heat. Reduce the heat to low and steam until the meat is tender without falling apart, adding more water if the pot starts to go dry, about 3 hours.

5. Transfer to a cutting board and cool for 10 minutes before slicing against the grain into thin, long strips.

Test Kitchen Notes

- If the corned beef is not low-sodium, soak it in a pot of water overnight in the fridge to remove excess salt that can mask the flavors of the pastrami.

- Discard any flavoring packets that come with the corned beef.

- Crack the mustard, coriander, and fennel seeds in a garlic press or under a heavy pot on a cutting board.

- A pastrami is tender when you can poke a meat fork into it and the tines come back out without any resistance.

- Some liquid smoke uses barley malt flour as a carrier for the smoky flavors. If concerned, search out gluten-free alternatives, most readily available online.

RECIPE CONTINUES

More!   To make pastrami in a pressure cooker, place the steamer rack or basket in a 6- to 8-quart pressure cooker, set the coated corned beef on the rack or in the basket, then add the liquid smoke and water as directed, letting the liquids come to about ¼ inch below the bottom of the rack or basket. For a stovetop cooker, lock on the lid, set the pot over high heat, and bring to high pressure (15 psi); then reduce the heat as low as possible to maintain high pressure and cook for 50 minutes. For an electric cooker, lock on the lid and set to cook at high pressure (9 to 11 psi) for 1 hour 10 minutes. In either case, use a natural release, removing the stovetop pot from the heat source or turning off the electric cooker. Unlock the lid, transfer the pastrami to a cutting board, and cool for 10 minutes before slicing as directed.

Want to make the best Reuben sandwich? Start by making the best Russian dressing: Whisk ¼ cup mayonnaise, 1 tablespoon ketchup, and 1 tablespoon pickle relish in a small bowl. For one Reuben, smear 1 tablespoon of the dressing on each of two slices of rye bread. Top one with ¼ cup drained sauerkraut and 3 to 4 ounces thinly sliced pastrami. Set the other slice of bread, dressing side down, on top. Lightly coat a large skillet with nonstick spray, then set it over medium heat for a minute or two. Add the sandwich and cook, turning once, until the bread is toasted golden brown, about 3 minutes. Notice what's missing? Cheese. A million kosher delis can't be wrong.

Make-Way-Ahead No-Knead Bread

Makes 3 loaves

No-knead bread is a culinary miracle: Stir the ingredients together and let the bread rise overnight in the refrigerator without any elbow grease. But here's an even bigger miracle: Form that dough into loaves and freeze them to be baked anytime you want.

4 cups bread flour

3 cups all-purpose flour

Two ¼-ounce packages instant yeast (about 1½ tablespoons)

2 to 3 teaspoons kosher salt

3 cups warm water, between 105°F and 110°F

1. Stir both flours, the yeast, and salt in a large bowl. Stir in the water to form a wet dough. Cover and refrigerate overnight, at least 12 hours or up to 16 hours.

2. Divide the mixture into three equal balls. Cover each with plastic wrap and freeze for up to 2 months.

3. The night before you bake your bread, unwrap one ball. Place it on a large lipped baking sheet. Cover the ball of dough with a mixing bowl and set in the refrigerator overnight to thaw, at least 12 hours or up to 24 hours.

4. The next day, uncover the ball of dough on the baking sheet and set aside in a warm, draft-free place or in an oven set to the proofing function, until it rises by about 50 percent of its original volume, about 2 hours.

5. Position the rack in the center of the oven; heat the oven to 425°F.

6. Bake the bread on its baking sheet until it is golden brown and sounds hollow when tapped, about 30 minutes. Transfer the bread to a wire rack and cool for at least 15 minutes before slicing and serving.

Test Kitchen Notes

- Use instant yeast, not quick-acting or active dry.

- The best way to tell if hot tap water is the right temperature for yeast is to use a cleaned instant-read meat thermometer to measure its temperature.

- The salt measurement is a range. How salty do you like your bread?

- If you like, mix up to ⅓ cup raisins, chopped nuts, and/or seeds into one of the balls before freezing.

Voilà! As a general rule for all oven recipes, heat your oven to 25°F or even 50°F more than the stated temperature in the recipe. Do this because when you open the door, the oven loses lots of heat. By upping the temperature at the start, you can afford to lose a few degrees. Turn the oven to the proper temperature once the food's inside.

EASIER

GLUTEN-FREE

Buy-in-Bulk Freezer-to-Oven Chicken Breasts and Pork Chops

Makes 2 servings per freezer bag

Test Kitchen Notes

- Take your pick from the six marinades to the right, depending on your whim or the contents of your fridge.

- Or you may want to make several of the marinades, so you have different types of chicken breasts or pork chops stored away for nearly instant entrees. The sky (or freezer space) is the limit.

- If you're using larger, 12-ounce chicken breasts or pork chops, they'll cook in 12 to 15 minutes, turning once. They will also need to be thawed overnight in the fridge.

- Because of food contamination issues, discard the remaining marinade from the bag; do not use it to mop the cooked breasts or chops as they cook.

- If gluten is an issue, make sure you use gluten-free soy sauce and Worcestershire sauce.

Go ahead and shop without fear at the big-box store. Buy those giant packages of boneless chicken breasts or pork chops, then make several batches of these marinades, each in a 1-quart plastic freezer bag. Add 2 breasts or chops to each bag, seal, and throw in the freezer.

In the morning, toss one (or more) of the bags in the fridge. Pick up a prepared salad after work. When you get home, the chicken or pork will be thawed and ready for the grill or grill pan.

And one more thing: If the chicken has been injected with a "solution containing..." (read the package), consider skipping the salt or halving the soy sauce in the marinade. This technique essentially brines the meat as it freezes and then thaws.

Spicy and Sour Chicken or Pork

1 small jalapeño chile, stemmed, seeded, and minced

1½ tablespoons soy sauce (gluten-free if that is a concern)

2 teaspoons peanut oil

2 teaspoons red wine vinegar

1 teaspoon granulated white sugar

1 teaspoon fresh thyme leaves

¼ teaspoon ground allspice

¼ teaspoon ground cinnamon

¼ teaspoon grated nutmeg

¼ teaspoon ground black pepper

Two 6-ounce boneless skinless chicken breasts or 6-ounce center-cut boneless pork loin chops

Nonstick spray

Garlic and Sesame Chicken or Pork

1 medium scallion, thinly sliced

2 tablespoons soy sauce (gluten-free if that is a concern)

1½ tablespoons red wine

1 tablespoon light brown sugar

2 teaspoons minced garlic

1½ teaspoons toasted sesame oil

¼ teaspoon ground black pepper

Two 6-ounce boneless skinless chicken breasts or 6-ounce center-cut boneless pork loin chops

Nonstick spray

Lemon and Fennel Chicken or Pork

1 teaspoon finely grated lemon zest

1½ tablespoons fresh lemon juice

1½ tablespoons olive oil

1 teaspoon minced fresh oregano leaves

1 teaspoon minced garlic

¼ teaspoon fennel seeds

½ teaspoon ground black pepper

¼ teaspoon table salt

1 small bay leaf

Two 6-ounce boneless skinless chicken breasts or 6-ounce center-cut boneless pork loin chops

Nonstick spray

Sage and Anchovy Chicken or Pork

1½ tablespoons Worcestershire sauce (gluten-free if that is a concern)

1½ tablespoons olive oil

1 tablespoon minced fresh sage leaves

1 packaged anchovy fillet, minced

1 teaspoon minced garlic

¼ teaspoon ground black pepper

Two 6-ounce boneless skinless chicken breasts or 6-ounce center-cut boneless pork loin chops

Nonstick spray

RECIPE CONTINUES ➤

Sour Orange and Cumin Chicken or Pork

The juice of 1 medium sour orange or 3 tablespoons bottled sour orange juice

2 teaspoons minced fresh oregano leaves

2 teaspoons olive oil

1 teaspoon minced garlic

½ teaspoon ground cumin

¼ teaspoon ground allspice

¼ teaspoon table salt

¼ teaspoon ground black pepper

Two 6-ounce boneless skinless chicken breasts or 6-ounce center-cut boneless pork loin chops

Nonstick spray

Dijon and Caper Chicken or Pork

1 tablespoon smooth Dijon mustard

1 tablespoon olive oil

1 tablespoon white wine vinegar

1 teaspoon capers, drained and minced

1 teaspoon minced garlic

½ teaspoon ground black pepper

¼ teaspoon table salt

Two 6-ounce boneless skinless chicken breasts or 6-ounce center-cut boneless pork loin chops

Nonstick spray

1. Mix the wet and dry ingredients for any marinade in a 1-quart plastic bag.

2. Add the chicken or pork. Squeeze out excess air and seal the bag closed. Massage the marinade for a few seconds against the meat, then place in the freezer where it can be stored for up to 3 months.

3. To prepare the chicken or pork, place the sealed bag to thaw in the refrigerator for at least 12 hours or up to 24 hours.

4. Brush a grill grate clean and coat it with nonstick spray, then prepare the grill for high, direct-heat cooking. Or lightly coat a cast-iron or nonstick grill pan with nonstick spray and set it over medium-high heat for a few minutes. Add the chicken or pork and cook, turning once, until an instant-read meat thermometer inserted into the thickest part of the meat registers 165°F for chicken or 155°F for pork, 6 to 8 minutes.

Voilà! It's a myth that you can't refreeze meat. You can—but only under specific conditions. The meat must have been thawed at or below 40°F (that is, in the refrigerator, not on the counter). And it can only have remained in its thawed state for at most 24 hours. If you've met both criteria, refreeze at will.

EASIER

GLUTEN-FREE

Make-Ahead Freezer-to-Oven Chicken Packets

Makes 4 packets per batch

Test Kitchen Notes

- If there's a packaged convenience product like marinated sun-dried tomatoes in the mix, the recipe leaves out any additional salt. Pass more at the table to season the meal to your taste.

- Use only chicken already prepared for stir-frying. Packages of precut chicken are readily available in almost all supermarkets. But only use unmarinated chicken, of course—and discard any seasoning packets.

- In any of these, you can use packaged pork cutlets or strips, if desired. Or buy 1½ pounds thinly sliced center-cut boneless pork loin chops and slice into ¼-inch-thick strips.

- Seal the packets well. Any drips mean moisture lost as they bake.

- Make sure the oven has reached 425°F before taking the packets out of the freezer. A standard oven can take up to 10 to 15 minutes to hit this mark.

Cooking from sealed packets has become something of a shortcut cliché. Most of us know that you can seal ingredients in parchment paper and aluminum foil and bake the individual servings on a baking sheet. But imagine this: a stack of packets in your freezer that you can take straight to the oven for a full dinner in 30 minutes. Consider this one of our best ideas for weekend power cooking: Build as many packets as you want and put a tasty dinner within easy reach for weeks to come. Each of the recipes to the right makes 4 packets—and you can make more than one batch, while you're at it. And one more thing: If you've pounded out your workout at the gym or skipped lunch, consider using 2 packets per serving.

Antipasto Chicken Supper

1½ pounds packaged sliced boneless skinless chicken breast for stir-fry

¼ cup drained marinated sun-dried tomatoes, roughly chopped

¼ cup drained pickled onions, roughly chopped

¼ cup pitted green olives, halved

¼ cup roasted red pepper strips

1 teaspoon dried thyme

¼ teaspoon red pepper flakes

Tomato and Herb Chicken Supper

1½ pounds packaged sliced boneless skinless chicken breast for stir-fry

16 grape tomatoes, halved

1 small yellow squash, cut in half lengthwise, then into ¼-inch-thick half-moons

1 medium shallot, cut in half, then sliced into thin half-moons

3 tablespoons olive oil

2 tablespoons dry white wine, vermouth, or chicken broth

Four 3-inch fresh rosemary sprigs

Four 3-inch multi-branched fresh thyme sprigs

½ teaspoon table salt

½ teaspoon ground black pepper

Chicken Stir-Fry Supper

1½ pounds packaged sliced boneless skinless chicken breast for stir-fry

1 medium red bell pepper, stemmed, cored, and cut into thin strips

4 ounces fresh green beans, trimmed and cut into 1-inch pieces

4 medium scallions, thinly sliced

⅓ cup roasted unsalted peanuts or cashews

2 tablespoons minced peeled fresh ginger

1 teaspoon minced garlic

2 tablespoons soy sauce (gluten-free if that is a concern)

2 tablespoons unseasoned rice vinegar

2 teaspoons toasted sesame oil

Up to 2 teaspoons hot red pepper sauce, such as Sriracha

Curried Chicken and Potato Supper

1½ pounds packaged sliced boneless skinless chicken breast for stir-fry

1 large Yukon Gold potato (about 8 ounces), shredded through the large holes of a box grater

1 medium globe tomato, chopped

1 small red onion, quartered and thinly sliced

¼ cup regular or low-fat plain yogurt

1 teaspoon granulated white sugar

1 teaspoon ground coriander

1 teaspoon ground ginger

½ teaspoon ground cinnamon

½ teaspoon ground cumin

½ teaspoon table salt

¼ teaspoon ground cloves

¼ teaspoon ground turmeric

RECIPE CONTINUES ▸▸

- To make sure the packets are cooked through, stick an instant-read meat thermometer at an angle through the top of a packet (not the sides or bottom) to make sure the chicken is at 165°F (or pork is at 155°F).

- All the versions are gluten-free (but check the soy sauce if you're making the Chicken Supper Stir-Fry).

1. Mix all the ingredients in a very large bowl until the meat is well-coated in a uniform sauce.

2. Place a 12-inch piece of aluminum foil on your work surface; top with a 12-inch piece of parchment paper. Spoon a quarter of the chicken mixture into the middle of the parchment paper.

3. Fold the long sides so they meet in the middle of the packet, then crimp these long edges together to make a tight seal, using the foil to catch and hold the waggly parchment paper in the seam. Roll both of the ends of the packet to seal as well. Continue to make 3 more packets.

4. Set the packets on a large baking sheet and freeze for at least 24 hours. Then remove the sheet and stack the packets flat in the freezer.

5. To bake, position the rack in the center of the oven and heat the oven to 425°F.

6. Place 1 or more of the packets straight from the freezer on a large lipped baking sheet. Bake for about 30 minutes, or until hot and steamy inside. Cool for 10 minutes before opening and serving.

Voilà! Although wine is a great cooking medium, it doesn't last long, no more than a few days even when well corked. A better alternative is dry (or white) vermouth. It should be a pantry staple. Although it offers a slightly more herbaceous finish, it can remain in good shape after opening for up to 2 months in a cool, dry pantry, or up to a year in the refrigerator.

MAKE-AHEAD FREEZER-TO-OVEN SLOW-COOKER BRAISES

Who doesn't love a deep, flavorful braise on a cold night? So here's comfort-food magic. Make a *no-cook* sauce mixture, then freeze it in a 1-gallon plastic freezer bag. When you're ready, empty the bag straight from the freezer into a slow cooker, then add the protein right on top of that frozen base. The protein requires no additional prepping: no browning, no slicing.

Each of these recipes was developed for a 5- to 6-quart slow cooker. If you don't have a machine that size, use our instructions for making the braise in a Dutch oven on the stove.

And we'd be remiss not to note that these are not "instant" dinners. They do need to cook for quite a while in the slow cooker. Of course, you can set one to cook at the start of the day and it'll be ready when you get home in the evening. Or you can plan on making one of these stews on the weekend.

Test Kitchen Notes

- Some of these no-cook braising sauces get mixed in a bowl before they're put in the freezer bag; some are just dumped straight into the bag. The difference is how important it is to get certain ingredients even throughout the mixture—thus, mix in the bowl first for those recipes.

- It's best to freeze the braise base flat so it's easier to work with.

- **Better:** Freeze the base in its bag that is set inside the removable insert of a 5- to 6-quart slow cooker. It'll then be the shape of your cooker.

- **Even better:** Stack several bags on top of each other in the insert to freeze them all to the right size.

- To get the braising base out of the bag, tear and peel away the plastic. If desired, use a pair of kitchen shears to make a few initial openings in the bag.

Artichoke and Dill Chicken Braise

Makes 6 servings

This is a great braise for a spring or fall evening when the weather's not dire, just chilly. If you can't find frozen artichoke heart quarters, substitute one 15-ounce can of artichoke hearts packed in water; drain and cut the hearts into quarters. Serve the braise over cooked white rice or orzo.

3 large tomatoes, roughly chopped

9 ounces frozen artichoke heart quarters (do not thaw)

1 small leek, pale and white green parts only, halved, rinsed, and thinly sliced

1 cup pitted green olives

¼ cup chopped fresh dill fronds

2 teaspoons minced garlic

1½ teaspoons fennel seeds

½ teaspoon table salt

¼ teaspoon red pepper flakes

3 pounds boneless skinless chicken thighs

1. Mix the tomatoes, artichoke hearts, leek, olives, dill, garlic, fennel seeds, salt, and red pepper flakes in a 1-gallon plastic freezer bag. Seal tightly, removing any excess air. Freeze flat for up to 4 months.

2. To cook, remove the frozen braise base from the bag, then set in a 5- to 6-quart slow cooker, chipping up any bits so that the frozen base essentially sits flat.

3. Arrange the chicken thighs on top of the base. Cover and cook on low for 8 hours. The braise can stay on the keep-warm setting for up to 3 hours.

More! To make this braise on the stovetop, remove the frozen base from its bag and set in a Dutch oven, chipping the corners to fit. Arrange the chicken over the frozen base and bring to a simmer over medium heat, stirring occasionally. Add 1 cup chicken broth. Reduce the heat to low and simmer, covered but stirring occasionally, for 1½ hours.

Chickpea Lamb Stew

Makes 6 servings

More! To make this braise on the stovetop, remove the frozen base from its bag and set in a Dutch oven, chipping the corners to fit. Arrange the lamb over the frozen base and bring to a simmer over medium heat, stirring occasionally. Add 1 cup chicken broth. Reduce the heat to low and simmer slowly, covered but stirring occasionally, for 2 hours.

The flavors of this braise are based on Moroccan tagines, highly spiced braises that are traditionally served over couscous. But you could also serve this over cooked quinoa or even millet, a tasty if unusual grain that's fantastic when dressed in melted butter and hot red pepper flakes. If desired, substitute 3 pounds boneless skinless chicken thighs or even beef stew meat, cut into 1½-inch cubes, for the lamb.

One 28-ounce can diced tomatoes

One 15-ounce can chickpeas, drained and rinsed

½ cup frozen chopped onion (do not thaw)

½ cup dry white wine, dry vermouth, or unsweetened apple cider

¼ cup loosely packed parsley leaves, finely chopped

2 tablespoons tomato paste

1½ tablespoons mild smoked paprika

1 teaspoon ground cinnamon

½ teaspoon ground cloves

½ teaspoon table salt

½ teaspoon ground black pepper

3 pounds lamb stew meat, trimmed and cut into 1½-inch pieces

1. Mix the tomatoes, chickpeas, onion, wine, parsley, tomato paste, smoked paprika, cinnamon, cloves, salt, and pepper in a large bowl until the tomato paste coats everything evenly.

2. Pour and scrape the contents of the bowl into a 1-gallon plastic freezer bag. Squeeze out the air, seal tightly, and freeze flat for up to 4 months.

3. To cook, remove the frozen braise base from the bag, then set in a 5- to 6-quart slow cooker, chipping up any bits so that the frozen base essentially sits flat.

4. Arrange the lamb pieces on top of the base. Cover and cook on low for 8 hours. The braise can stay on the keep-warm setting for up to 3 hours.

Coconut Curry Shrimp

Makes 4 to 6 servings

This curry will mellow quite a bit after freezing. For a brighter flavor, squeeze lemon juice over each bowl before serving. You can substitute 2 pounds boneless white-fleshed fish fillets, cut into 2-inch pieces, for the shrimp. And feel free to substitute 2 cups frozen bell pepper strips (do not thaw) for the fresh bell pepper. Try the braise over cooked and drained rice noodles.

One 13½-ounce can regular coconut milk

2 medium red bell peppers, cored, seeded, and cut into thin strips

¼ cup unsalted roasted peanuts

¼ cup chopped fresh cilantro leaves

3 tablespoons fish sauce

2 tablespoons light brown sugar

2 tablespoons minced peeled fresh ginger

Up to 2 tablespoons store-bought yellow curry paste

2 teaspoons minced garlic

2 pounds peeled and deveined medium shrimp (about 30 per pound)

1. Mix the coconut milk, bell pepper strips, peanuts, cilantro, fish sauce, brown sugar, ginger, curry paste, and garlic in a large bowl until the curry paste evenly coats everything.

2. Pour and scrape the mixture into a 1-gallon plastic freezer bag. Squeeze out excess air, seal, and freeze flat for up to 4 months.

3. To cook, remove the frozen braise base from the bag, then set in a 5- to 6-quart slow cooker. Cover and cook on low for 6 hours. The sauce at this point can be kept on the keep-warm setting for up to 1 hour.

4. Stir in the shrimp, cover, and cook on low for 10 minutes or until the shrimp are pink and firm. (Do not let the sauce and shrimp sit on the keep-warm setting because the shrimp will become overcooked and tough.)

 More! To make this braise on the stovetop, remove the frozen base from its bag and set in a Dutch oven, chipping the corners to fit. Bring to a simmer over medium heat, stirring occasionally. Reduce the heat to low and simmer slowly, covered but stirring occasionally, for 20 minutes. Stir in the shrimp and continue cooking until the shrimp are pink and firm, about 10 minutes.

Porcini and Orange Braised Short Ribs

Makes 6 servings

This sweet-and-sour braise is a great meal on a very cold night. Make sure you crumble the dried porcini so they contribute the most flavor to the stew, providing an earthy contrast to the vinegary orange sauce. The baby carrots called for are not true immature carrots, the micro vegetables you can sometimes find at high-end markets. Rather, they're standard carrots, cut into short cylinders and sold in bags at almost every grocery store. If you like, substitute 3 pounds boneless country-style pork ribs for the beef short ribs.

2 cups reduced-sodium chicken broth

1 cup frozen pearl onions (do not thaw)

12 baby carrots

¼ cup raisins

3 tablespoons white balsamic vinegar

1 tablespoon finely grated orange zest

½ ounce dried porcini mushrooms, crumbled

2 teaspoons dried sage

½ teaspoon ground allspice

3 pounds boneless beef short ribs

1 bay leaf

1. Mix the broth, onions, carrots, raisins, vinegar, orange zest, mushrooms, sage, and allspice in a 1-gallon plastic freezer bag. Seal tightly and freeze flat for up to 4 months.

2. To cook, remove the frozen braise base from the bag, then set in a 5- to 6-quart slow cooker, chipping up any bits so that the frozen base essentially sits flat.

3. Arrange the short ribs pieces and the bay leaf on top of the base. Cover and cook on low for 10 hours. The braise can stay on the keep-warm setting for up to 3 hours. Discard the bay leaf before serving.

More! To make this braise on the stovetop, remove the frozen base from its bag and set in a Dutch oven, chipping the corners to fit. Arrange the short ribs and bay leaf over the frozen base and bring to a simmer over medium heat, stirring occasionally. Add 1 cup beef broth. Reduce the heat to low and simmer slowly, covered but stirring occasionally, until the beef is tender, 2½ to 3 hours. Discard the bay leaf before serving.

TASTIER

GLUTEN-FREE

Coffee-Braised Beef Stew with Parsnips

Makes 6 servings

 More! To make this braise on the stovetop, remove the frozen base from its bag and set in a Dutch oven, chipping the corners to fit. Arrange the beef over the frozen base and bring to a simmer over medium heat, stirring occasionally. Add 1 cup beef broth. Reduce the heat to low and simmer slowly, covered but stirring occasionally, for 2½ hours. Discard the cinnamon stick before serving.

Coffee is unbelievable for braises. It mellows into an earthy sweetness with nary a bitter note. If you like, use brewed espresso for a more sophisticated (if still mellow) flavor. If you've bought espresso powder for another recipe, here's a good use for it. Feel free to substitute 3 pounds boneless pork shoulder, trimmed and cut into 1½-inch pieces.

1 large red onion, halved and sliced into thin half-moons

3 large parsnips, peeled and cut into 1-inch chunks

1½ cups strong brewed coffee, cooled to room temperature

¼ cup tomato paste

3 tablespoons Worcestershire sauce (gluten-free if that's a concern)

2 tablespoons brown sugar

1 teaspoon ground allspice

½ teaspoon table salt

½ teaspoon ground black pepper

One 4-inch cinnamon stick

3 pounds boneless beef chuck cubes, about 1½ inches each

1. Mix the onion, parsnips, coffee, tomato paste, Worcestershire sauce, brown sugar, allspice, salt, and pepper in a 1-gallon plastic freezer bag. Add the cinnamon stick, squeeze out any excess air, seal the bag, and freeze flat for up to 4 months.

2. To cook, remove the frozen braise base from the bag, then set in a 5- to 6-quart slow cooker, chipping up any bits so that the frozen base essentially sits flat.

3. Arrange the beef cubes on top of the base. Cover and cook on low for 9 hours. The braise can stay on the keep-warm setting for up to 3 hours. Discard the cinnamon stick before serving.

MAKE-AHEAD
BEAN SUPPERS

Canned beans suffer from, um. . . squishiness. Sure, they're a great convenience. But there's no doubt about it: Rehydrated dried beans have better texture and flavor. So here's an idea for a make-ahead meal: Soak those dried beans overnight, then toss them in a bag with lots of other ingredients and freeze them for a freezer-to-pot supper that's less hassle with more toothsome bean goodness.

Yes, these are not ready-in-minutes meals. They must cook for a good while. So consider these as make-aheads for a chilly weekend evening. Make sure you pick up a sturdy red wine or a hoppy IPA to round out the meal.

White Bean and Lamb Shank Stew

Makes 4 to 6 servings

Test Kitchen Notes

- This recipe makes a thick stew. For a lighter soup, add 2 to 4 additional cups of broth.

- So-called "baby carrots" are not immature carrots; they're larger carrots cut down to smaller shapes, better for a snack in a little kid's hand.

- Want to go over the top? Substitute 2 duck leg quarters for the lamb shank. Remove the skin and any large blobs of fat from the quarters before adding them to the stew mix.

☛ **More!** A word about dried beans: They should look plump, or at least rounded, and maybe a little shiny. They should not be wrinkled, cracked open, chipped, or broken. Unfortunately, dried beans can sit on store shelves for a long time. The longer they sit, the more moisture they lose. And sometimes, they're so old that they'll never rehydrate properly, despite all the care you can give them. The best dried beans look firm and "fresh."

Super-rich and filling, this stew is a version of cassoulet, the traditional French casserole with lots of white beans. For a terrific topping, toast fresh breadcrumbs with some minced garlic in a little olive oil in a skillet set over medium-low heat, stirring until golden brown. Sprinkle these over each serving. Look for fresh breadcrumbs in the bakery of most large supermarkets.

1¼ cups dried cannellini or great northern beans

1 cup frozen pearl onions (do not thaw)

10 baby carrots

3 celery stalks, thinly sliced

2 teaspoons minced garlic

1½ teaspoons dried sage

1 teaspoon dried thyme

½ teaspoon table salt

½ teaspoon ground black pepper

One 1- to 1¼-pound lamb shank

4 cups (1 quart) chicken broth

1 bay leaf

1. Place the beans in a large bowl, then add enough water to cover by 2 inches. Set aside to soak for 12 hours.

2. Drain the beans and pour into a 1-gallon plastic freezer bag. Add the pearl onions, carrots, celery, garlic, sage, thyme, salt, and pepper. Then drop in the lamb shank and seal closed, squeezing out any excess air. Freeze flat and store in the freezer for up to 4 months.

3. To cook the stew, remove the frozen block from the plastic bag and place in a Dutch oven, chipping it to fit in one layer. Add the broth and bay leaf. Cover and melt over medium heat, stirring often.

4. Bring to a simmer, then reduce the heat to low and simmer slowly, covered, until the beans are tender, about 3 hours. Before serving, discard the bay leaf, then transfer the lamb shank to a cutting board and cool for a few minutes. Shred the meat off the shank and stir these bits back into the stew.

EASIER

VEGETARIAN

GLUTEN-FREE

Three-Bean Chili with Squash and Cinnamon

Makes 4 servings

Test Kitchen Notes

- Make it easier with frozen diced butternut squash. Do not thaw before using.

- Easier still, also use 1 cup frozen chopped onion. Again, do not thaw.

- For a slightly thicker chili, add ¼ cup raw buckwheat groats in step 2.

Hardly a traditional chili, this version is Tex-Mex made simple (and vegan at that) for a satisfying meal. Yes, of course, you can cut down on the number of kinds of beans, but not the total amount. Use 1½ cups total volume of any two of the beans (or even just one of them to make it very easy).

½ cup dried red kidney beans

½ cup dried cannellini or great northern beans

½ cup dried pink beans

One 28-ounce can no-salt-added crushed tomatoes

2 cups diced seeded peeled butternut squash

One 12-ounce bottle amber ale

1 medium yellow onion, chopped

One 4½-ounce can mild or hot diced green chiles (do not drain)

2½ tablespoons chile powder

1 teaspoon oregano

1 teaspoon ground cinnamon

1 teaspoon table salt

1 cup water, plus more if needed

1. Pour the kidney, cannellini, and pink beans into a large bowl, add enough water to cover by 2 inches, and set aside to soak for 12 hours.

2. Drain the beans in a colander set in the sink. Pour them into a 1-gallon plastic freezer bag. Add the tomatoes, squash, beer, onion, chiles, chile powder, oregano, cinnamon, and salt. Seal, squeezing out any excess moisture, and freeze flat. Store in the freezer for up to 4 months.

3. To make the chili, remove the block of bean mixture from its bag and chip it to fit inside a Dutch oven in one layer. Add the water, then set over medium heat to thaw, stirring occasionally. Bring to a simmer.

4. Reduce the heat to low, cover, and simmer until the beans are tender, stirring occasionally, about 3 hours, adding up to 1 cup of water if the chili gets too thick.

More! Unfortunately, you can't prepare these make-ahead bean dishes in a slow cooker without a big alteration. Many beans, particularly kidney beans, contain a chemical compound, phytohaemagglutinin, that can cause severe gastric upset, not just the usual "bean problem" some experience. This compound is destroyed when beans are boiled, which never happens in a slow cooker. In fact, there's some evidence to suggest that the relatively low heat of a slow cooker exacerbates the effect of this compound. If you want to make these dishes in a slow cooker, soak the beans as directed, drain, then boil in a big pot of water for 10 minutes. Drain again, cool, and build the chili, soup, or stew in the freezer bag. Cook in a slow cooker from the frozen state, covered and on low, for 10 hours, or until the beans are tender.

Black Bean Soup with Dried Apples and Sausage

Makes 4 servings

Here's an American twist on a Cuban classic, made even easier by freezing the soup in a bag so it's ready when you are. The broth is added to the pot, rather than the bag, to make the bag easier to handle. That said, you could just pour the quart of broth right into the bag and freeze the whole thing: Put the bag in a big bowl to catch spills—and put all the other ingredients into the bag first to weight it down, then pour in the broth. Garnish the bowls of soup with sour cream, if desired. And have tortillas on hand.

1 cup dried black beans

1 cup unsweetened apple juice

1 cup chopped dried apples

8 ounces smoked kielbasa (gluten-free if that is a concern), thinly sliced

1 small green bell pepper, stemmed, seeded, and chopped

½ cup frozen chopped onion (do not thaw)

1 tablespoon dried oregano

1 teaspoon ground cumin

½ teaspoon table salt

One 4-inch cinnamon stick

4 cups (1 quart) chicken broth

1. Place the beans in a large bowl and add enough water to cover by 2 inches. Set aside to soak for 12 hours.

2. Drain the beans and pour them into a 1-gallon plastic freezer bag. Add the juice, dried apples, kielbasa, bell pepper, onion, oregano, cumin, salt, and cinnamon stick. Seal closed, squeezing out any excess air. Freeze flat, then store in the freezer for up to 4 months.

3. To cook the soup, remove the frozen block from the plastic bag and place it in a Dutch oven, chipping it to fit in one layer. Pour in the broth, cover, and melt over medium heat, stirring often.

4. Bring to a simmer, then reduce the heat to low and simmer slowly, covered, until the beans are tender, 2 to 2½ hours. Before serving, discard the cinnamon stick.

SLOW-COOKER
CONFIT

To confit meat—to preserve it in fat—is the essence of old-school, slow-food cooking, a way to preserve food for the long haul. But the process doesn't have to be difficult, thanks to the shortcut of a slow cooker. So get ready to slow cook amazingly luxurious tuna, salmon, and chicken confit.

These are definitely make-ahead meals, since the confits can be stored for days (or up to a year, in the case of the chicken), ready when you are. No, these are not everyday fare. In fact, they're a little over the top—even self-consciously "fancy food." But the recipes may well represent the best of shortcut cooking: not just saving time but also saving effort, something we use all too much of to get by in this modern world.

TASTIER

GLUTEN-FREE

Salmon Confit

Makes 8 servings

This is undoubtedly an extravagant dish, made with lots of olive oil (that you can't use again). It could be the best Mother's Day treat ever—or maybe the perfect thing as a first course for that big anniversary dinner you've been planning. The salmon becomes almost absurdly rich, ready to be turned into an unbelievable salmon salad with a little mayonnaise, minced red onion, and thinly sliced celery.

One 2-pound skin-on salmon fillet

At least 2 quarts olive oil

2 medium garlic cloves, peeled and smashed

2 teaspoons finely grated lemon zest

3 fresh thyme sprigs

1. Set the salmon fillet in a 4- to 6-quart slow cooker. Pour in enough oil to cover the salmon by ½ inch.

2. Lift the (still raw) fillet out of the oil, letting any excess oil drain back into the cooker. Set the fillet, skin side down, on a large lipped baking sheet. Cover with plastic wrap and refrigerate while you complete the next step.

3. Stir the garlic, lemon zest, and thyme into the oil in the cooker. Cover and cook on high for 2 hours.

4. Slip the (cold) fillet, skin side down, into the oil. Cover and cook on low for 2½ hours or until the thickest part of the fillet flakes when pricked with a fork. Use a wide spatula (or two!) to lift the fillet from the oil and onto a serving platter—or into a large baking dish which you can cover and refrigerate for up to 3 days.

Test Kitchen Notes

- This dish does not call for the lean, wild-caught, West coast salmon. It's better with fatty, Atlantic salmon.

- The skin is left on to flavor the confit. It also helps hold the salmon fillet together after it's cooked.

- You'll need to lift the salmon fillet out of the oil *before* it's cooked. It's a messy task but you need to have the fish in the slow cooker to determine the right amount of oil—then you'll infuse that oil with the aromatics for 2 hours on low before putting the salmon back into the cooker.

- Double the garlic for a more flavorful confit.

 More! To serve, make a simple aioli for the salmon and serve it like cold poached salmon on a platter surrounded by salad greens. The fastest aioli is made with an immersion blender: Crack a large egg into a 1-quart measuring cup. Add about 2 teaspoons minced garlic and 2 teaspoons fresh lemon juice. Pour about ¾ cup olive oil on top and let it settle. Set the blade end of the immersion blender at the bottom of the measuring cup, turn on the blender, and slowly start to lift it out, tilting the head this way and that, until the aioli is creamy. To make sure all the oil has blended, you'll need to lift the immersion blender slowly to the top of the ingredient mixture before turning it off. Remove the blender and whisk in an additional ¼ cup olive oil in a slow, steady stream. Season with table salt and pepper to taste.

Chicken Confit

EASIER

GLUTEN-FREE

Makes 4 to 8 servings

Chicken confit is one of the richest dishes around. It's savory and very satisfying, a wonderful treat. Best of all, the chicken confit can be stored in the freezer for quite a while. If you don't want to make a meal out of the leg quarters (with a salad on the side), you can crisp one quarter and shred the meat to serve on crackers for an easy, fancy snack with cocktails.

4 bay leaves

4 fresh thyme sprigs

4 medium garlic cloves, peeled and halved

4 small skin-on bone-in chicken thigh-and-leg quarters (10 to 12 ounces each)

2 tablespoons kosher salt

About 2½ quarts olive oil

1. Make four piles of a bay leaf, a thyme sprig, and two halves of a garlic clove on a large lipped baking sheet. Set one chicken quarter, skin side up, on top of each pile of aromatics. Sprinkle the skin of each with ½ tablespoon salt. Cover the tray loosely with plastic wrap and refrigerate for 24 hours.

2. Rinse the salt off each chicken quarter; pat dry. Transfer all the bay leaves and half of the garlic halves to a 4- to 6-quart slow cooker. (Discard the remaining garlic and the thyme sprigs.) Lay the quarters skin side up in the cooker. Pour in enough olive oil to cover the meat by 1 inch.

3. Cover and cook on low for 8 hours or until the meat is quite tender.

4. Use large tongs and a spatula to transfer the fragile quarters, skin side up, to a large baking dish. Make sure they lie as flat as possible. Fish out and discard the bay leaves and garlic. Ladle the oil from the cooker over the chicken quarters, submerging them fully. (You may need to add even more oil, depending on the size of the baking dish.)

5. Cover and refrigerate for at least 4 days or up to 2 weeks. Afterward, remove the chicken from the solidified oil, scrape off as much as possible, and freeze the quarters in sealed plastic bags for up to 1 year.

Test Kitchen Notes

- You'll need the full thigh-and-leg quarters of a chicken, not just drumsticks.

- Look for small, 10- to 12-ounce chicken quarters, not the giant, 1¼-pound ones that are common in supermarkets. The larger ones will end up tough and stringy with this technique. You may have to ask the butcher for the correctly sized quarters.

- Don't be afraid of the amount of salt. It cures the chicken, keeping it tender and allowing it to poach in the oil without falling apart.

 More! To serve, thaw one or two quarters, then unwrap if necessary. Set them skin side up on a large, lipped baking sheet and bake in a 400°F oven until crisp, about 20 minutes. Serve them whole or shredded on a warm lentil salad, a crunchy green salad, or on their own with toasted bread and a spicy, fruit-laced chutney.

Italian-Style Tuna Confit

Makes 6 servings

If you love Italian tuna preserved in olive oil but are sick of paying up to 20 bucks for a tiny portion, here's good news: You can make this luxurious treat yourself in a slow cooker with almost no work. Tuna confit will make the best tuna salad you've ever had. It's also great seared and served on buns with coleslaw—a tuna burger for the ages. For more ideas, see the **More!** section below.

Six 4-ounce tuna fillet steaks

1 teaspoon kosher salt

1 teaspoon ground black pepper

Two 4-inch fresh rosemary sprigs

2 garlic cloves, peeled

Two 2 x ½-inch strips orange zest

Enough olive oil to cover the tuna (at least 1 quart, maybe more)

1. Season the tuna steaks on both sides with the salt and pepper. Place them in one layer in a 4- to 6-quart slow cooker. Tuck the rosemary, garlic, and orange zest among the fillets.

2. Pour in enough oil to cover the tuna by ½ inch. Cover and cook on low for 4 hours. The tuna can stay on the keep-warm setting for up to an additional 4 hours.

3. Either set the covered bowl of the slow cooker on a kitchen towel directly in the refrigerator; or transfer the tuna steaks, aromatics, and almost all the oil to a 9 x 13-inch baking dish, then cover and refrigerate. Either way, the confit will keep in the fridge for up to 4 days.

Test Kitchen Notes

- The olive oil will not be good for much else after this. Don't buy the expensive stuff, just a solid store brand.

- In like manner, there's no need for sushi-grade tuna here. Buy frozen tuna fillets and thaw them in the fridge.

Voilà! Even if they're not turned into tuna confit, three-ounce frozen tuna steaks, thawed, are the perfect size for tuna burgers on hamburger buns.

More! To serve, remove as many fillets as you'd like from the oil. It will have solidified so scrape off as much oil as possible without uncovering any of the other fillets. Set the chosen fillet(s) aside at room temperature on a large plate until the oil melts away. Break apart the tuna meat and serve over salad greens tossed with a creamy dressing, or make tuna salad by mixing the chopped tuna confit with some chopped celery, chopped red onion, some drained and rinsed canned white beans, and lemon juice to taste. You won't need mayonnaise because the tuna is so rich. Or sear the tuna steaks in a smoking cast-iron skillet set over medium-high heat or on a grill grate directly over a high-heat source, turning once, just until there are several char marks on each side. Serve with a dollop of olive tapenade on each fillet.

5

DINNER MADE
EASIER

Here's the first of two dinner chapters, this one with slightly easier fare, including more cooking right out of the freezer (although this time with frozen store-bought chicken breasts, pork chops, steaks, and more, rather than the make-ahead mix of ingredients in freezer bags featured in chapter 4). There are also sheet-pan suppers and broiler meals, as well as a technique to cook skewers in the oven over a baking dish of vegetables so you make a full meal—and so the kebabs don't turn gray on their undersides against the baking sheet.

But before the recipes themselves, on your next trip to a big box store or just the neighborhood grocery store, consider for a moment the rule for most shortcut cooking: Think small. In general, the bigger something is, the longer it takes to cook and (often) the more complicated the preparation. To that end, baby vegetables cook more quickly than their full-grown counterparts; very small potatoes more quickly than large ones.

The smaller-is-faster rubric really comes into play with proteins. Yes, in this chapter there's a shortcut way to make a whole turkey and a whole chicken. There's even a standing rib roast in the next chapter. But beyond these recipes, here's a handy guide to what's easier on a weeknight:

HOW TO "THINK FAST" AT THE STORE

A little planning pays off on a trip to the store to stock up.
But a little know-how pays off even more.

QUICK	NOT QUICK
BEEF: flank steak, sirloin, strip steaks, rib-eye steaks, T-bone and porterhouse steaks, tenderloin steaks (aka filet mignon), London broil	**BEEF:** brisket, chuck roast, blade steaks, bottom round, oxtails, eye round, stew meat, shanks, whole tenderloin roast, standing rib roast
CHICKEN: boneless skinless chicken breasts, including chicken tenders	**CHICKEN:** all other cuts
DUCK: breasts	**DUCK:** legs, whole birds
LAMB: loin chops, rib chops, loin, sirloin, rack of lamb	**LAMB:** shoulder chops, leg, stew meat, breast, shanks
PORK: loin chops, rib chops, tenderloin, bacon, boneless center-cut chops	**PORK:** whole pork loin, ham, shanks, shoulder, Boston butt, belly, rib roasts
TURKEY: scaloppini, turkey London broil	**TURKEY:** whole breast, leg quarters, wings, whole birds
VEAL: scaloppini, rib chops, loin chops (also known as veal porterhouse steaks or veal T-bone steaks)	**VEAL:** brisket, leg, breast, rib roast, stew meat

Nutty-Crunchy Oven-Fried Cutlets

Makes 6 servings

Call it "better cooking with a rolling pin"! In a blender or food processor, the coating for oven-frying gets too powdery to yield a good crunch. But by pounding the breadcrumb mixture in a plastic bag by hand, you create a coarser texture, with little bits of nuts and spice throughout. Toss the sealed bags with the pulverized bits in the freezer to keep for up to 6 months. You don't even need to thaw them when you're ready to dredge the cutlets. And as a final bonus, with nuts in the mix, you don't need to brush the meat with egg before coating (just coat with nonstick spray), saving you a bowl and a step, too.

Walnut, Lemon, and Sage Cutlets

1 cup plain panko breadcrumbs

⅔ cup walnut pieces

2 tablespoons cornstarch

1 tablespoon dried sage

2 teaspoons finely grated lemon zest

1 teaspoon table salt

Nonstick spray, preferably an olive oil spray

Six 6-ounce thin turkey breast cutlets, veal cutlets, or skinless catfish fillets

Spicy Pecan and Cornmeal Cutlets

1 cup yellow cornmeal

⅔ cup pecan pieces

2 tablespoons all-purpose flour

1 teaspoon garlic powder

1 teaspoon onion powder

1 teaspoon ground dried mustard

1 teaspoon mild paprika

1 teaspoon table salt

Up to 1 teaspoon cayenne

Nonstick spray, preferably an olive oil spray

Six 6-ounce thin turkey breast cutlets, veal cutlets, or skinless catfish fillets

Hazelnut and Chive Cutlets

1 cup plain dried breadcrumbs

½ cup peeled roasted hazelnuts

6 tablespoons finely grated Parmigiano-Reggiano (about ¾ ounce)

1 tablespoon dried chives

1 tablespoon fennel seeds

½ teaspoon ground black pepper

Nonstick spray, preferably an olive oil spray

Six 6-ounce thin turkey breast cutlets, veal cutlets, or skinless catfish fillets

Test Kitchen Notes

- For Sunday power cooking, make one batch of any of the three coating variations to the left (without the cutlets in tow—and without pouring the coating mixture onto a plate). Or make two, or all three coatings. Maybe even a bag or two each. These can then be stored in the freezer for up to 6 months, ready to go when you are. There's no need to thaw before use.

- Dried herbs work much better than fresh in this technique, as they won't singe and turn bitter.

- Squeeze out any excess air from the plastic bag with the coating or it will pop when pounded.

- The cutlets or fish fillets must be thin, under ½ inch thick.

- Do not use an insulated baking sheet. It will actually slow down the cooking and render the coating soggy.

- Because the coating is lighter than most other breaded coatings, do not turn the cutlets on the baking sheet—and remove them gingerly with a thin metal spatula.

RECIPE CONTINUES ➤➤

More! To make these with pork cutlets, buy 6-ounce center-cut boneless pork loin chops, put them between two sheets of plastic wrap, and pound with the flat side of a meat pounder, a heavy rolling pin, or the bottom of a heavy pot until each is ¼ inch thick. Work gently at first, then more aggressively as they start to spread out, taking care not to tear the cutlets.

1. Position the rack in the center of the oven; heat the oven to 400°F.

2. Place all the ingredients for your desired coating (except, of course, the nonstick spray and the cutlets) in a large plastic freezer bag. Squeeze out the excess air and seal.

3. Pound the bag on a counter with a rolling pin, lightly at first until you get the hang of it, then harder and harder, until the nuts are coarsely pulverized, but not powdery. At least twice, shake the bag to rearrange the ingredients so they're uniformly distributed. Pour the coating into a pie plate or a 9-inch square baking dish.

4. Lightly coat a large lipped baking sheet with nonstick spray. Also lightly coat each cutlet on both sides with the spray. Dredge each cutlet on both sides in the coating, shaking off any excess. Lay in a single layer on the baking sheet.

5. Spray the tops of the cutlets one more time. Bake until the cutlets are golden and crunchy, about 18 minutes. Set the baking sheet on a wire rack and cool for 5 minutes before serving.

Dry-Aged Strip Steaks Without Drying or Aging

Makes 2 servings (can be doubled)

Test Kitchen Notes

- You must use a cast-iron skillet for this technique. The temperatures will go well above any regarded as safe for nonstick coatings. Even a more standard skillet can begin to warp under these temperatures.

- The steaks must be boneless—indeed, must be flat—so all the meat rests against the hot cast iron.

- The meat should also be fairly well marbled since the fat helps carry this flavor trick forward. Look for thin but noticeable fat caps around the sides of the steaks.

- You must use ground *white* pepper, which has a far muskier flavor than black pepper.

- You won't get the soy sauce to stick to a wet steak. If there's any surface moisture, blot the steak dry with paper towels.

Dry-aging steaks gives them a mineral, earthy flavor—not sweet, but more savory, even umami— that is highly prized among steak lovers. It's ordinarily a many-months process in a special, humidity- and temperature-controlled chamber. Having someone else do it for you quadruples the price of the steak, but you can do it on your own tonight with this easy rub that mimics those flavors.

1½ ounces dried porcini mushrooms

1 teaspoon kosher salt

½ teaspoon granulated white sugar

½ teaspoon ground white pepper

Two 10-ounce boneless New York strip steaks, about 1 inch thick

2 tablespoons soy sauce (gluten-free if that is a concern)

3 tablespoons unsalted butter

2 tablespoons balsamic vinegar

1. Grind the porcini, salt, sugar, and pepper into a fine powder in a spice or coffee grinder.

2. Rub the steaks with the soy sauce, then coat with the mushroom powder. Set aside for 20 minutes at room temperature.

3. Meanwhile, position the rack in the center of the oven; heat the oven to 400°F.

4. Set a cast-iron skillet over medium-high heat until smoking. Add the butter, wait a couple of seconds until it melts, then set the steaks in the skillet. Sear well without moving the steaks for 3 minutes.

5. Flip the steaks and transfer the cast-iron skillet to the oven. Roast until an instant-read meat thermometer inserted into the thickest part of each steak registers 125°F for rare or 130°F for medium-rare, about 4 or 6 minutes.

6. Transfer the steaks to serving plates. Pour the vinegar into the superhot skillet and scrape up any browned bits. Drizzle this mixture over the steaks and serve.

Voilà! Clean out spice or coffee grinders by grinding raw white rice to a fine powder, then wiping it out with a damp paper towel. As a bonus, the ground rice powder will absorb any oils that may lurk in the corners or under the blades.

Mixer Meatball Parmesan

Makes 4 servings

A mixer is the perfect solution for anyone who doesn't want to stick their hands into raw meat to mix up meatballs. A stand mixer works best, but you can even use a handheld, provided you also use a very large bowl (so there's plenty of room to move the mixer blades around with the meat mixture). And there's no need to form the meatballs in your palms if you've got a large, ¼-cup ice cream scooper.

1 cup fresh breadcrumbs

⅓ cup whole, low-fat, or fat-free milk

1 pound lean ground beef, at least 93 percent lean

1 pound bulk sweet or spicy Italian sausage meat

1 large egg

¼ cup finely grated Parmigiano-Reggiano (about ½ ounce)

3 cups plain marinara sauce, store-bought or homemade (page 98)

2 cups shredded mozzarella (about 8 ounces)

1. Stir the breadcrumbs and milk in the bowl of a stand mixer or a large bowl. Set aside for 10 minutes. Meanwhile, position the rack in the center of the oven and heat the oven to 400°F.

2. Add the beef, sausage meat, egg, and cheese to the breadcrumb mix. Using the stand mixer with the paddle attachment or an electric handheld mixer at *low* speed, mix the ingredients until uniform and well blended.

3. Lightly oil the inside of a 9 x 13-inch baking pan. Use a ¼-cup ice cream scooper to create about 16 meatballs from the meat mixture. One by one, plop them directly into the pan.

4. Bake the meatballs until lightly browned and cooked through, about 20 minutes.

5. Pour the marinara sauce over the meatballs and turn the meatballs very gently while scraping up any browned bits in the baking dish. Sprinkle the cheese over the meatballs. Bake until the cheese has melted and the sauce is bubbling hot, 10 to 15 minutes longer. Cool a couple of minutes before serving.

Test Kitchen Notes

- This recipe's not just about solving a gross-out factor. A mixer makes a more homogenous blend, better than you could ever create with a wooden spoon—and in less time, too.

- By using bulk sausage, you don't have to add other seasonings.

- For more flavor, use 1½ pounds lamb merguez sausage, casings removed, and ½ pound lean ground beef.

- You can also substitute finely grated Manchego for the mozzarella.

- The meatballs will still be a bit fragile when you add the marinara sauce. A metal spatula in one hand and a wooden spoon in the other are the best tools for turning them.

Voilà! You can find fresh breadcrumbs in the bakery department of most large supermarkets. But if you want to make your own, there's no need to drag out a food processor. Let a kaiser or hoagie roll go very stale, then grate it through the large holes of a box grater.

THREE SECRET WEAPONS
IN THE KITCHEN

1. Balsamic Vinegar

Made from Trebbiano grapes, balsamic vinegar adds a sweet/sour pop to dishes from appetizers to desserts. It's thicker, richer, and sweeter than other vinegars, almost like a sauce in a bottle. Consider these pantry staples:

- **Plain balsamic vinegar,** a go-to ingredient, sturdy and reliable

- **Aged, syrupy balsamic vinegar,** a true splurge—not for cooking, but used solely as a condiment

- **White balsamic vinegar,** a sweeter version, made from grape pressings mixed with white wine vinegar

WITH THESE, YOU CAN...

- Marinate steaks, chicken breasts, or pork loin chops in plain balsamic vinegar before grilling.

- Drizzle fresh berries with aged, syrupy balsamic for dessert. Or drizzle the aged stuff over peach frozen yogurt.

- Add a few drops of any variety to melted chocolate to drizzle on pound cake.

- Use white balsamic vinegar as a finishing condiment for fish off the grill.

- Add a drizzle of white balsamic to pie crusts to give the crust a sweet/sour pop.

- Stir a little balsamic or white balsamic vinegar into any non-dairy braise at the end of cooking to revive buried flavors.

- Spike any non-cream or non-milk dip, French onion to hummus, with syrupy, aged balsamic.

- Stir white balsamic and fresh thyme leaves into goat cheese for a sandwich spread.

- Brighten any tuna or salmon salad with standard balsamic vinegar.

- Stir a little balsamic vinegar into a pot of mussels or clams before serving to mute the brininess and bring forward the sweetness.

- Deglaze a pan of roasted vegetables with white balsamic vinegar.

- Whisk balsamic vinegar into any store-bought barbecue sauce to make it more complex.

2. Honey

Honey is a complex sweetener with a depth of flavor: woody, floral, fruity, spicy, or herbaceous, depending on the type of honey. Beyond clover or wildflower honey, look for:

- **Orange-blossom honey** for an intense floral taste

- **Buckwheat honey** for a dark, rich, slightly bitter flavor

- **Single-flower honeys** like eucalyptus or star thistle

- **Herb honeys,** made from the likes of sage, rosemary, or thyme flowers

- **Tree honeys** from oaks or chestnuts—dark and bitter, not for the novice

- Whisk a teaspoon or two into any vinaigrette to balance the vinegar or lemon juice.

- Brighten tomato-based sauces at the end of cooking.

- Make fruit salads more floral.

- Take grilled cheese over the top by smearing honey on the inside of the bread, particularly with sharp Cheddar or goat cheese.

- Mix a bit into melted chocolate for an elegant dip for sliced bananas.

- Add to pancake and waffle batters for a more intense sweetener (reduce the volume from that originally stated for the sugar by 25 percent).

- Perk up a pot of chili by stirring in a couple of teaspoons.

- Bring depth to the flavors of a slow-cooker braise with a little honey at the end.

- Make a mop for grilled chicken breasts with equal parts honey, soy sauce, and lemon juice.

- Make a barbecue rub by mixing your favorite dried herb blend into equal parts honey and vinegar.

3. Lemons

Lemon juice brightens flavors, brings salty notes to the fore, and even makes whatever's sweet seem a little sweeter. When you're using lemon zest, use only the zest itself, the bright yellow bit on the outer skin of the lemon, not the bitter white pith underneath (except for the lemon muffins on page 321). The best tool for removing the zest is a Microplane. Look for:

- **Fresh lemons** for zesting and juicing
- **Bottled lemon juice** (quality varies, so it may be better to juice your own)
- **Lemon extract,** a wallop of flavor to be used sparingly

NOW YOU CAN...

- Brighten the flavors of any non-dairy soup or stew with a drizzle of lemon juice before serving.
- Replace half the vanilla extract in almost any cookie or cake recipe with lemon extract.
- Spike pesto with finely grated lemon zest for a fresher taste.
- Bake whole fish or fish fillets on a bed of thin lemon slices and dill.
- Substitute lemon juice for vinegar in almost any non-dairy salad dressing.
- Perk up mayonnaise for a sandwich spread with finely grated lemon zest
- Bring steamed green vegetables back to their fresh-picked flavor with a drizzle of lemon juice.
- Mix finely grated lemon zest into the cheesy filling in any lasagna or stuffed pasta shell recipe.
- Whisk finely grated lemon zest and all-fruit spread into ricotta for a spread on toast.
- Spike guacamole or any avocado dip with lemon juice.
- Keep trimmed artichokes and sliced apples fresh by immersing them in water with a little lemon juice.

COOK IT RIGHT OUT OF THE FREEZER

It seems like a dream, right? You're home from your day, you're hungry, you didn't go to the store, and you don't want to order in... but you've got stuff in the freezer. Here are six solutions: six dinners with ingredients that go directly from freezer to oven, including one that won't save your Tuesday evening but may save your Thanksgiving.

In all cases, if you've bought the protein in bulk at a big box store or on sale at your local supermarket, don't store it in a big lump in the freezer—or even in the original packaging. Individually wrap each piece, even just in plastic wrap, making sure it freezes as flat as possible to save space.

No-Fuss Chicken Parmesan Casserole

EASIER

GLUTEN-FREE

Makes 6 servings

In North America, the "Chicken Parmesan" thing is something of a misnomer. It's always made with melted mozzarella, not Parmigiano-Reggiano. And it's alleged to be a dish from Parma. (Spoiler alert: It's not.) But nomenclature aside, this recipe gets you a pretty fantastic dinner without much fuss: chicken breasts straight from the freezer baked with marinara. Always keep jars of plain marinara sauce in the pantry, or containers of your homemade in the freezer, for these and other emergencies.

1 tablespoon olive oil

Six 8-ounce frozen boneless skinless chicken breasts

3 cups plain marinara sauce, store-bought or homemade (page 98)

2 cups shredded mozzarella (about 8 ounces)

½ teaspoon dried oregano

Up to ½ teaspoon red pepper flakes

1. Position the rack in the center of the oven; heat the oven to 350°F.

2. Pour the oil into a 9 x 13-inch baking pan; spread it to coat the bottom evenly. Set the frozen chicken breasts in the pan in one layer.

3. Pour the marinara sauce over the chicken, cover the dish with parchment paper, then seal with aluminum foil. Bake for 30 minutes.

4. Uncover the baking dish and use an instant-read meat thermometer to take the temperature in the thickest part of a couple of the chicken breasts. The temperature should be 125°F. If not, cover the baking dish again and continue baking, testing the temperature every 10 minutes.

5. Once the chicken's at the right temperature, sprinkle the pieces evenly with the cheese, dried oregano, and red pepper flakes.

6. Bake, uncovered, until the cheese has melted and lightly browned and an instant-read meat thermometer inserted into the thickest part of a couple of the breasts registers 165°F, about 15 minutes longer. Cool in the baking dish for 10 minutes before serving.

Test Kitchen Notes

- This recipe will only work with smaller boneless skinless chicken breasts, *not* the giant ones that sometimes weigh nearly 1 pound each.

- Parchment paper puts a necessary barrier between the acidic marinara sauce and the reactive aluminum foil.

- This recipe assumes that the marinara sauce carries the salt. Bring more to the table and salt to taste.

- If gluten is a concern, make sure your store-bought marinara sauce is indeed gluten-free.

- As a bonus, this recipe is a lighter version of the usual, since the chicken isn't first breaded and fried.

Voilà! Before shredding cheese with the large holes of a box grater, spray the grater with nonstick spray to cut down on sticking.

Crunchy Herb-Coated Chicken Breasts

Makes 6 servings

Test Kitchen Notes

- Make sure the chicken breasts have been frozen flat without rounded corners or folded bits. If there is a rounded-down corner, set the frozen breast in the baking dish with the rounded side down and the flatter surface up and exposed.

- The mustard actually sticks more easily to frozen chicken breasts than to thawed.

- Panko breadcrumbs can withstand the long baking better than standard breadcrumbs.

There are plenty of pre-breaded, frozen chicken breast cutlets on the market. However, the coatings are stocked with preservatives and sometimes trans fats, none good for you. Here's a way to make your own with just about as much convenience but far fewer unpronounceables—and by cooking the chicken right from the freezer.

⅔ cup plain panko breadcrumbs

2½ tablespoons olive oil

1 teaspoon dried thyme

1 teaspoon dried chives

½ teaspoon table salt

½ teaspoon ground black pepper

Six 8-ounce frozen boneless skinless chicken breasts

3 tablespoons Dijon mustard

1. Position the rack in the center of the oven; heat the oven to 350°F.

2. Stir the breadcrumbs, 1½ tablespoons of the oil, the thyme, chives, salt, and pepper in a medium bowl until the herbs and oil are uniform throughout.

3. Pour the remaining 1 tablespoon oil into a 9 x 13-inch baking dish and smear it around to coat the bottom. Place the chicken breasts in one layer in the pan. Smear each with ½ tablespoon mustard, then sprinkle the breadcrumb mixture evenly over the breasts so it sticks to the mustard.

4. Cover the baking dish with aluminum foil and bake for 30 minutes.

5. Uncover the dish and continue baking until an instant-read meat thermometer inserted into the thickest part of a couple of the breasts registers 165°F, about 15 minutes. Tent loosely with foil if there's any danger of the coating getting too browned. Cool in the baking dish for 10 minutes before serving.

Weeknight Tangy Lemon Chicken

Makes 6 servings

Although there's no sugar in this basting sauce, it's still a sweet/sour mix. Lemon juice, despite being tart, carries lots of natural sugar—which will reduce and caramelize to add intense flavor to the chicken. Serve this one alongside roasted potatoes (page 278) or long-grain white or brown rice.

¼ cup olive oil

Six 8-ounce frozen boneless skinless chicken breasts

2 tablespoons fresh lemon juice

1 tablespoon red wine vinegar

4 teaspoons minced garlic

1 tablespoon minced fresh oregano leaves

2 teaspoons fresh thyme leaves

1 teaspoon table salt

½ teaspoon ground black pepper

1. Position the rack in the center of the oven; heat the oven to 350°F.

2. Pour half the oil into a 9 x 13-inch baking dish. Tip it this way and that to coat the bottom.

3. Place the frozen chicken breasts in one layer in the baking dish. Drizzle the remainder of the oil evenly over the breasts, as well as the lemon juice and red wine vinegar. Sprinkle the garlic, oregano, thyme, salt, and pepper evenly over the chicken.

4. Cover with parchment paper, then aluminum foil. Bake for 30 minutes.

5. Uncover and continue baking, basting the meat occasionally with the juices in the dish, until an instant-read meat thermometer inserted into the thickest part of a couple of the breasts registers 165°F, about 20 minutes longer. Cool the chicken in the baking dish for 10 minutes before serving.

Test Kitchen Notes

- The fresh herbs won't burn because a) they're cooked covered, and b) there's so much liquid in the dish.

- Don't stint on basting. You want to glaze the chicken, not let the juices burn in the baking dish.

- Don't worry if the herbs come off as the chicken is basted. They'll get picked back up as part of the sauce with the basting.

Voilà! Throughout the recipes in this book the assumption is that you'll be using store-bought minced garlic and ginger, available in little jars from the produce section. These are not lasts-forever ingredients. At the store, they should not be brown or even a dark beige. Minced garlic should be pale, creamy white; ginger should have a slightly pink luster. There should be some liquid in the jar but not a lot. At home, store the jars in the fridge but plan on using them before tossing them out after a couple of months. And if you're chopping your own garlic, 1 small clove will give you about 1 teaspoon minced.

EASIER

GLUTEN-FREE

Maple and Sage Chicken with Butternut Squash

Makes 6 servings

Not only does the chicken start out frozen, the butternut squash and pearl onions do, too. It adds up to an absurdly luscious dish for a fall evening. This would also make a great dinner for the holidays or Thanksgiving, particularly if you've got family members who don't like turkey. Have mashed potatoes (page 264) at the ready.

1 tablespoon canola or vegetable oil

Six 8-ounce frozen boneless skinless chicken breasts

4 cups frozen butternut squash cubes (do not thaw)

½ cup frozen pearl onions (do not thaw)

¼ cup maple syrup

1 tablespoon apple cider vinegar

1 tablespoon minced fresh sage leaves

½ teaspoon table salt

½ teaspoon ground black pepper

¼ teaspoon grated nutmeg

1. Position the rack in the center of the oven; heat the oven to 375°F.

2. Pour the oil into a 9 x 13-inch baking dish; tilt the dish to coat the bottom with the oil.

3. Place the chicken breasts in a single layer in the baking dish. Scatter the squash and onions over and around the chicken.

4. Whisk the maple syrup, vinegar, sage, salt, pepper, and nutmeg in a small bowl until uniform. Drizzle over the top of everything.

5. Cover the baking dish with aluminum foil and bake for 30 minutes.

6. Uncover and toss the vegetables a bit. Continue baking until the squash is tender and an instant-read meat thermometer inserted into the thickest part of a couple of the breasts registers 165°F, about 20 minutes longer. Cool in the baking dish on a wire rack for 10 minutes before serving.

Test Kitchen Notes

- The oven temperature is higher here than in other recipes in this set because the frozen vegetables take longer to heat up.

- Because the sauce is less acidic and won't come into contact with the foil, there's no need for parchment paper between the food and the foil.

Voilà! Before you prep the ingredients for even moderately complicated recipes, fill muffin tin indentations with paper muffin cups, then fill these with measured spices and small, dry ingredients for the dish at hand. (Wet ingredients like canned chipotles in adobo sauce or prepared horseradish will stick to the paper.)

Perfect Strip Steaks

Makes 2 steaks (2 or 4 servings)

Strip steaks are actually better when they start out frozen. The technique is first to sear the frozen steaks in a lot of oil (so they get crunchy), then roast them in a relatively low-temperature oven to preserve that texture. A cast-iron skillet is the best tool for the first steps. After that, you'll need a heat-safe rack in a roasting pan. Why? The steaks will continue to thaw a bit, even after they're in the oven. If you put the frozen steaks into the oven in that same skillet you used to sear them, or if you set them directly on a baking sheet in the oven, they'll still give off enough moisture to begin to burble in their own juices, hardly a good way to get a good crunch on a steak. The rack in the pan lifts them out of the moisture and gives them a better texture.

About ¼ cup canola oil

Two 10-ounce frozen boneless beef strip steaks

Kosher salt and ground black pepper, to taste

1. Position the rack in the center of the oven. Set a shallow roasting rack in a roasting pan. Set this pan in the oven and heat the oven to 275°F.

2. Pour enough oil into an 8- or 10-inch cast-iron skillet to come to a depth of ⅛ inch. Set the skillet over medium-high heat just until smoking.

3. Add the frozen steaks and cook for 90 seconds. Turn and cook for another 90 seconds.

4. Transfer the steaks to the rack in the roasting pan. Season them with salt and pepper.

5. Roast until an instant-read meat thermometer inserted into the thickest part of the steak registers 125°F for rare, 130°F for medium-rare, or 135°F for medium, 15 to 20 minutes. Let the steaks stand at room temperature for 5 minutes before serving.

Test Kitchen Notes

- Use only boneless strip steaks so that the entire surface of one side of the steak lies flat against the hot skillet.

- Turn on your vent hood or open a window. And maybe disable the smoke alarm. It's going to get smoky.

- To prevent a big mess, set a mesh splatter shield over the skillet as the steaks sear.

- Season the steaks after they're browned so the salt and pepper don't get lost in the oil.

Voilà! There's a reason your stove's burners go up to high. You can cook more quickly at higher temperatures—within reason, of course. The best cooking shortcut is often a little more heat.

Freezer-to-Oven Whole Turkey

Makes 8 to 24 servings, depending on the size of the bird

Here's a nightmare: It's Thanksgiving morning and you forgot to thaw the turkey. Don't worry. A turkey roasts beautifully even in its frozen state. Yes, it takes longer. But the skin will get browner and even crunchier, a definite plus. Or if it's a long way from the holiday but you've got unexpected houseguests coming this weekend, pick up that frozen turkey at the market and roast it tonight. You'll have sandwiches for days!

One 8- to 24-pound frozen whole turkey

½ cup (1 stick) unsalted butter, melted

2 teaspoons kosher salt

Ground black pepper, to taste

Chicken broth or water, as needed

1. Position the rack as high as it can go in the oven and still accommodate the turkey, probably around the bottom third. Heat the oven to 325°F.

2. Unwrap the frozen turkey and place it breast side down on a roasting rack inside a large roasting pan. Roast for 2½ hours.

3. Use kitchen tongs to find and remove the giblets and neck inside the bird. If they're still stuck inside the bird, continue roasting, checking every 15 minutes until you can remove them.

4. Once the giblets are out, tip the bird to allow any hot juices to run out into the roasting pan. Turn the bird breast side up. Brush the breast with the melted butter. Season with the salt and pepper to taste.

Test Kitchen Notes

- Substitute olive oil for butter, if desired.

- Kosher turkeys are, in effect, pre-brined. Use a kosher bird for even better flavor with this technique—which, unfortunately, does *not* work well with wild turkeys or many heritage breeds.

- To get the giblets out of the hot bird, use a very long pair of kitchen tongs. Or wear silicone gloves.

- If the giblets don't come free in step 3, subtract the additional time until they do from the long roasting time in step 5.

RECIPE CONTINUES ➤➤

- Hot juices can pour out of a cooked bird. Send any children or dogs out of the room for step 4.

- Some turkeys have been injected with various brining solutions—and a few of these contain gluten or gluten-based additives. Most of the big brands are gluten-free, but check the labels to be sure.

5. Continue roasting, adding a little broth or water to the pan if it dries out or the drippings are burning, and tenting the bird loosely with aluminum foil if it browns too deeply, until an instant-read meat thermometer inserted into both the thigh and the thickest part of the breast (without touching bone) registers 165°F. Use the following chart as a rough guide to timing:

- **8- to 12-pound turkey:** 1½ to 2 hours longer

- **12- to 14-pound turkey:** 2 to 3¼ hours longer

- **14- to 18-pound turkey:** 3¼ to 3¾ hours longer

- **18- to 20-pound turkey:** 3¾ to 4¼ hours longer

- **20- to 24-pound turkey:** 4¼ to 5 hours longer

6. Transfer the (hot!) turkey to a carving board and let stand at room temperature for at least 20 minutes or up to 45 minutes before carving.

More! All poultry may be "injected with no more than ten percent of a solution containing…." Read the labels. If so, the chicken or turkey has been (sort of) brined and cooks up juicier, although you're also paying upfront for additional water weight. If you buy either injected or kosher birds, consider omitting the salt from any recipe and passing extra at the table.

THE RIGHT WAY TO MAKE A SHEET-PAN SUPPER

They're popular, no doubt. But sheet-pan suppers are often less than satisfying because varied ingredients don't often cook at the same rate, despite our wishing it were so. We end up with a baking sheet of overcooked vegetables and perfectly cooked meat—or dried out chicken breasts and crunchy potatoes. In these recipes, we stagger additions to the baking sheet based on their proper cooking times. Yes, the techniques are still streamlined a bit to save time overall. And no doubt about it, this technique is "cheffier." Frankly, it seems worth it for a better dinner. The recipes work best with a standard, 11 x 17-inch or 13 x 18-inch lipped baking sheet, not a nonstick or an insulated one, and certainly not a rimless cookie sheet, from which the rendered juices will cascade onto your oven's floor—which is no one's idea of a shortcut meal.

TASTIER

GLUTEN-FREE

Sheet-Pan Fennel-Crusted Pork Loin with Potatoes and Shallots

Makes 6 servings

Test Kitchen Notes

- For even serving slices, tie the roast with butchers' twine in two places to hold it into an even cylinder as it roasts.

- The lemon zest is really the key ingredient here. It provides a little sweet-and-sour pop against the fennel. Make sure it's truly *finely grated*. Mince any large bits.

- The hot surface of the baking sheet is what delivers golden-brown meat and crispy vegetables. Make sure the ingredients have good contact with it.

- To go over the top, drizzle with a fine, finishing olive oil before serving.

Here's Italian country cooking at its best. Since the pork roast gets a head start in the oven, it's cooked perfectly by the time the potatoes are browned and crunchy. And by raising the oven's temperature partway through, you won't gray the meat (but rather brown it) or undercook the vegetables.

1 tablespoon fennel seeds, crushed lightly under a pot on a cutting board

1 tablespoon finely grated lemon zest

1 teaspoon table salt

1 teaspoon freshly ground black pepper

3 pounds boneless pork loin

1 pound golf ball–size Yukon Gold potatoes, halved

4 tablespoons olive oil

8 large shallots, peeled and halved

8 medium garlic cloves, peeled

1 tablespoon minced fresh rosemary leaves

1. Position the rack in the center of the oven and heat the oven to 350°F.

2. Mix the crushed fennel seeds, lemon zest, salt, and pepper in a small bowl. Massage this mixture evenly over the pork.

3. Set the meat fat side down on a large lipped baking sheet. Roast for 30 minutes.

4. Turn the pork over. Scatter the potatoes around the baking sheet and drizzle everything with 2 tablespoons of the olive oil. Roast for another 30 minutes.

5. Scatter the shallots, garlic, and rosemary around the baking sheet. Drizzle the remaining 2 tablespoons of olive oil over everything.

6. Turn up the oven's temperature to 375°F. Continue roasting until the vegetables are browned, the potatoes are tender, and an instant-read meat thermometer inserted into the thickest part of the pork registers 150°F, about 30 minutes longer. Cool on the baking sheet for 10 minutes before carving and serving.

Sheet-Pan Five-Spice Chicken Tenders with Bok Choy and Shiitake Mushrooms

TASTIER

GLUTEN-FREE

Makes 4 servings

Roasting mushrooms and bok choy gives them a super-satisfying flavor burst. Bok choy is often sandy, so rinse the heads before chopping—or fill a cleaned, stoppered sink with cool water, put the halves in it, agitate a bit, and then leave them alone for 5 minutes. Scoop them out without disturbing the water, then drain and rinse the sink.

1½ pounds chicken tenders

1 tablespoon peanut oil or canola oil

1 teaspoon table salt

½ teaspoon five-spice powder

1¼ pounds baby bok choy, each cut in half through the stem and rinsed as necessary

4 ounces fresh shiitake mushrooms, stems removed and discarded

1 tablespoon soy sauce (gluten-free if that is a concern)

1½ teaspoons Worcestershire sauce (gluten-free if that is a concern)

1½ teaspoons balsamic vinegar

2 teaspoons sesame seeds

1. Position the rack in the center of the oven and heat the oven to 375°F.

2. Toss the chicken, oil, salt, and five-spice powder on a large lipped baking sheet until the chicken is evenly and thoroughly coated. Roast for 10 minutes.

3. Toss the bok choy, shiitakes, soy sauce, Worcestershire sauce, and balsamic vinegar in a second bowl. Scatter the coated bok choy around the chicken tenders, scraping any remaining marinade from that bowl onto the baking sheet.

4. Roast for another 15 minutes, until the chicken is cooked through and the bok choy stems are tender. Cool on the baking sheet for 5 minutes at room temperature and sprinkle the sesame seeds over everything just before serving.

Test Kitchen Notes

- You must use the smaller chicken tenders for this recipe, not chicken cutlets. Make sure you buy ones that are not already breaded or seasoned.

- If you don't want to buy five-spice powder, use ¼ teaspoon ground dried ginger and ¼ teaspoon ground cinnamon.

- If you can only find large bok choy, buy 1¼ pounds, core the heads, and chop into 2-inch pieces.

EASIER

Sheet-Pan Turkey Caesar Salad

Makes 4 servings

Test Kitchen Notes

- The turkey breast cutlets should be no more than ¼ inch thick.

- Rather than rolling the cutlets in the breadcrumb mixture, spoon it onto them and pat into place. Dredging them without egg or added oil will be an exercise in inefficiency, leaving too much of the coating behind. No, the bottom of the cutlets, sitting right on the metal pan, will not be coated. The meat itself will be in closer contact to the hot surface to cook even more quickly.

- Hearts of Romaine are often sold in bags in the produce section. If you buy standard heads, remove the dark green outer leaves and cut off the thick core.

Sheet-pan...*Caesar salad?* Definitely, because roasted Romaine is a thing of beauty. The natural sugars caramelize a bit, making this classic salad even tastier. Here, all the traditional flavors are built into the coating for the turkey cutlets, so you don't need any additional dressing.

Four 6-ounce thin turkey breast cutlets

½ cup finely grated Parmigiano-Reggiano or Pecorino (about 1 ounce)

½ cup plain panko breadcrumbs

4 tablespoons olive oil, plus more for the baking sheet and for serving

2 tablespoons chopped fresh parsley, preferably flat-leaf

1 teaspoon minced garlic

½ teaspoon table salt

½ teaspoon freshly ground black pepper

2 large hearts of Romaine, halved lengthwise

4 anchovy fillets packed in oil

1 tablespoon fresh lemon juice

¼ teaspoon red pepper flakes

1. Position the rack in the center of the oven and heat the oven to 450°F. Lightly oil the inside of a large lipped baking sheet.

2. Place the turkey cutlets on the baking sheet. Combine the cheese, panko, 2 tablespoons of the oil, the parsley, garlic, salt, and pepper in a small bowl. Spoon this mixture evenly onto the cutlets and pat into place with clean, dry hands.

3. Roast until the crumb topping begins to turn golden, about 10 minutes.

4. Place the Romaine cut side up on the baking sheet. Drizzle the lettuce with the remaining 2 tablespoons oil.

5. Continue roasting until the turkey is cooked through and the lettuce is a bit browned at the edges, about 5 minutes. Let stand at room temperature for 5 minutes.

6. To serve, set a cutlet on each serving plate and top with a Romaine wedge, then with an anchovy fillet. Sprinkle the lemon juice and red pepper flakes over the top. If desired, drizzle a little olive oil over each salad.

Sheet-Pan No-Fry Kung Pao Shrimp

Makes 4 servings

Stir-frying on a baking sheet? Not exactly. Instead, you'll first infuse the oil with the flavors of the Chinese-American favorite, and use that oil to oven-fry the shrimp right on the baking sheet. After that, the dish comes together quickly, so be prepared. Have cooked white or brown rice on hand.

3 tablespoons peanut oil

4 medium scallions, white and green parts separated, each thinly sliced

1 tablespoon shredded fresh ginger

2 medium garlic cloves, slivered

8 dried red chiles, preferably chiles de árbol

½ teaspoon Sichuan peppercorns, optional

1 pound medium shrimp (about 30 per pound), peeled and deveined

2 medium red bell peppers, stemmed, seeded, and cut into 1-inch squares

½ cup unsalted roasted peanuts

2 tablespoons soy sauce (gluten-free if that is a concern)

2 tablespoons Shaoxing, dry sherry, or unsweetened apple juice

2 tablespoons unseasoned rice vinegar

2 teaspoons granulated white sugar

1 teaspoon bottled hot red pepper sauce, such as sambal oelek or Texas Pete

1 teaspoon cornstarch

1. Mix the oil, the white parts of the scallions, the ginger, garlic, chiles, and peppercorns (if using) on a large lipped baking sheet until the aromatics are slick with oil.

2. Position the rack in the center of the oven. Set the baking sheet on the rack in the cool oven and heat the oven to 400°F.

3. When the aromatics are sizzling and fragrant, after about 15 minutes, add the shrimp, bell pepper squares, and peanuts. Toss well to coat with the oil, then roast until the shrimp are pink and firm, about 5 minutes.

4. Whisk the soy sauce, Shaoxing, rice vinegar, sugar, hot sauce, and cornstarch in a small bowl. Pour over the shrimp, toss well, and roast for 1 to 2 minutes, just until the sauce is bubbling and coating everything. Sprinkle the scallion greens over the baking sheet just before serving.

Test Kitchen Notes

- Shaoxing is a Chinese cooking wine made from rice. You can usually find it in Asian markets and most large North American supermarkets, but feel free to substitute an equivalent amount of dry sherry. Once opened, Shaoxing can be stored in a cool pantry for about 6 months.

- Shred fresh ginger through the large holes of a box grater. If the ginger's husk isn't dry and fibrous, you needn't peel it (for this or any recipe).

- Substitute 1 pound boneless skinless chicken breasts cut for stir-fry for the shrimp; increase the cooking time in step 3 to 8 minutes.

Voilà! Need cooked rice but don't have the time to make it? Stop by any Chinese restaurant. They'll sell you a container or two.

Sheet-Pan Mole-Crusted Pork with Yellow Squash and Sweet Onions

Makes 4 servings

Test Kitchen Notes

- The fig jam will give the pork a somewhat earthy flavor; the marmalade will make it sweeter and more summery.

- If your market doesn't have a pork tenderloin large enough, ask the butcher to tie two together to make an evenly sized roast.

- Do not use so-called "pure" chile powder (like ancho or jalapeño powder). You want the flavor of the oregano that is mixed into standard chili powder.

The flavors of mole, the Oaxacan sauce made with unsweetened chocolate and spices, get turned into a rub for pork loin in this sheet-pan supper. Since the onions don't roast very long, look for Vidalias or other sweet onions. Their caramelized sugars will complement the complex flavors in the rub. Serve with white or Spanish rice.

1 tablespoon fig jam or orange marmalade

1 tablespoon chili powder

1 teaspoon unsweetened cocoa powder

1 teaspoon dried oregano

1 teaspoon white sesame seeds, optional

1 teaspoon table salt

1½ pounds pork tenderloin

1½ pounds yellow summer squash, cut into 1-inch-thick rings

2 medium sweet white onions, peeled and sliced into ½-inch-thick rings

2 tablespoons olive oil

½ teaspoon ground cumin

½ teaspoon freshly ground black pepper

1 medium lime, cut into wedges, for serving

1. Position the rack in the center of the oven and heat the oven to 400°F.

2. Make a paste by combining the jam, chili powder, cocoa powder, oregano, sesame seeds (if using), and ½ teaspoon salt in a small bowl until uniform.

3. Smear this mixture evenly over the pork tenderloin and set it on a large lipped baking sheet. Roast for 10 minutes.

4. Scatter the squash and onions around the roast. Drizzle the vegetables with the olive oil and sprinkle with the cumin, pepper, and remaining ½ teaspoon salt.

5. Continue roasting until the vegetables are tender and an instant-read meat thermometer inserted into the center of the pork tenderloin registers 150°F, about 15 minutes. Set aside at room temperature for 5 minutes, then carve and serve with the lime wedges to squeeze over each slice of pork.

TASTIER

Sheet-Pan Individual Turkey Meat Loaves with Lemon-Garlic Vegetables

Makes 4 servings

These are small meat loaves, about the same weight as standard, homemade hamburger patties. If you don't need to feed four tonight, save the leftovers in the fridge for meat loaf sandwiches the next day.

Test Kitchen Notes

- You'll have a better chance finding the right size potatoes in the bulk bin.

- Ground turkey gives off less gray, cloudy fat than beef would, making the vegetables more appetizing.

- In step 5, spoon the chutney mixture over the loaves—or use a pastry brush.

12 ounces large Brussels sprouts, any brown leaves removed, halved through the stems

12 ounces golf ball–size red potatoes, quartered

1 large leek (about 8 ounces), white and pale green parts only, sliced into thin rings

5 tablespoons olive oil

1 teaspoon finely grated lemon zest

2 tablespoons fresh lemon juice

2 teaspoons minced garlic

1 teaspoon table salt

1 teaspoon ground black pepper

1½ pounds ground turkey breast meat

1 medium carrot (about 2 ounces), grated through the large holes of a box grater

1 small yellow onion, peeled and grated through the large holes of a box grater

6 tablespoons plain panko breadcrumbs

1 large egg, lightly beaten in a small bowl

½ cup mango or cranberry chutney

2 tablespoons soy sauce

1. Position the rack in the center of the oven and heat the oven to 400°F.

2. Mix the Brussels sprout halves, potatoes, leek, oil, lemon zest and juice, garlic, ½ teaspoon salt, and ½ teaspoon pepper on a large, lipped baking sheet until the vegetables are evenly and thoroughly coated. Arrange them in one layer on the sheet. Roast for 10 minutes.

3. Meanwhile, gently mix the ground turkey, carrots, onion, breadcrumbs, egg, remaining ½ teaspoon salt, and remaining ½ teaspoon pepper in that same bowl until uniform. Shape into four, small, even loaves.

4. Nestle these loaves among the vegetables on the baking sheet. Continue roasting until an instant-read meat thermometer inserted into the thickest part of one loaf registers 150°F, about 25 minutes.

5. Mix the chutney and soy sauce in a small bowl until uniform. Spread over the meat loaves. Continue roasting until the loaves are irresistibly glazed and an instant-read meat thermometer inserted into the center of at least two of the loaves registers 165°F, about another 10 minutes. Cool on the baking sheet at room temperature for 10 minutes before serving.

Voilà! What's the deal with peeling carrots? Probably to get rid of brown spots. If a carrot's to be cooked in some way, there's no need to peel it. Just wash off any grit, then prep as directed.

ONE-PAN
SKEWER SUPPERS

Oven-roasted skewers and kebabs are a waste! Well, not exactly. They're a simple, easy supper. But so much of the juice gets wasted as the flavors concentrate in the oven. So why not roast them over a 9 x 13-inch baking dish of vegetables? You'll transfer the benefit of their juices to a flavorful side dish or condiment.

More importantly, don't sit the skewers *in* the pan on top of the vegetables, or the whole thing will get mushy. Instead, rest the ends of each skewer on the sides of the baking dish so they stay airborne—sort of like a foosball table. (See the photograph on page 208.) The skewered protein will brown evenly, and the vegetables will have enough contact with the hot air of the oven to crisp up. Since you don't want those skewers to roll around (or off !) the baking dish, thread each piece on two skewers for stability.

And one little bit of warning: Take extra care when turning those skewers over the baking dish. Don't use your fingers! The pan is already hot—and right below the skewer. Use kitchen tongs to grab hold of the meat or fish and then turn the skewer over.

One-Pan Swordfish Kebabs with Spicy Roasted Pineapple

EASIER

GLUTEN-FREE

Makes 4 servings

Swordfish offers a terrifically meaty texture for kebabs—but can get overcooked as the pieces rest right against a baking sheet or even against a grill grate. By giving them a little heft over a 9 x 13-inch baking pan, they'll stay toothsome and evenly cooked. Roasting pineapple (below those kebabs) gives it an even sweeter flavor—and allows you to create a warm pineapple salsa as a side dish for fish kebabs.

1 medium fresh pineapple, peeled, cored, and cut into 1-inch chunks (about 3 cups)

1 tablespoon honey

1 medium shallot, minced

1 teaspoon minced garlic

½ teaspoon dried thyme

½ teaspoon red pepper flakes

¼ teaspoon ground allspice

¼ teaspoon table salt

1½ pounds thick-cut skinless swordfish steaks, cut into 1-inch cubes

2 tablespoons soy sauce (gluten-free if that is a concern)

1 teaspoon ground black pepper

1. Position the rack in the center of the oven; heat the oven to 450°F.

2. Toss the pineapple, honey, shallot, garlic, thyme, red pepper flakes, allspice, and salt in a 9 x 13-inch baking dish. Roast for 10 minutes.

3. Meanwhile, gently toss the fish with the soy sauce and black pepper in a large bowl until the chunks are well coated. Working slightly off-center, thread the swordfish cubes onto four 10-inch bamboo skewers. Then insert a second skewer through the chunks so each batch is on two parallel skewers.

4. After 10 minutes, set the skewers side by side crosswise on the roasting pan so the bamboo ends rest on the pan and the fish hangs over the pineapple mixture.

5. Roast for 5 minutes, then turn the skewers over and continue roasting until the fish is hot and cooked through, about 5 minutes longer. Transfer the skewers to serving plates or a platter; dish up the hot pineapple salsa below as its condiment.

Test Kitchen Notes

- Look in the produce section's refrigerator case for whole fresh pineapple that's been peeled and cored.

- If you can only find swordfish with the skin on, ask the fishmonger at your market to skin it for you (and maybe cut it into cubes while she or he is at it).

- For a heftier meal, prepare rice noodles, then toss them with the pineapple mixture in the baking dish.

Voilà! Consider investing in a mini food processor. It can mince herbs, shallots, scallions, or ginger in seconds.

One-Pan Tuna Skewers with Miso Butter and Kale

Makes 4 servings

Test Kitchen Notes

- For greater ease, buy bagged, pre-shredded kale.

- The tuna steaks should be 1 inch thick to make cubes more easily.

- Buy tuna with bands of meat that are compact and tight, not separating.

- Use a very sharp knife to cube the tuna. Or ask the fishmonger to do it.

- For a much more piquant meal, substitute wasabi paste for the miso paste.

- It's hard to tell the exact moment when the tuna cubes are done. We often follow chef Eric Ripert's technique (in fact, for most fish): Stick a sharp paring knife into the fish, hold it there for a couple of seconds, then remove it and touch the *flat* of the blade to your lips. (Be very careful of sharp edges.) The metal should be slightly warm, not cool but certainly not hot.

Miso paste is a fermented soy bean paste, available in most large supermarkets and from health-food stores. Combined with butter, it's the ultimate East/West fusion, a wonderfully salty match-up that makes the tuna and the accompanying kale rich and satisfying.

6 cups shredded stemmed kale

1 tablespoon unseasoned rice vinegar

1 tablespoon soy sauce (gluten-free if that is a concern)

1 tablespoon mirin

1½ pounds thick-cut tuna steaks, cut into 1-inch cubes

3 tablespoons unsalted butter, melted

2 teaspoons white miso paste

1. Position the rack in the center of the oven; heat the oven to 450°F.

2. Toss the kale, vinegar, soy sauce, and mirin in a 9 x 13-inch baking dish until the kale is evenly coated. Roast for 5 minutes.

3. Working slightly off-center, thread the tuna chunks onto four 10-inch bamboo skewers. Then insert a second skewer through the chunks so each batch is on two parallel skewers. Mix the butter and miso paste in a small bowl.

4. Toss the kale in the pan. Set the skewers side by side crosswise on the roasting pan so the bamboo ends rest on the pan sides and the chunks hang over the kale mixture. Brush the tuna skewers with half the miso butter, letting any excess fall onto the kale below.

5. Roast for 5 minutes, then turn the skewers over and brush them with the remaining miso butter. Continue roasting until the tuna is medium-rare, about 5 minutes longer. Transfer the skewers to serving plates or a platter; dish up the kale mixture below as the side dish.

One-Pan Lamb Kebabs with White Beans and Artichokes

Makes 4 servings

These kebabs are roasted over a wonderful mix of vegetables, a Mediterranean-style side dish in the pan below. While the lamb will be cooked through by the times in the recipe, take its internal temperature periodically while it roasts to be sure. It should be for 130°F for medium-rare, or 145°F for medium. (However, understand that 130°F is not within the safety standards set by the USDA.)

One 15-ounce can white beans, such as great northern beans, drained and rinsed

1 pound frozen artichoke heart quarters, thawed

¼ cup dry vermouth, dry white wine, or chicken broth

2 tablespoons olive oil

1 tablespoon dried herbes de Provence

½ teaspoon table salt

½ teaspoon ground black pepper

1½ pounds boneless lamb loin, cut into 1-inch cubes

2 tablespoons Dijon mustard

2 teaspoons white balsamic vinegar

½ cup minced fresh parsley leaves

1. Position the rack in the center of oven; heat the oven to 400°F.

2. Combine the beans, artichoke quarters, vermouth, olive oil, herbes de Provence, salt, and pepper in a 9 x 13-inch baking dish. Roast for 10 minutes.

3. Meanwhile, toss the lamb chunks with the mustard and vinegar in a large bowl until the chunks are evenly and thoroughly coated. Working slightly off-center, thread the lamb onto four 10-inch bamboo skewers. Then insert a second skewer through the chunks so each batch is on two parallel skewers.

4. Set the skewers crosswise on the roasting pan so the bamboo ends rest on the pan sides and the lamb hangs over the bean mixture.

5. Roast for 10 minutes, then turn the skewers over and continue roasting until the lamb is medium-rare or medium, about 5 or 10 minutes longer.

6. Transfer the skewers to serving plates or a platter. Sprinkle the parsley over the bean mixture in the baking dish, stir well, and serve alongside the skewers.

Test Kitchen Notes

- You can substitute boneless leg of lamb for the more expensive lamb loin, but it's more of a chore to cut it into 1-inch cubes. The texture will be firmer, less like tenderloin and more like sirloin.

- If you don't like lamb, use cubed boneless pork loin.

- For more flavor, add halved peeled medium garlic cloves with the artichoke heart quarters.

Voilà! Put raw meat in the freezer for up to 1 hour or raw fish in the freezer for up to 30 minutes before slicing to make it easier to cut.

One-Pan Beef Kebabs with Warm Garlicky Corn and Bean Salsa

EASIER

GLUTEN-FREE

Makes 4 servings

Here's a new take on Tex-Mex. The salsa that roasts under the kebabs is something like a cross between salsa and baked beans. It's spicy and not too sweet, despite the tiny amount of brown sugar which aids in caramelization. Serve the beef and salsa with tortillas and jarred pickled jalapeño slices for easy homemade tacos.

One 28-ounce can diced tomatoes, drained

1 cup fresh corn kernels or thawed frozen corn kernels

1 cup canned pink beans, drained and rinsed

2 tablespoons sherry vinegar

2 medium garlic cloves, thinly sliced

2 teaspoons dried oregano

½ teaspoon table salt

2 teaspoons dark brown sugar

2 teaspoons ground cumin

2 teaspoons mild smoked paprika

1½ pounds beef sirloin, cut into 1-inch cubes

1. Position the rack in the middle of the oven; heat the oven to 400°F.

2. Stir the tomatoes, corn, beans, vinegar, garlic, oregano, and salt in a 9 x 13-inch baking dish. Roast for 12 minutes.

3. Meanwhile, mix the brown sugar, cumin, and smoked paprika in a large bowl. Add the beef cubes and stir until evenly coated. Working slightly off-center, thread the beef onto four 10-inch bamboo skewers. Then insert a second skewer through the chunks so each batch is on two parallel skewers.

4. After 12 minutes, stir the corn mixture, then set the skewers crosswise on the roasting pan so the bamboo ends rest on the pan sides and the beef hangs over the corn mixture.

5. Roast for 8 minutes, then turn the skewers over and continue roasting until an instant-read meat thermometer inserted into one of the cubes registers 130°F for medium-rare or 140°F for medium, about 3 or 6 minutes longer. Transfer the skewers to serving plates or a platter; dish up the hot corn and bean salsa as the condiment.

Test Kitchen Notes

- To drain canned diced tomatoes, use a fine-mesh sieve or line a standard colander with paper towels.

- If you'd like, substitute apple cider vinegar for the sherry vinegar, but increase the brown sugar to 1 tablespoon.

Voilà! Nothing slows you down like washing cutting boards. Buy two or three, so you can stash a dirty one in the dishwasher or a sudsy sink and use another without stopping to clean up.

EASIER

One-Pan Pork Skewers with Sweet and Sticky Broccoli

Makes 4 servings

Voilà! To keep a chef's knife from sticking to raw pork, chicken, or lamb, mist it with water before slicing.

In this oven-roasted version of takeout Chinese sweet and sour pork, the hoisin sauce caramelizes and makes the sauce irresistible. If desired, sprinkle chopped cashews over each plate for added crunch.

4 cups small broccoli florets

3 medium scallions, trimmed and thinly sliced

2 tablespoons hoisin sauce

1 tablespoon minced peeled fresh ginger

1 tablespoon unseasoned rice vinegar

1½ pounds boneless pork loin, cut into 1-inch cubes

1 tablespoon toasted sesame oil

1 teaspoon five-spice powder

1. Position the rack in the center of the oven; heat the oven to 400°F.

2. Combine the broccoli florets, scallions, hoisin sauce, ginger, and vinegar in a 9 x 13-inch baking pan, stirring until the broccoli is evenly coated.

3. Toss the pork with the sesame oil and five-spice powder in a large bowl. Working slightly off-center, thread the pork pieces onto four 10-inch bamboo skewers. Then thread a second skewer through the chunks so each batch sits on two parallel skewers. Set the skewers crosswise on the roasting pan so the bamboo ends rest on the pan sides and the pork hangs over the broccoli.

4. Roast for 12 minutes. Turn the skewers and gently toss the broccoli. Continue roasting until the pork is cooked through, about 12 minutes longer.

5. Transfer the skewers to serving plates or a platter; serve the broccoli alongside.

BROILER SUPPERS

The broiler may be the most underused kitchen tool in your arsenal. It provides an intense, searing heat for culinary possibilities way beyond browning meringues or turning the sugary topping on crème brûlée crunchy. In fact, it can work wonders in the caramelization of natural sugars in all sorts of savory ingredients. Make sure you work with broiler-safe equipment, and avoid nonstick baking sheets that may indeed heat beyond the safe temperature of the coating.

Because you'll cook the meal under the broiler, not just brown something quickly, the oven rack will be set slightly lower than in many traditional broiler recipes. The lower setting allows greater time under the intense heat, the better to reduce the sauce in the pan, without burning. If your oven rack does not allow for the dish to be 6 inches from the broiler, err on the side of greater distance, not less.

Broiler Salmon Fillets with Red Onion and Asparagus

Makes 4 servings

Test Kitchen Notes

- Use thicker-cut salmon fillets for more even cooking.

- Set the salmon fillets on the baking sheet with the flat side (that is, the skinned side) down.

Salmon fillets cook quickly—but also dry out easily. The intense broiler heat works in their favor: less time in the oven, more sear on the surface. Beyond that, the point here is to get a little char on the onions and asparagus as well as a nice glaze on the salmon from the reduction of the soy-honey sauce.

2 tablespoons honey

1 tablespoon soy sauce (gluten-free if that is a concern)

1 tablespoon Dijon mustard

1 tablespoon balsamic vinegar

½ teaspoon red pepper flakes

1½ pounds thin asparagus spears, trimmed and cut into 2-inch pieces

1 large red onion, roughly chopped

2 tablespoons olive oil

½ teaspoon kosher salt

½ teaspoon ground black pepper

Four 6-ounce skinless salmon fillets

1. Mix the honey, soy sauce, mustard, balsamic vinegar, and red pepper flakes in a small bowl until uniform. Set aside.

2. Position the oven rack 6 inches away from the broiler element. Heat the broiler.

3. Toss the asparagus, onion, oil, salt, and black pepper on a large lipped baking sheet until uniform. Nestle the salmon among the vegetables.

4. Broil the salmon and vegetables for 2 minutes. Remove the baking sheet from the oven and brush the salmon with the honey mixture, allowing it to drizzle over the vegetables, too. Toss the vegetables one more time around the fish.

5. Broil until the salmon is glazed and almost cooked through, 3 to 4 minutes. Serve hot.

FASTER

Broiler Kofta with Peppers, Onions, and Tahini Sauce

Makes 4 servings

Test Kitchen Notes

- Kofta is usually made only with ground lamb. However, ground beef adds a definite sweetness, more appetizing with this mix of flavors.

- Kofta is usually formed around a metal skewer. Since you're not using such a tool here, make these logs compact so they'll hold together over the heat.

- Mince the onion into tiny bits, no more than ⅛ inch each.

- If you like, skip the tahini sauce and substitute a store-bought yogurt ranch salad dressing.

Kofta is a highly flavored Middle-Eastern dish of ground meat, sometimes shaped into a sausage or meatball shape without a casing. Here, it's broiled with vegetables and served with a traditional Middle Eastern sauce. While you can serve this supper alongside pita rounds, you can also offer it right inside pita pockets: Put the kofta and roasted vegetables in the pockets, include chopped iceberg lettuce if you want, and serve with tahini sauce for drizzling or dipping.

For the Kofta and Vegetables

1 pound lean ground lamb

1 pound lean ground beef

1 large egg

1 small yellow onion, finely minced

⅔ cup unseasoned dried breadcrumbs

¼ cup chopped fresh mint leaves

¼ cup chopped fresh dill fronds

2 tablespoons tomato paste

2 teaspoons minced garlic

1 teaspoon ground cumin

1 teaspoon table salt

½ teaspoon ground cinnamon

½ teaspoon ground allspice

½ teaspoon ground cloves

½ teaspoon red pepper flakes

2 large red onions, thinly sliced and broken into rings

2 large yellow bell peppers, stemmed, cored, and cut into thin strips

¼ cup olive oil

For the Tahini Sauce

⅓ **cup tahini**

¼ **cup regular or low-fat plain yogurt**

¼ **cup fresh lemon juice**

2 **tablespoons minced fresh parsley leaves**

½ **teaspoon table salt**

½ **teaspoon ground black pepper**

Water, as needed

To Serve

4 **pitas**

To Make the Kofta and Vegetables

1. Mix the lamb, beef, egg, minced yellow onion, breadcrumbs, mint, dill, tomato paste, garlic, cumin, salt, cinnamon, allspice, cloves, and red pepper flakes in a medium bowl until uniform. Form into eight sausage-like logs.

2. Set the logs, red onion rings, and pepper strips on a large lipped baking sheet. Drizzle the olive oil over everything.

3. Position the rack 6 inches from the broiler element; heat the broiler for a couple of minutes.

4. Broil, turning the kofta and tossing the vegetables once, until the meat is cooked through, about 8 minutes. Cool on the baking sheet for a few minutes.

To Make the Tahini Sauce

5. Whisk the tahini, yogurt, lemon juice, parsley, salt, and pepper in a small bowl until uniform. Add additional water, 1 tablespoon at a time, to create a sauce with the consistency of pancake batter.

To Serve

6. Transfer the contents of the baking sheet to a serving platter. Drizzle the kofta and roasted vegetables with the tahini sauce and serve with the pitas.

Broiler Blood Orange and Rosemary Chicken

Makes 4 servings

By starting the chicken thighs skin side down, you cook them quite a bit before turning them over and crisping the skin under the hot broiler element. The chicken, of course, takes much longer than the fennel—and thus the vegetable is added later.

2 pounds small bone-in skin-on chicken thighs (about 8 ounces each)

1 tablespoon finely grated blood orange zest

⅔ cup freshly squeezed blood orange juice (from about 3 blood oranges)

⅓ cup olive oil

1 tablespoon white wine vinegar

1 tablespoon minced fresh rosemary

½ teaspoon table salt

¼ teaspoon ground black pepper

2 medium fennel bulbs, thinly sliced into strips

1 medium garlic head, broken into cloves but not peeled

1 baguette loaf, cut into slices and toasted

1. Position an oven rack 6 to 8 inches from the broiler element; heat the broiler.

2. Place the chicken thighs skin side down on a large lipped baking sheet and broil for 10 minutes, until the meat and even the exposed bone have browned, maybe even blackened in a couple of places.

3. Meanwhile, whisk the blood orange zest and juice, the olive oil, vinegar, rosemary, salt, and pepper in a small bowl until uniform.

4. Turn the chicken pieces over (now skin side up) and sprinkle the fennel strips and garlic cloves around the pan (but not on the chicken). Pour the juice mixture over everything.

Test Kitchen Notes

- Use only smaller 8-ounce chicken thighs for this recipe, not the larger 12-ounce or even 1-pound thighs.

- Blood oranges add a slight "berry" flavor to the dish. If you can't find blood oranges, substitute fresh orange juice, but mash about 2 tablespoons fresh raspberries into it for the right flavor.

- To thinly slice a fennel bulb into strips, trim off the stalks and fronds, as well as any browned outside leaves. Slice the bulb in half top to bottom, then thinly slice these halves, breaking up the slices into strips with your fingers.

- Since you're using medium fennel bulbs (8 to 10 ounces each), there's no need to remove their cores.

5. Continue broiling, basting everything twice, until the chicken skin has browned and an instant-read meat thermometer inserted into the thickest part of a couple of pieces (without touching bone) registers 165°F, about 10 minutes. Cool on the baking sheet for 5 minutes. To serve, squeeze the soft garlic onto the bread slices (discarding the skins) and serve the chicken and vegetables with any remaining pan juices drizzled over them. When eating, feel free to use the garlic-coated bread rounds to sop up those juices.

Voilà! Use scissors for mincing fresh herbs directly into soups, stews, and pan sauces.

6

MORE SUPPER
SHORTCUTS

A few of these supper shortcut recipes are a little more challenging, or perhaps a little fancier, than others in the book: roast duck, roast beef, even pulled pork. They go beyond the realm of the everyday. That's not the worst thing, of course. It's just a consideration.

But most of the recipes are still easy and quick. For example, there's a set of recipes to discover the untapped possibilities of the brine left over in a pickle jar. Another set turns a Bundt pan into a vertical roaster. And there are recipes for the best way to cook fish fillets on the grill.

Before heading off to the last of the supper recipes, let's take a quick review of a few of the most common cooking mistakes.

1. The heat's too low. Leading hands-on cooking classes over the years across the U.S. and on cruise ships around the world, we've noticed that many people are afraid of the stove's heat—not out of a fear of burning themselves, but because of a basic timidity when it comes to the task of cooking. To be frank, searing, caramelizing, or (most of the time) even grilling on low is like driving 35 mph at the Indy 500. Crank up that heat! If a recipe calls for medium heat, consider it to be the very middle of your burner's dial, not nudged back down toward the low side. If you watch your skillets and pans carefully, you can nudge the heat a little higher than medium, on toward medium-high. And if you know your stove is sluggish, you should also bump up the dial a bit. Of course, there are lots of times when you should use a very low heat: simmering, reducing something over several hours, keeping a covered soup warm.

2. The skillet is packed. If so, the moisture that meat, fish, and veggies give off over the heat has no place to go. It pools in the pan and then turns to steam which softens the food's outer edges and prevents proper browning. You need a fair amount of hot, exposed surface area in a skillet to burn it off quickly. Of course, you can go overboard. Two little boneless skinless chicken breasts can actually burn more quickly in a 14-inch skillet since all the protective moisture is almost instantly burned off. So use a small skillet only to cook small things: a single pork chop, a two-egg omelet, a turkey cutlet.

3. The meat is cold. Your refrigerator—and hence the food in it—is around 40°F. (Or it *should* be, or even a degree or two colder, for proper food safety.) But your oven is at 350°F, maybe higher. By the time a chicken breast or pork loin in the oven finally warms up at its center, it's desiccated at the edges. So take meat and poultry out of the fridge 10 to 20 minutes before cooking it. That said, we do have recipes in this book that are cooked directly from the freezer. These have been calibrated with more liquids, lower cooking temperatures, and other culinary tricks to make sure they're satisfying when they're ready.

4. The pan or pot (or grill grate) is cool. Food on a hot surface immediately starts to sizzle and sputter. The road to caramelization may be noisy, but it yields a crisp crust and beautifully browned edges. Put ingredients in a room-temperature or even barely warm pan or pot *only* when a recipe specifically says to do so.

Slow-Roast No-Watch Standing Rib Roast

Makes 6 to 8 servings

Rib roasts are a holiday treat. But let's face it: They can be a tad, well, *boring* for such an expensive cut of meat. What can you do besides the salt-and-pepper treatment, especially since any flavorful rubs or sauces will burn in a high-heat oven? Here's the solution. After massaging a flavorful rub into the meat and roasting it very slowly for a long time at a low temperature, you can then sear it to a crunch right before serving and the spices won't char during cooking. Bonus: You can roast a spectacular piece of beef without worrying about it, checking on it, or fussing with it. And here's the best news of all: This technique will result in a rib roast that's rare (or medium-rare) right to the edge, no overcooked bits around the center eye. So, you might ask, is a recipe that takes longer than the traditional method still a kitchen shortcut? Yes! Because there's minimal effort with much better results. And this recipe's something of a holiday miracle, given that there's an hour lag built into the middle of it. You'll have time to make a side dish, build a playlist, and open the wine.

Test Kitchen Notes

- Pick one of the three spice-rubbed or seed-coated rib roasts below.

- To infuse the flavor of the roasting bones into the meat, do not buy a rib roast where the eye of meat has been cut off the bones and tied back on. Instead, buy one with the meat still attached to the bones. You may have to *insist* on this at the store. Butchers love to cut the meat off the bones and tie it back on. But when left intact, the rib roast will benefit from the added flavor the bones bring to the meat as it roasts. Even the small barrier of the cut cells between the bones and the eye of meat makes a big difference.

- For the meatiest slices (with less fat and gristle), ask your butcher for bones 1 through 3 (or 4, depending on how many you'd like to feed). And again, insist. This is the preferred part of the rack of ribs. Butchers love to try to get rid of bones 5 through 7 or even 8 when they can.

Four-Seed Rubbed Rib Roast

One 4- to 6-pound (3- to 4-bone) beef standing rib roast

2 tablespoons olive oil or canola oil

1 tablespoon yellow mustard seeds

1 tablespoon coriander seeds

1 tablespoon caraway seeds

1 teaspoon celery seeds

2 teaspoons kosher salt

1 teaspoon ground black pepper

Southwestern Rubbed Rib Roast

One 4- to 6-pound (3- to 4-bone) beef standing rib roast

2 tablespoons olive oil or canola oil

1 tablespoon cumin seeds

1 tablespoon dried oregano

1 tablespoon dark brown sugar

2 teaspoons kosher salt

1 tablespoon ground black pepper

Garlic-and-Fennel Rubbed Rib Roast

One 4- to 6-pound (3- to 4-bone) beef standing rib roast

2 tablespoons olive oil or canola oil

Up to 3 tablespoons minced garlic

2 tablespoons fennel seeds, crushed in a garlic press or under a pot on a cutting board

2 teaspoons kosher salt

Up to ½ teaspoon red pepper flakes

RECIPE CONTINUES ➡➡

- Kosher salt makes for a crunchier and more flavorful rub.

- An instant-read meat thermometer is crucial to the success of this recipe. Go by the meat's internal temperature in step 3. The stated timings there are mere suggestions.

- In step 3, take the temperature after 3½ hours, then again at the 4-hour mark, to see where the meat's at, the better to judge how long it should continue to roast.

- If your oven has a convection setting, use it in step 5 for the best crunchy crust.

1. Position the rack in the center of the oven or as close as you can get to its center while still accommodating the beef in a roasting pan. Heat the oven to 175°F (or 200°F, if your oven will not go that low).

2. Rub the beef with the oil. Mix together the seasonings from the rub of your choice, then sprinkle it over the meat, pressing any dried spices so they stick.

3. Set the rib roast in a roasting pan bone side down. Roast until an instant-read meat thermometer inserted into the thickest part of the meat (without touching bone) registers 124°F for rare, 127°F for medium-rare, or 135°F for medium, 4 to 5 hours.

4. Remove the beef from the oven and let it stand at room temperature for 1 hour (while you do other things). Meanwhile, increase the oven's temperature to 500°F.

5. Return the beef in its roasting pan to the oven and roast for 10 minutes to crisp the exterior.

6. Transfer the roast to a cutting board and leave it alone for 10 to 15 minutes. To carve, slice the eye of meat off the bones by running a large, thin carving knife along the interior curve of those bones. Remove the eye and carve it into ½-inch-thick slices. Slice between the bones for roasted beef ribs.

Voilà! Couscous stocked with lots of vegetables makes a much faster veggie side than potatoes or leafy greens. Packaged couscous cooks in about 5 minutes. Once ready, add lots of salad fixings: sliced broccoli florets, sliced sugar snap peas, halved seedless grapes, quartered cherry tomatoes, baby kale, and/ or an antipasto selection of pitted olives and marinated artichoke hearts. Add additional olive oil for a dressing.

Cast-Iron Paella

Makes 6 to 8 servings

The problem with making an authentic Spanish paella is the traditional pan: a concave, shallow pan, a bit like a super-wide wok, that fits into a fire well. Who has such a pan? Who has a fire well? Here's a way to adapt the technique for a dinner party–worthy dish with a standard pan, stove, and oven. You'll start the paella on top of the stove and stir the rice just a bit to rub some of its starch into the sauce. After that, the whole thing goes in the oven to finish off while you open the wine. It's an adaptation shortcut to turn a once-in-a-lifetime dish into a weekend staple. One warning: The skillet is heavy when full. You'll need two hands to move it, as well as dry pot holders.

4 cups (1 quart) chicken broth

Up to ½ teaspoon saffron threads

3 tablespoons olive oil

1 pound fresh mild pork or turkey sausage, cut into 1½-inch pieces

1 pound boneless skinless chicken thighs

1 medium yellow onion, chopped

1 medium fennel bulb, trimmed and chopped

½ cup dry sherry or rosé wine

One 14-ounce can diced tomatoes

1½ tablespoons mild smoked paprika

1½ teaspoons dried thyme

1½ teaspoons dried oregano

Up to 1 teaspoon red pepper flakes

½ teaspoon ground dried yellow mustard

½ teaspoon table salt

1½ cups uncooked white Valencia, bomba, arborio, or other medium-grain white rice

1 pound medium shrimp (about 30 per pound), peeled and deveined

12 mahogany or other thin-shelled small clams

½ pound mussels, debearded and scrubbed if necessary

Test Kitchen Notes

- Either Valencia or bomba is the traditional Spanish rice for paella. If you can't find either at your grocery store, white arborio will work just as well. (Lately, brown arborio rice has shown up at high-end supermarkets. It will not work with this technique.)

- Scrub the clams before using to remove excess grit. Do not use any open raw clams or mussels that do not close when tapped.

- Don't ignore the 10-minute resting period at the end of the recipe. The rice needs time to fully absorb the excess liquid.

RECIPE CONTINUES ➤➤

1. Position the rack in the center of the oven; heat the oven to 350°F.

2. Mix the broth and saffron in a medium saucepan. Set over low heat to warm but do not bring to a simmer.

3. Heat the oil in a heavy-bottomed 14- or 15-inch skillet, preferably cast-iron. Add the sausage and chicken thighs; brown well on all sides, turning occasionally, about 6 minutes. Transfer to a large bowl.

4. Add the onion and fennel to the skillet; cook, stirring often, until the onion turns translucent and begins to soften, about 4 minutes. Add the sherry and scrape up any browned bits on the bottom of the skillet. Bring to a full simmer and reduce until the liquid is half its original volume, 1 to 2 minutes.

5. Add the tomatoes, smoked paprika, thyme, oregano, pepper flakes, mustard, and salt. Stir well and cook until bubbling, probably less than 1 minute. Add the rice and stir constantly until the liquid has been absorbed, about 5 minutes.

6. Pour in the broth and continue to cook, stirring constantly, until the mixture begins to look like a very wet risotto, about 15 minutes.

7. Stir in the sausage and chicken thighs. Artfully arrange the seafood on top of the rice, setting the clams and mussels hinge side down in the saucy rice.

8. Slip the skillet into the oven and bake until the rice is tender, the meat is cooked through, and the bivalves have opened, about 20 minutes. To test if the paella is ready, use a small spoon to pull it back from the pan's side. Check to make sure there's just the barest amount of liquid left. Then scoop up a few grains of rice and taste them for tenderness.

9. Set the skillet aside for 10 minutes at room temperature. Discard any unopened bivalves just before serving.

More! Paella often has a crunchy bottom, called the *socarrat*. To achieve that here, set the finished paella on the stove over medium-high heat for a couple of minutes—but no more or the rice will start to burn. Keep checking by pulling some of the paella away from the side of the skillet and looking at the rice on the bottom to see if it's developed a lightly browned, dried out crust. But be careful: Because of an abundance of natural sugars, the rice will quickly burn thereafter.

No-Cutting-Board No-Prep Arroz con Pollo

Makes 6 servings

It's hard to believe you don't have to chop or mince to make the classic Spanish chicken and rice casserole—at least, not in this shortcut version. The technique saves time by working with frozen chopped vegetables. It's important to add them in a different order than if you were building the dish off a cutting board. Given that, it's certainly a weeknight possibility, even if you're dog-tired from the day.

2 tablespoons olive oil

1 pound sweet Italian sausage links

2¾ pounds (about 6) boneless skinless chicken thighs

1 teaspoon table salt

½ teaspoon ground black pepper

1 cup frozen pearl onions (do not thaw)

1½ cups frozen artichoke heart quarters (do not thaw)

2 teaspoons minced garlic

2 teaspoons dried oregano

1 teaspoon mild smoked paprika

Up to ½ teaspoon saffron threads

½ cup dry sherry or unsweetened apple cider

2½ cups chicken broth

One 14-ounce can diced tomatoes, preferably fire-roasted

1½ cups uncooked white arborio or Valencia rice

1 cup frozen bell pepper strips (do not thaw)

Test Kitchen Notes

- Some Italian sausage links use wheat filler. Check the label if gluten is an issue.

- If you'd like, substitute fresh chorizo sausage for a bigger flavor.

- If you can't find frozen artichoke heart quarters, use 5 artichoke hearts packed in water from a can or a jar. Drain and cut these in half.

- To plump the rice and blend the flavors, set the casserole aside, covered but off the heat, for 10 minutes before serving.

- To take the dish over the top, clean the shells of a handful of very small, raw clams and set them on top of the casserole before you set it aside for the final 10 minutes. They'll open in the residual steam.

1. Heat the oven to 325°F.

2. Warm 1 tablespoon of the oil in a Dutch oven, cast-iron casserole, or oven-safe deep sauté pan set over medium-high heat. Add the sausage and brown well, turning occasionally, about 4 minutes. Transfer to a plate.

3. Season the chicken with the salt and pepper. Add the remaining 1 tablespoon oil to the pan, then add the chicken and brown on both sides, turning once, about 4 minutes. Transfer to the plate as well.

4. Add the pearl onions to the pan and cook in the rendered fat and residual oil, stirring frequently, until lightly browned, about 3 minutes. Add the artichoke quarters; cook, stirring often, until they begin to soften, about 3 minutes.

5. Stir in the garlic, oregano, smoked paprika, and saffron until aromatic, about 20 seconds. Pour in the sherry and bring it to a simmer, scraping up all the browned bits in the pan.

6. Pour in the broth, tomatoes, rice, and bell pepper strips. Stir well as it comes to a full simmer. Nestle the sausages and chicken into the rice and vegetables.

7. Cover, transfer to the oven, and bake until the rice is tender and the liquid has been absorbed, about 40 minutes. Remove from the oven and set aside, covered, for 10 minutes before serving.

TASTIER

GLUTEN-FREE

No-Splatter Roast Duck

Makes 4 servings

The dispiriting part of cooking a duck, frankly, is the mess. First off, there's fat splattered all over the oven. And to add insult to injury, the meat's tough, particularly at the thighs, because the skin gets overdone before the meat is tender. Maybe that's why people don't make duck as often as they should. But with this two-step technique (steam it, then roast it), the mess mostly disappears and you're left with the crispest skin and the most tender meat underneath. No, this isn't everyday fare. But it's a holiday treat.

One 5- to 6-pound whole duck, any giblets and neck removed from the inner cavities, any excess skin trimmed away

1 teaspoon kosher salt

1 teaspoon ground black pepper

Test Kitchen Notes

- Save the fat in the bottom of the pan. Refrigerate the fat and liquids until solid, then scrape off the fat, discard the liquids, and freeze the fat in a sealed container to use for scrambled eggs or in place of butter or oil in any chicken braise. Or use it in place of olive oil for roast potatoes.

- This recipe works best in a large, deep, covered, oval roasting pan, a bit of a specialty tool. Most of these are sold with a rack that fits inside. Hint: The best place to find deals on specialty kitchen tools is eBay!

- You can jury-rig a covered roasting pan from a more standard, rectangular or even oval roasting pan (not the more shallow broiler pan that used to come with every oven). Make a lid by tightly crimping two or three long sheets of aluminum foil lengthwise. The makeshift cover should be wide and long enough to reach down the sides of the roasting pan where you can bunch it into a tight fit around the corners or the ends of the pan. The foil must not extend under the pan. It can actually melt and fuse to the stove under high heat.

1. Prick the duck repeatedly with a fork, concentrating on the fattier bits.

2. Pour 1 inch of water into a large roasting pan that has a cover. Place a shallow roasting rack in the bottom of the pan. Set the duck breast side down on the rack. Cover the pan and set it over high heat to bring the water to a boil.

3. Reduce the heat to low so the water simmers slowly but steadily. Steam the duck for 75 minutes, adding more water to the pan if it dries out or the rendered fat starts to burn.

4. Set the roasting pan off the heat and cool the duck for 30 minutes. Meanwhile, position the rack in the center of the oven and heat the oven to 375°F.

5. Use oven mitts to pick up the hot duck. Being very careful, pour out any juices inside the large cavity of the duck, preferably catching them in the pan if you intend to save them or in a bowl so you can later discard them in a sealed plastic bag. (Duck fat down a drain can be quite a mess—and quite expensive, given that it quickly solidifies into a lump and then leads to an expensive plumber bill. Trust us.) Set the duck on a shallow roasting rack in a shallow roasting pan. Season the duck all over with the salt and pepper.

6. Roast until the skin is brown and crisp, about 45 minutes. There's no need to take the duck meat's internal temperature since the steaming will have essentially cooked the meat.

7. Transfer the duck to a carving board and let stand at room temperature for 15 minutes before carving. To carve, start it breast side down and remove the leg-thigh quarters. Then turn it breast side up and slice the breast meat off the breast bone in one chunk. Slice that breast meat into 1-inch-thick pieces.

Voilà! But what if you don't have a steamer for this duck recipe or even fresh vegetables as a side dish? Easy! Slice a baking potato into 2-inch rounds, then place cut side down (and up) in a deep skillet or Dutch oven. Add water and set a pie plate on top of the potatoes. Instant steamer! You can even eat the cooked potatoes underneath.

EASIER

GLUTEN-FREE

No-Boil Corned-Beef-Stuffed Cabbage

Makes 4 to 6 servings

Test Kitchen Notes

- There's no added salt because corned beef is salty (as is the mustard in the sauce).

- This recipe will only work with a savoy cabbage because its leaves are more tender from the get-go. The round savoy looks a bit like a regular green cabbage, except its leaves are frilled and crinkled. Do not confuse it with napa cabbage.

- The oats add a smooth texture to the stuffing, better than little grains of rice throughout.

Stuffed cabbage, that famed Eastern European comfort food, is glorious—but we don't love the many pots needed to make it. Here's how to cut down on the cleanup: First, eliminate the step of boiling the cabbage leaves. Instead, freeze the head. The thawing process will soften the leaves so they're ready to be stuffed and baked without an extra pot of water. And second, don't chop or sauté to build the filling. Instead, use store-bought corned beef, already flavorful enough to stand up to our easy tomato sauce. Squirrel away a cabbage in the freezer for several months so you're never far away from this Old World favorite.

1 large head savoy cabbage

1 pound store-bought low-sodium corned beef (either packaged raw in the meat counter or a chunk of deli corned beef)

1 pound lean ground beef

½ cup rolled oats (certified gluten-free if that is a concern)

2 tablespoons minced fresh dill fronds

2 teaspoons caraway seeds

One 28-ounce can crushed tomatoes

1 tablespoon Dijon mustard

1 tablespoon honey

1 tablespoon white wine vinegar

More! Don't throw out the rest of that cabbage. Make a Russian-inspired cabbage soup: Roughly chop the remaining cabbage (you should have 3 or 4 cups), then place it in a large soup pot with 1 pound beef sirloin, trimmed and cut into ½-inch pieces; 1 cup chopped onion; ¼ cup raisins; 1 quart chicken broth; one 28-ounce can diced tomatoes; ¼ cup red wine vinegar; 2 tablespoons granulated white sugar; 1 teaspoon table salt; and ½ teaspoon ground black pepper. Bring to a simmer over medium-high heat, stirring occasionally. Then cover, reduce the heat to low, and simmer slowly for 1 hour, stirring occasionally. To serve, garnish the bowls of soup with sour cream.

1. Wrap the cabbage tightly in plastic wrap and freeze for at least 24 hours or up to 4 months.

2. Unwrap the cabbage, place it in a large bowl, and thaw overnight in the refrigerator, about 12 hours.

3. Cut off the stem and core the cabbage. The leaves will now peel off easily, as if they've been blanched. Remove 16 leaves. Reserve the rest of the head for another use (see **More!**).

4. Place the corned beef in a food processor, cutting the meat into several chunks to fit. Pulse until coarsely chopped. Scrape into a large bowl.

5. Add the ground beef, oats, dill, and caraway seeds to the corned beef. Mix until uniform.

6. Place a cabbage leaf, veins down, on a clean, dry work surface. Cut out the thick middle vein, maybe as far as halfway up the leaf. Set ¼ cup of the corned beef mixture at the thicker end of the leaf, fold the sides over the meat and into the leaf, then roll it up into a neat packet. Set aside and make 15 more rolls.

7. Place the 16 rolls in one layer in a large Dutch oven or a large, high-sided sauté pan. Whisk the tomatoes, mustard, honey, and vinegar in a medium bowl until the honey dissolves. Pour over the rolls.

8. Set the pot or pan over medium heat and bring to a simmer. Cover, reduce the heat to low, and simmer slowly for 1 hour, or until the meat filling is cooked through.

BETTER LIVING WITH PICKLE BRINE

Don't throw out the juice from the pickle jar. It's a terrific marinade. Want proof? Before you try any of these recipes, put boneless skinless chicken breasts or thin-cut center-cut boneless pork loin chops in the leftover brine from a jar of just about any pickle, cover, and refrigerate for an hour. If you use relatively small chicken breasts or pork loin chops, they'll fit right in the jar without having to dirty a bowl. You won't believe the flavor when you grill them up.

These recipes, however, move beyond that—and around the world, too, from Southeast Asia to South America to North American delicatessens. That jar has all the flavor you need to make some fantastic suppers. That said, these recipes were designed specifically for certain types of brines: bread-and-butter pickles, dill pickles, etc. You can mix-and-match with those simple grilled chicken breasts or pork chops. But for the recipes below, follow the type of brine specifically for the right set of flavors.

Finally, you can freeze leftover pickle brine in a sealed container until you're ready to use it. (But don't reuse it once you've put meat or other matter in it for these recipes.)

Pickle-Brine Chicken Pastrami

FASTER

GLUTEN-FREE

Makes 6 servings

You've already learned about a great way to make beef pastrami (page 145). But you haven't lived until you've made chicken pastrami—terrific in sandwiches for lunch. (Given the size of the boneless skinless chicken breasts, you don't even need to slice them. Just one per sandwich, particularly on an onion or kaiser roll.) What's more, you don't have to drag out a smoker!

1 cup dill pickle brine

Six 6-ounce boneless skinless chicken breasts

1½ teaspoons ground coriander

1½ teaspoons ground dried mustard

1½ teaspoons mild smoked paprika

1 teaspoon ground dried ginger

½ teaspoon garlic powder

1½ teaspoons ground black pepper

1. Stir the pickle brine and the chicken in a large bowl. Cover and refrigerate, tossing at least one time, for at least 6 hours, but not more than 8 hours.

2. Mix the coriander, mustard, smoked paprika, ginger, garlic powder, and pepper in a small bowl. Remove the chicken breasts from the brine, pat dry, and coat evenly with the spice mixture. Set aside at room temperature.

3. Position the rack in the center of the oven; heat the oven to 275°F. Set an oven-safe wire rack (such as a cookie cooling rack without rubber feet) on a large lipped baking sheet. Set the coated chicken breasts on the rack.

4. Bake until an instant-read meat thermometer inserted into the thickest part of more than one breast registers 160°F, 1 to 1½ hours. Set aside for at least 10 minutes at room temperature before serving. If desired, cool to room temperature, then store, tightly covered, in the refrigerator for up to 1 week.

Test Kitchen Notes

- Look for smaller boneless skinless chicken breasts, sometimes sold individually packaged in bags.

- The rack on the baking sheet lets air circulate around the bottom of the chicken, keeping the bottom from getting soggy.

- You can also use the brine from a jar of pickled green tomatoes. A 32-ounce jar will yield 2 cups (or more) of brine.

- If you don't have a rack that fits into a baking sheet, set the spice-rubbed breasts directly on the oven rack, then put a large lipped baking sheet on a rack below them to catch any drips.

Voilà! Act like a chef and tuck a clean kitchen towel into your waistband. You won't have to search for one to wipe up spills—which then won't have a chance to dry into gunky blobs on the counter.

FASTER

GLUTEN-FREE

Indonesian Chicken Lettuce Wraps

Makes 4 servings

This recipe uses the brine from a jar of sweet-and-sour pickles, which, along with the curry paste, mimics the flavors of Southeast Asian grilling. You'll even make some quick radish pickles to go in the wraps with the chicken.

1½ cups bread-and-butter pickle brine

12 large radishes, thinly sliced

1 tablespoon red Thai curry paste

1 tablespoon fish sauce

Four 8-ounce boneless skinless chicken breasts

2 heads Boston or Bibb lettuce, leaves separated and rinsed

1. Combine ½ cup of the brine and the radishes in a small bowl. Cover and refrigerate while you make the rest of this recipe.

2. Whisk the remaining 1 cup of the brine with the curry paste and fish sauce in a large bowl until smooth. Add the chicken and toss well to coat thoroughly. Cover and refrigerate for 1 hour, tossing a couple more times.

3. Brush the grill grates clean and prepare the grill for high-heat, direct cooking; or heat a large nonstick grill pan over medium-high heat. Drain the chicken and set the meat on the grate over the heat source or in the pan. Grill until cooked through, turning once, about 8 minutes.

4. Transfer the chicken to a cutting board; slice lengthwise into ½-inch-thick strips. To serve, use the lettuce leaves as wraps, filling them with the sliced chicken and cold pickled radishes drained of their brine. (Cover and save any remaining pickled radishes in the fridge for sandwiches in the next 3 or 4 days.)

Test Kitchen Notes

- Red Thai curry paste is available in most large supermarkets. Some pastes contain only chiles and salt; others have lots of aromatics. Look at the ingredient label to get the latter type. Pastes that list chiles as the first ingredient will be the hottest.

- The amount of brine required is a little less than what's left over from a 32-ounce jar of bread-and-butter pickles. If you are using smaller, 16-ounce jars, save the brine in a covered container in the freezer until you have enough.

- Not all bottled fish sauce is gluten-free. Again, check the label to be sure.

Voilà! Did you know that many butchers at large supermarkets, so long as they're not too busy, will sharpen a knife or two for you while you shop? Make sure you tip that butcher.

FASTER

GLUTEN-FREE

Five-Ingredient Swordfish Escabeche

Makes 4 servings

Test Kitchen Notes

- Giardiniera is an Italian relish of vinegared vegetables, usually a mix of cauliflower, carrots, and other vegetables. Some giardiniera are spicy; others, mild. Use your preference.

- For an easy way to tell if fish is cooked through, see the Test Kitchen Notes at the One-Pan Tuna Skewers recipe on page 206.

- Do not use aluminum bakeware to store the fish. It can react poorly with the marinade.

Voilà! There's no substitute for freshly ground black pepper. It may seem faster to use the pre-ground stuff, but it's usually missing the citrus and musk pop of the real thing. There's no point in saving a few seconds to make a shoddier meal.

Many cultures pickle fish—Japanese, Jewish, Scandinavian, and others. But this South American technique leaves the fish firmer, not slimy, with a better texture all around. Escabeche is a cold dish: Once cooked, the fish is put into a sweet-and-sour mixture, then chilled to be served on its own as an appetizer, or on salads, even in tortillas with sour cream and thinly sliced onions. It's a fantastic summer make-ahead.

Four 4-ounce swordfish steaks

1 teaspoon ground black pepper

2 tablespoons olive oil

One 8-ounce jar Italian giardiniera

One 6-ounce jar marinated artichokes

1. Season the swordfish steaks evenly with pepper.

2. Heat the oil in a large skillet set over medium heat. Add the fish and cook, turning once, until cooked through, about 8 minutes. Transfer the swordfish to a 9-inch square glass or Pyrex baking dish.

3. Pour the contents of the jars of giardiniera and artichoke hearts over the fish. Cover and refrigerate for at least 8 hours or up to 24 hours. Cut the swordfish into cubes or strips before serving with the marinated vegetables.

Five-Ingredient Trout Escabeche

FASTER

GLUTEN-FREE

Makes 4 servings

There may be no better lunch for a day on the patio. Serve the trout alongside a chopped salad of Romaine lettuce, carrots, cauliflower florets, and other crunchy, raw vegetables. Use some of the shallots from the marinade and a squeeze of one of the lemon wedges as the dressing. Or set the drained trout pieces on top of a Caesar salad (page 81) for an easy meal.

2 tablespoons olive oil

Four 6-ounce skin-on trout fillets

1 medium lemon, washed and sliced into paper-thin rounds, any seeds removed

1 medium shallot, sliced into paper-thin sheets

1½ cups dill pickle brine

1. Warm 1 tablespoon oil in a large nonstick skillet set over medium heat. Add two trout fillets, skin side down, and cook until the skin is crisp, about 5 minutes. Gently turn the fillets and cook for 1 minute. Transfer to a 9-inch baking pan.

2. Add the remaining 1 tablespoon oil to the skillet and cook the remaining two fillets in the same manner before getting them into the baking pan.

3. Arrange the fillets in one layer (as well as you can). Top them with the lemon and shallot slices.

4. Gently pour the brine over everything, taking care not to dislodge the slices. Cover and refrigerate for at least 8 hours or up to 24 hours. Slice the fillets into squares or larger pieces to serve.

Test Kitchen Notes

- Leave the trout in the pan mostly undisturbed as it cooks. The skin has to crisp so the fillet can turn easily.

- Use a nonstick skillet to keep the fillets intact.

- When you turn them, they should be beginning to flake, with the meat opaque and firm—in other words, just about cooked through.

Voilà! Speaking of vinegary, bright meals, nothing beats ceviche for an easy dinner on a hot night. For 2 servings, toss 4 ounces thinly sliced sea scallops and 4 ounces diced, skinned, sushi-grade red snapper fillet with ½ cup fresh lime juice in a medium glass bowl. Cover and refrigerate until the fish becomes opaque, about 45 minutes. Drain, then toss with 1 large tomato, diced; ½ medium avocado, pitted, peeled, and diced; 1 small red onion, minced; 2 tablespoons chopped fresh cilantro; 2 tablespoons fresh lime juice; 3 dashes hot sauce, and table salt and ground black pepper to taste. Serve cold on a bed of shredded iceberg lettuce.

THE UNTAPPED DEPTHS
OF PEANUT BUTTER

Because of the way peanuts are roasted and ground, peanut butter offers a depth of flavor that is the equivalent of a long-simmered base to use in stews and braises, even in some fine no-cook sauces. In fact, for the most intense flavor, look for the darkest colored peanut butter on the store's shelf. Some brands (like Laura Scudder's on the West Coast of the U.S. or Santa Cruz Organic) are particularly dark because they're made from peanuts roasted far beyond a light toasting. But there can even be color variations within the same brand.

In North America, peanut butter is sold as two types: natural-style and so-called "regular" (or "standard") peanut butter. Natural-style peanut butter is made solely from peanuts (and maybe salt), whereas regular (or standard) peanut butter has additional fat to help emulsify the mixture (and sometimes added sugar, too).

Natural-style peanut butter often separates, leaving an oil slick on the top. Do not pour off that oil for these recipes! Instead, turn the jar upside down and leave it alone for a few days, then turn it right side up and stir with a flatware knife to incorporate the oil (which is now sitting at the bottom of the jar).

Both sorts of peanut butters are sold in creamy and chunky versions. All these recipes (indeed, all the recipes in this book that use peanut butter) call for natural-style creamy peanut butter.

No-Prep Butternut Squash, Kale, and Peanut Soup

Makes 4 to 6 servings

Salty, spicy, sweet, and savory—this soup covers all the bases! Plus, there's no chopping or slicing beforehand, so you can cook a fast meal on a wintry night. Consider serving it over cooked long-grain white or brown rice.

2 tablespoons peanut oil

1 cup frozen chopped onion (do not thaw)

1 cup frozen bell pepper strips (do not thaw)

Up to ¼ teaspoon cayenne

One 28-ounce can diced tomatoes, preferably no-salt-added

1 pound frozen diced butternut squash (do not thaw)

2 cups vegetable broth

¼ cup natural-style creamy peanut butter

4 cups (about 6 ounces) packed bagged shredded kale

Kosher salt, for garnishing

1. Warm a medium saucepan over high heat. Swirl in the oil, then add the onion and bell pepper. Cook, stirring quite frequently, until they give off their liquid and it mostly evaporates, about 4 minutes.

2. Stir in the cayenne and cook for a couple of seconds. Dump in the tomatoes, squash, broth, and peanut butter. Stir well until the peanut butter melts, then bring the soup to a simmer, stirring often.

3. Reduce the heat to low, cover, and simmer slowly until the squash is tender, 20 to 25 minutes.

4. Stir in the kale, cover again, and continue cooking, stirring occasionally, until the kale is tender and the squash pieces start to fall apart and thicken the soup, about 10 minutes. Sprinkle a little crunchy kosher salt over the bowlfuls just before serving.

Test Kitchen Notes

- If you don't need the soup to be vegan, you can add more heft by substituting chicken broth for the vegetable broth.

- In other no-chop recipes, we've staggered the addition of the frozen vegetables. Here, they're going into a soup and can all go into the pot at once.

EASIER

GLUTEN-FREE

Peanut Chicken Curry

Makes 4 servings

Test Kitchen Notes

- It's easier to first cut the onions into wedges, then peel off the dry, outer layer.

- In step 4, stir fairly frequently and keep the heat very low (only a few bubbles at a time) to prevent scorching. If you can't get the heat low enough, use a heat diffuser or a "simmer mat" under the pot.

- There's no salt in the recipe because peanut butter is salty. Pass more at the table if you've used salt-free peanut butter.

Voilà! You can cut down the cooking time for rice as a side dish by using a two-step process: Set a large pot over high heat for a couple of minutes, add at least 1 cup long-grain rice (white or brown) and stir a minute or two to toast the grains. Then add two times the amount of water as the rice (which will come to a boil very quickly), cover, reduce the heat a little, and cook at a good boil until tender, maybe 10 minutes for white rice, 25 for brown. Drain in a fine-mesh sieve set in the sink. The rice will be chewier, less fluffy, and actually a better companion to rich curries and stews.

You might not even know there's peanut butter in this curry. It melts into the sauce, making it savory and salty with an unrivaled depth of flavor. Because there's that secret weapon in the ingredients, you've given yourself plenty of time to build a much more flavorful homemade curry from an assortment of spices, a more aromatic mixture than the standard premade yellow curry.

2 tablespoons peanut oil

3 medium yellow onions, halved, each half cut into three wedges

2 teaspoons minced garlic

2½ teaspoons ground ginger

2 teaspoons ground coriander

1 teaspoon ground cinnamon

Up to ¼ teaspoon cayenne

⅛ teaspoon ground cloves

1½ pounds boneless skinless chicken thighs

¼ cup dry vermouth, dry white wine, or water

¾ cup full-fat, low-fat, or fat-free plain Greek yogurt

¼ cup natural-style creamy peanut butter

¼ cup golden raisins

1. Warm a large Dutch oven over medium heat for a minute or so. Swirl in the oil, then add the onions. Cook, stirring occasionally, until lightly browned at the edges, about 3 minutes. Stir in the garlic and cook for a few seconds.

2. Add the ginger, coriander, cinnamon, cayenne, and cloves. Stir well, cook a few more seconds, then add the chicken. Stir until it is coated thoroughly and evenly with the spices.

3. Pour in the vermouth and bring to a simmer, stirring all the while to scrape up any browned bits on the bottom of the pot.

4. Stir in the yogurt, peanut butter, and raisins until the peanut butter dissolves. Bring to a low simmer, stirring quite often; then reduce the heat to very low, cover the pot, and cook at a very low bubble, stirring fairly often, until the meat is tender when pierced with a fork, 25 to 30 minutes.

5. Let rest, covered, off the heat for 5 minutes before serving.

Superfast Mongolian-Style Beef Stew

Makes 4 servings

Basically, this is a three-step version of a classic, all-day braise: Make a braising base from peanut butter, cook the meat with various aromatics, simmer the two together. The stew can be quite spicy—or you can tame it with less hot sauce and add more at the table as you wish.

½ cup natural-style creamy peanut butter

¼ cup dry vermouth, dry white wine, or unsweetened apple juice

2 tablespoons white wine vinegar

2 tablespoons soy sauce (gluten-free if that is a concern)

2 tablespoons light brown sugar

Up to 1½ tablespoons Sriracha or other hot chile sauce

2 tablespoons vegetable oil

1½ pounds sirloin steak, cut into thin ½-inch strips (as for stir-fry)

1 medium red onion, halved, then each half sliced into thin half-moons

2 medium red bell peppers, stemmed, cored, and cut into ¼-inch-thick strips

2 teaspoons minced garlic

Roasted unsalted peanuts and chopped fresh cilantro leaves, for garnish

1. Use a fork to mix the peanut butter, vermouth, vinegar, soy sauce, brown sugar, and Sriracha in a small bowl until smooth.

2. Set a large saucepan over medium heat for a couple of minutes. Swirl in the oil, then add the meat. Cook, stirring occasionally, until it loses its raw color, about 5 minutes.

3. Add the onion and bell peppers to the pan. Cook, stirring often, until the onion begins to soften, 3 to 4 minutes. Add the garlic and cook for a few seconds.

4. Stir in the peanut butter mixture until everything is evenly coated. Cover, reduce the heat to very low, and simmer slowly, stirring quite often, until the meat is tender, about 15 minutes. Garnish with peanuts and cilantro.

Test Kitchen Notes

- To cut the meat into strips, work against the grain. Run your fingers over the cut to determine the direction of the fibers. Slice at a 90-degree angle to these fibers. Or have the butcher at your supermarket slice the meat for you. Or look for beef precut for stir-fry.

- For a heartier meal, serve the stew over rice noodles.

Creamy Eggplant and Tomato Stew

Makes 4 servings

If you haven't tried the combo, eggplant and peanut butter may be the surprise of this book. It's a creamy, rich duo that has salty/savory notes aplenty. Here, those flavors are taken further with sweet tomatoes and then a little cream just for good measure. This hearty, vegetarian stew calls out for flatbread or pita.

¼ cup peanut oil

2 medium shallots, sliced into paper-thin rings

2 tablespoons minced peeled fresh ginger

1 to 2 fresh jalapeños, seeded and minced

3 medium Italian eggplants (about 12 ounces), peeled and diced

1 teaspoon ground coriander

1 teaspoon ground cumin

½ teaspoon ground turmeric

Up to ¼ teaspoon cayenne

One 14-ounce can diced tomatoes, preferably fire-roasted

2 tablespoons tomato paste

Up to 3 cups vegetable broth

½ cup natural-style creamy peanut butter

½ cup heavy cream

1. Set a Dutch oven over medium heat for a minute or two, then swirl in the oil. Add the shallots, ginger, and chiles; cook, stirring often, until the shallots soften, about 2 minutes.

2. Add the eggplant; cook, stirring occasionally, until the pieces begin to soften at their corners, about 3 minutes. Stir in the coriander, cumin, turmeric, and cayenne until the spices evenly coat the eggplant pieces.

3. Stir in the tomatoes and tomato paste until the paste has coated everything, then add 2 cups of the broth and the peanut butter, stirring until the peanut butter has dissolved.

4. Cover, reduce the heat to low, and simmer slowly, stirring fairly frequently to prevent scorching and adding more broth by ¼-cup increments if the stew gets too thick, until the vegetables are tender, about 20 minutes.

5. Stir in the cream and simmer, uncovered, for 1 minute to remove its raw taste. Serve hot.

Test Kitchen Notes

- If you can't find eggplants that are exactly 12 ounces, err on the larger side, not the smaller (for more moisture in the soup).

- If you're in the market for a new vegetable peeler, look for one with a serrated edge which will make peeling eggplants (as well as tomatoes and even peaches) much easier.

- The amount of broth is given as a range because the eggplant will have varying amounts of natural moisture based on the time of year, how long it's sat on the store shelf, and even its specific hybrid varietal.

- This recipe has no added salt, on the notion that the peanut butter is salty. Add some at the table, if desired.

Voilà! In general, look for canned tomatoes, tomato paste, and broths without added salt. Why let someone else control the sodium content of your food—and often with inferior-quality salt?

Three No-Cook Blender Peanut Sauces

Makes 1¼ to 1⅔ cups per batch, enough for
8 ounces dried pasta or 12 ounces fresh pasta

Test Kitchen Notes

- Depending on your mood, make just one or all of the variations detailed in the ingredient list. Store them separately in covered containers.

- Don't want to dirty another container? Simply store the sauce in the covered blender canister in the refrigerator for up to 1 week.

- If the sauce separates in the fridge, whisk it back to uniformity before using. If it thickens too much, whisk in water in 1-tablespoon increments until it has the right consistency.

- Of course, these sauces are gluten-free if you are careful about certain ingredients—and then only if you put them over gluten-free noodles!

These three sauces are incredibly versatile. Use them to sauce cooked noodles, as a dressing for shredded chicken salad, as a dip for grilled shrimp or cut-up vegetables, as a sauce for kebabs off the grill, or even as a spread with ham or turkey sandwiches.

Spicy and Crunchy Peanut-Sesame Sauce

MAKES ABOUT 1¼ CUPS

½ cup natural-style creamy peanut butter

3 tablespoons vegetable broth

3 tablespoons toasted sesame oil

2 tablespoons soy sauce (gluten-free if that is a concern)

2 tablespoons unseasoned rice vinegar

1 tablespoon Worcestershire sauce (gluten-free if that is a concern)

2 teaspoons granulated white sugar

1 teaspoon Sriracha, Texas Pete, or other hot red chile sauce

Coconut and Peanut Sauce

MAKES ABOUT 1½ CUPS

⅔ cup natural-style creamy peanut butter

¼ cup regular or low-fat coconut milk

¼ cup vegetable broth

2 tablespoons fish sauce

2 tablespoons light brown sugar

1 small shallot, minced

1 small fresh jalapeño, stemmed, seeded, and minced

1 teaspoon minced garlic

Creamy Peanut Sauce

MAKES ABOUT 1⅔ CUPS

¾ cup (6 ounces) silken firm tofu

½ cup natural-style creamy peanut butter

3 tablespoons soy sauce (gluten-free if that is a concern)

3 tablespoons white balsamic vinegar

1 tablespoon minced peeled fresh ginger

2 teaspoons granulated white sugar

1. For any sauce, put all the ingredients in a large blender, cover, and blend until smooth, stopping the machine at least once to scrape down the inside of the canister.

2. Pour and scrape the sauce into a small container, seal, and store in the fridge for up to 1 week.

More!

To make your own nut butter: Place about 1 pound raw, shelled nuts—that is, pecans, walnuts, skinned hazelnuts, almonds, or pistachios, as well as any nut pretenders like cashews or peanuts—in a large food processor. Cover and process until creamy and smooth, scraping down the interior of the bowl often while waiting patiently for the mixture to break down and emulsify, anywhere from 12 to 18 minutes depending on the oil content of the nuts.

There are distinct phases to a nut butter as it processes: After a minute or so, the mixture will look like a dry, loose sand; next, that sand begins to clump; then the clumps turn oily, almost like sticky cookie batter; and finally, the released oils emulsify the mixture into a creamy paste. Stop the processor at least once during each phase to scrape down the bowl—or anytime the mixture clumps to the side or bottom of the bowl and is not actively mixing with the blades.

For a deeper flavor, toast the nuts before processing: Scatter them on a large baking sheet and roast in a 350°F oven for 10 to 15 minutes until lightly browned and fragrant. However, nut butters made with toasted nuts are in general a little grainier and even drier than nut butters made with raw nuts.

Finally, one caution: Without professional rollers and grinders, a homemade nut butter will never be as creamy as a commercial jar. There will always be flecks and specks of nuts in the paste.

BUNDT-PAN CHICKEN SUPPERS

There's a cool gadget called a vertical roaster that makes a fine roast chicken: It lifts the chicken skin out of the juices, allowing air to circulate around the bird and crisping the skin. But you don't need a fancy tool. A 10- to 12-cup Bundt pan is a vertical roaster in the making. Better yet, the high sides can hold vegetables or sides right under the chicken, allowing them to baste in the juices and turning this once-in-a-while cake pan into an everyday kitchen tool.

Test Kitchen Notes

- Remove any visible excess fat from the chicken before roasting for cleaner flavors.

- Removing the small "flippers" from the last joint of the chicken wings exposes more surface area of the skin, and yields better crispness.

- Don't use an angel-food cake pan, or any pan with a removable bottom. The hot juices will leak out.

- Even so, you must put the Bundt pan on a lipped baking sheet to catch the juices that drop through the center hole of the pan.

- The easiest way to remove a hot chicken from the Bundt pan is to pick it up using silicone baking gloves.

Bundt-Pan Chicken and Israeli Couscous

EASIER

Makes 4 servings

Israeli couscous is a par-cooked pasta, small little balls that will soften in the pan as the chicken roasts above it. If you have any chicken left over, remove and discard the skin, then take the meat off the bones. Chop it into small bits and stir it into the remaining Israeli couscous mixture to make an on-the-go chicken salad lunch for the next day. (Drain any fat and juices from the couscous before storing in a sealed container in the fridge.)

1½ cups Israeli couscous

1 medium yellow or red bell pepper, stemmed, cored, and chopped

2 medium shallots, chopped

1 teaspoon minced garlic

1 teaspoon dried oregano

1 teaspoon table salt

½ teaspoon ground black pepper

One 3- to 3½-pound whole chicken, any giblets and neck removed, the small wing tips removed, and trimmed of excess fat

2 tablespoons olive oil

3 cups chicken broth

1. Position one oven rack as high as it can go while still accommodating the chicken atop a 10- to 12-cup Bundt pan. Heat the oven to 350°F. Cover the hole at the center of the Bundt pan with aluminum foil.

2. Mix the couscous, bell pepper, shallots, garlic, oregano, ½ teaspoon of the salt, and the black pepper in the Bundt pan, forming an even layer.

3. Set the chicken in the Bundt pan, legs down, so that the large opening fits over the center of the pan and the chicken stands up in the pan. Rub the exposed skin with the olive oil and sprinkle with the remaining ½ teaspoon salt.

4. Pour 1½ cups of the broth over the couscous mixture. Set the entire Bundt pan operation on a large lipped baking sheet. Roast for 1 hour.

5. Add the remaining broth to the pan. Continue roasting until the chicken is well browned and an instant-read meat thermometer inserted into the thickest part of a thigh (without touching bone) registers 165°F.

6. Let sit at room temperature for 10 minutes, then take the chicken off the top of the Bundt pan. Carve, and serve with the couscous mixture.

Test Kitchen Notes

- Double the garlic at will.

- For a spicy kick, add up to ½ teaspoon red pepper flakes to the couscous mixture.

EASIER

GLUTEN-FREE

Bistro Bundt-Pan Chicken with Shallots and Potatoes

Makes 4 servings

Test Kitchen Notes

- For a silkier finish, substitute melted unsalted butter for the olive oil.

- Single-lobed shallots are sometimes called "French shallots."

More! The best tool for carving a roast chicken is a pair of kitchen shears, but you can also use a knife. Either way, start by pulling a thigh-and-leg quarter away from the main section of the bird, then pushing down to reveal the thigh joint. Cut or clip right through the joint. Repeat on the other side. In the large opening, cut on either side of the spine to remove it from the bird. Slice the breast in half lengthwise, then cut each of these halves widthwise in two. Of course, remove any meat from the bones for children.

There's actually a fair amount of "classical" French cookery here: the chicken roasted with a mustard glaze, the potatoes done in a little chicken fat (as it runs off the bird). Serve this rich meal alongside a shredded lettuce and carrot salad with a vinegary dressing.

3 tablespoons olive oil

1 tablespoon smooth Dijon mustard

1 teaspoon dried thyme

1 teaspoon table salt

½ teaspoon ground black pepper

One 3- to 3½-pound whole chicken, any giblets and neck removed, the small wing tips removed, and trimmed of excess fat

8 large whole shallots (preferably long, single-lobed shallots), peeled

2 large Yukon Gold potatoes (about ½ pound each), cut into 6 wedges each

1. Position one oven rack as high as it can go while still accommodating the chicken atop a 10- to 12-cup Bundt pan. Heat the oven to 350°F. Cover the hole at the center of the Bundt pan with aluminum foil.

2. Mix 1 tablespoon of the oil, the mustard, thyme, ½ teaspoon of the salt, and the pepper in a large bowl until smooth.

3. Set the chicken in the Bundt pan, legs down, so that its large opening fits over the center of the pan and the chicken stands up in the pan. Rub the mustard mixture over the exterior of the bird.

4. Add the remaining 2 tablespoons oil and ½ teaspoon salt to that same large bowl, then add the shallots and potatoes. Toss well to coat.

5. Position the shallots and potatoes around the chicken, using the flutes of the pan to stand them up where possible. Set the entire Bundt pan operation on a large lipped baking sheet.

6. Roast until the potatoes are tender, the chicken is well browned, and an instant-read meat thermometer inserted into the thickest part of a thigh (without touching bone) registers 165°F, about 2 hours.

7. Let sit at room temperature for 10 minutes, then take the chicken off the top of the Bundt pan. Carve and serve with the potatoes and shallots, discarding any juices in the pan.

EASIER

Bundt-Pan Hen and Dressing

Makes 4 servings

Test Kitchen Notes

- Use the full amount of broth, basting the dressing repeatedly as it cooks.

- For a Yankee interpretation, substitute small, plain croutons for the cornbread.

 More! **To make a simple homemade cornbread** (with some left over for breakfast): Butter a 9 x 13-inch baking dish. Mix 1½ cups yellow cornmeal, 1⅓ cups all-purpose flour, 2 tablespoons granulated white sugar, 1 teaspoon baking powder, 1 teaspoon baking soda, and ½ teaspoon table salt in a large bowl. Add 2 large eggs, 1½ cups buttermilk, and 6 tablespoons unsalted butter, melted and cooled. Stir with a wooden spoon until well combined, then pour into the prepared pan. Bake in a 350°F oven until set, about 35 minutes.

Hen and dressing is an old-school Southern treat: a chicken roasted right on top of a pan of cornbread dressing. In this version, the chicken sits *above* the dressing, allowing the bird to get browner all around. You'll also still end up with a rich dressing underneath—although more of the cornbread will be exposed to the heat, creating a firmer texture and crunchier edges.

6 cups crumbled, premade cornbread (about 3 large cornbread muffins—or see the recipe just to the left.)

4 celery stalks, thinly sliced

1 small yellow onion, chopped

2 teaspoons dried sage

1 teaspoon dried thyme

1 teaspoon table salt

One 3- to 3½-pound whole chicken, any giblets and neck removed, the small wing tips removed, and trimmed of excess fat

1 tablespoon unsalted butter, melted and cooled

2 cups chicken broth

1. Position one oven rack as high as it can go while still accommodating the chicken atop a 10- to 12-cup Bundt pan. Heat the oven to 350°F. Cover the hole at the center of the Bundt pan with aluminum foil.

2. Mix the cornbread, celery, onion, 1 teaspoon of the sage, ½ teaspoon of the thyme, and ½ teaspoon of the salt in a large bowl. Place this mixture loosely in the bottom of the Bundt pan.

3. Set the chicken in the Bundt pan, legs down, so that the large opening fits over the center of the pan and the chicken stands up in the pan.

4. Mix the butter with the remaining 1 teaspoon sage, ½ teaspoon thyme, and ½ teaspoon salt in a small bowl. Brush evenly over the chicken.

5. Drizzle ¾ cup broth over the cornbread mixture. Set the entire Bundt pan operation on a large lipped baking sheet.

6. Bake, basting the dressing with more broth every 15 minutes after the first half hour, until the chicken is well browned and an instant-read meat thermometer inserted into the thickest part of a thigh (without touching bone) registers 165°F, about 2 hours in all.

7. Let sit at room temperature for 10 minutes, then take the chicken off the top of the Bundt pan. Carve, and serve with the dressing.

CLASSIC BARBECUE... IN A SLOW COOKER OR A PRESSURE COOKER

You can make wonderful barbecue in a slow cooker or a pressure cooker with two shortcut tricks. First, use ingredients that offer many of the smoky notes that come from cooking the meat over a wood fire. Liquid smoke is a start, but supplement it with smoked paprika, canned chipotles, and even fire-roasted cumin or tomatoes to get unexpected depth of flavor.

Second, create a rub to offer a big hit of flavor in the relatively moist environment of either sort of cooker. Since some of that rub slips off during cooking, don't waste the liquid in the pot. Turn it into a fine barbecue sauce.

All these recipes can be made in a slow cooker—or much more quickly in a pressure cooker.

EASIER

Fast or Slow Spiced Pulled Pork

Makes 6 to 8 servings

Test Kitchen Notes

- For more flavor, use smoked brown sugar, often found at specialty cookware stores.

- Or use fire-roasted ground cumin, available at large supermarkets.

- Go way over the top by using smoked salt.

- You can skip step 3 if you're in a hurry, but the flavor will be more intense if the meat rests overnight.

Nope, you don't have to build a barbecue pit or man a smoker all day to make pulled pork. True, you won't have any "burnt ends"; but you will have a terrific meal on a day when you've got other things to do. Because a slow cooker pulls so much moisture from the pork, there's no need for additional liquid. However, the pressure cooker *must* have that additional liquid to create steam—and thus gets some added beer in this technique. In the end, the pressure-cooker sauce will be soupier and need to reduce longer in step 7. Serve the pulled pork on hamburger (or slider) buns with lots of pickled jalapeño rings and coleslaw.

1 tablespoon adobo sauce from a can of chipotle chiles in adobo sauce

1 tablespoon liquid smoke

One 4-pound bone-in skinless pork shoulder

2 tablespoons mild smoked paprika

2 tablespoons dark brown sugar

1 tablespoon ground cumin

1 tablespoon ground dried mustard

1 teaspoon onion powder

1 teaspoon garlic powder

1 teaspoon table salt

½ teaspoon ground cinnamon

½ teaspoon ground cloves

Up to one 12-ounce beer, preferably a porter or even a smoked porter (for the pressure cooker only)

1½ tablespoons apple cider vinegar

1. Combine the adobo sauce and liquid smoke in a small bowl. Smear and rub this mixture all over the pork.

2. Combine the smoked paprika, brown sugar, cumin, dried mustard, onion powder, garlic powder, salt, cinnamon, and cloves in a medium bowl. Rub this mixture all over the pork.

3. Place the pork shoulder in a 9 x 13-inch baking dish. Cover with plastic wrap and refrigerate overnight.

4. **To cook the pork in a slow cooker:** Place the pork in a 4- to 6-quart slow cooker, scraping every last drop from the baking dish into the cooker. Add ½ cup beer. Cover and cook on high for 6 hours or on low for 10 hours, until the meat is falling off the bone.

To cook the pork in a pressure cooker: Place the pork and the whole bottle of beer in a 6- to 8-quart pressure cooker. Lock the lid onto the pot and cook at high pressure for 1 hour in a stovetop pot (15 psi) or 1 hour 20 minutes in an electric pot (9 to 11 psi). Remove the stovetop pot from the heat or turn off the electric pot. Let the pressure come back to normal naturally, about 20 minutes. Unlock the lid and open the pot.

5. Transfer the meat to a carving board; discard the bones. Shred the meat with two forks and place these shreds in a large bowl or a deep serving platter.

6. Skim the fat from the liquid in the cooker, then pour it into a medium saucepan and stir in the vinegar.

7. Bring the sauce to a boil over high heat, stirring occasionally. Boil until reduced to half its volume, about 6 minutes for the slow-cooker sauce and 10 minutes for the pressure-cooker sauce. Pour the sauce over the pork and serve.

Voilà! Here's an easy, mayonnaise-less slaw to go with barbecue: Whisk equal parts vinegar and olive oil in a bowl until smooth, then add a pinch of sugar, table salt, and lots of ground black pepper. Stir in some bagged slaw mix, then shred an apple or two into the mix through the large holes of a box grater. Add a little sliced red onion and parsley leaves, then taste again. More cabbage? More salt? A little more olive oil?

Fast or Slow Tikka-Style Pulled Chicken

Makes 6 to 8 servings

Tikka is a Punjabi specialty: chunks of meat marinated in a spicy mix. This recipe fuses those flavors with American barbecue to create a very aromatic version of the pulled classic. Serve in seeded buns (gluten-free, if that is a concern) with a little pickle relish or even store-bought India relish (less sweet and tangier). Or stuff in pita pockets and top with shredded cucumber, chopped fresh cilantro, Greek yogurt, and minced red onion. Or for a fusion mix-and-match dinner, serve it in corn tortillas with sour cream and pickled jalapeño rings.

One 14-ounce can diced tomatoes

One 4½-ounce can chopped mild green chiles

3 tablespoons red wine vinegar

2 tablespoons Worcestershire sauce (gluten-free if that is a concern)

2 tablespoons tomato paste

2 tablespoons mild smoked paprika

1 tablespoon red curry powder

1 tablespoon minced garlic

3 pounds boneless skinless chicken thighs, any globs of fat removed

1. Mix the tomatoes, chiles, vinegar, Worcestershire sauce, tomato paste, smoked paprika, red curry powder, and garlic in a 4- to 6-quart slow cooker or a 6-quart stovetop or electric pressure cooker.

2. Add the chicken thighs and toss well to coat.

3. To cook the chicken in the slow cooker: Cover and cook on high for 2½ hours or on low for 6 hours, until the meat is beyond fork-tender. Shred the meat with two forks right in the cooker, mixing it with the sauce. Serve warm.

To cook the chicken in the pressure cooker: Lock the lid onto the pot and bring to high pressure. Cook at high pressure for 12 minutes in the stovetop pot (15 psi) or for 18 minutes in the electric pot (9 to 11 psi). Remove the stovetop pot from the heat or turn off the electric pot. Let the pressure come back to normal naturally, 7 to 10 minutes. Unlock the lid and remove it. Shred the chicken with two forks in the cooker. Mix with the sauce and serve warm.

Test Kitchen Notes

- Red curry powder is far spicier than yellow. Look for it in the spice rack of most large supermarkets. Or use an equivalent amount of yellow curry powder plus ¼ teaspoon cayenne.

- Since the Worcestershire sauce is salty, it's best to use no-salt-added tomato paste.

Voilà! There are two ways to heat tortillas. The best way is over an open gas flame, setting them one by one right on the metal grating and turning them with kitchen tongs until very lightly charred just in spots. But it's laborious. The fast way is in stacks in a microwave. Put no more than five in a stack on a microwave-safe plate and cover with a slightly damp paper towel. Microwave on high for 15-second bursts, or until they are warm but not hot.

EASIER

GLUTEN-FREE

Fast or Slow Barbecued Shredded Beef with Coffee and Vinegar

Makes 6 to 8 servings

Test Kitchen Notes

- The coffee should be quite strong. Use 50 percent more grounds than you might—or make espresso.

- Or make very strong coffee by whisking together equal parts water and instant espresso powder.

- Skirt steak may have a thin, translucent membrane on one side. Peel it off before using, or have the butcher do it for you.

- The mixture is itself gluten-free—and will definitely be so if served on gluten-free buns.

Voilà! To keep raisins fresh, remove them from their original packaging and place in a sealable plastic bag. Squeeze out all the excess air and seal tightly. Store in a cool pantry for 6 months, maybe more.

Coffee makes an amazing barbecue sauce. It's got the right mix of bitter- and savory-ness to set off the sweet undertones in barbecued brisket. There's also plenty of sweetness in the raisins and even the balsamic vinegar. Want to go nuts? Ladle the shredded beef over a bowl of Fritos and top with some shredded Cheddar. Or just serve it over brown rice with some bottled hot sauce on the side.

1½ cups strong black coffee

2 tablespoons balsamic vinegar

2 tablespoons finely grated orange zest

2 tablespoons packed fresh oregano leaves

1 tablespoon ground cumin

1 canned chipotle chile in adobo sauce, stemmed, seeded if desired, and minced

2 teaspoons minced garlic

1 teaspoon table salt

½ teaspoon ground allspice

½ teaspoon ground black pepper

3 pounds beef flank steak or skirt steaks, cut into 4 or 5 portions

1 medium red onion, halved and sliced into thin half-moons

⅓ cup raisins

1. Combine the coffee, vinegar, orange zest, oregano, cumin, chile, garlic, salt, allspice, and pepper in a 4- to 6-quart slow cooker or a 6-quart stovetop or electric pressure cooker.

2. Add the beef, then the onions and raisins. Toss well to coat in the sauce.

3. To cook the beef in the slow cooker: Cover and cook on high for 5 hours or on low for 9 hours, until the meat is fork-tender. Shred the meat with two forks right in the cooker. Mix it with the sauce and serve warm.

To cook the beef in the pressure cooker: Lock the lid onto the cooker and cook at high pressure for 35 minutes in a stovetop pot (15 psi) or for 42 minutes in an electric pot (9 to 11 psi). Remove the pot from the heat or turn off the electric pot; let the pressure come back to normal naturally, 15 to 20 minutes. Unlock the lid and remove it. Shred the meat with two forks right in the cooker, toss with the sauce, and serve warm.

NO-STICK
GRILLED FISH

Stop lining the grill grate with aluminum foil to keep fish fillets from sticking. First off, the foil can melt over high heat and fuse to those grates. And secondly, it insulates the fish fillets too much, leaving them unappealingly mushy.

Instead, here are three recipes that use citrus as a bed to protect fish fillets from the hot grates. There'll be no sticking, and in one of the recipes you can even use that charred citrus to create a condiment for the fish.

These recipes work best with medium heat at the grill. (Every other grill recipe in this book works with high heat.) In general, medium heat is somewhere between 350°F and 400°F. On a gas grill, turn on fewer ranks or burners than you ordinarily might and space them out: one on, one off. For a charcoal grill, let the coals become well-ashed, no longer searingly hot, then spread them out with a grill rake.

In two of these recipes, there's no need to grease the grill grate, since you'll coat the citrus slices with nonstick spray. (In the last recipe, you'll need to spray the grate, not the citrus, as an extra step of protection against the heat.) However, always brush the grate clean to remove excess char and any burned food bits that are now none too savory.

Grilled Swordfish Steaks with Grapefruit and Tarragon

Makes 4 servings

Swordfish stuck on a grill grate is a tragedy! You're not just losing skin; you're losing the meat itself. Swordfish cooks longer than other sorts of fish, so it's imperative the heat be kept at medium, not nudged up toward high (which is sometimes around 500°F, even higher).

1 large grapefruit

Nonstick spray

4 fresh tarragon sprigs, stemmed (leaves only)

Table salt as needed

Two 12-ounce swordfish steaks, sliced in half horizontally

1 fresh medium jalapeño, stemmed and thinly sliced

2 tablespoons olive oil

Test Kitchen Notes

- Most swordfish steaks are cut quite thick. Even 6-ounce steaks are too thick for this recipe, so we suggest you slice your steaks in half horizontally to make two thinner steaks.

- To slice swordfish steaks horizontally, set them on a cutting board and bend down so they're at eye level. Start at the side nearest you, and use a long, thin knife that is parallel to the board to slice the steak in two.

1. Slice the grapefruit in half through its "equator" (assuming the stem end is one of the poles). Cut two ¼-inch-thick rounds from each half.

2. Brush the grate clean and prepare the grill for direct, medium-heat cooking.

3. Generously coat one side of the four grapefruit slices with nonstick spray. Lay each of these over the heat on the grate sprayed side down. Top each with a quarter of the tarragon leaves and a pinch of salt. Place a fish steak and several jalapeño rings on top of the tarragon. Place the remaining sections of the grapefruit halves (the "ends") cut side down on the grill grate.

4. Cover and grill until the fish is firm and cooked through, about 10 minutes.

5. Using a large metal spatula, transfer each grapefruit-based stack to a serving plate. Remove the grapefruit ends and wait a minute or two to let them cool down. Squeeze their juice over the servings. Drizzle each serving with ½ tablespoon olive oil.

Grilled Salmon Fillets
with Orange, Basil, and Pine Nuts

Makes 4 servings

Skinless salmon fillets are almost impossible on the grill. The meat flakes and chips into nothing in no time. By putting them on orange slices, you can get them on and off the grill with all the juicy flesh intact. Wild-caught sockeye or king salmon is leaner than farmed and perhaps a better choice for this technique since there will be less salmon fat to leak into the orange slices below.

2 large navel oranges

Nonstick spray

2 tablespoons minced fresh basil leaves

Table salt as needed

Ground black pepper

Four 6-ounce skinned salmon fillets (thawed if frozen)

2 tablespoons olive oil

2 tablespoons pine nuts

1. Slice one orange into ¼-inch-thick rounds. Seed these rounds. Slice the other orange in half.

2. Brush the grill grate clean and prepare for direct, medium-heat cooking.

3. Spray one side of each orange slice with nonstick spray. Place two orange slices, sprayed side down, side by side on the grate to make a "platform." Make three more platforms, then sprinkle each with a quarter of the basil, as well as a pinch of salt and pepper. Set one salmon fillet, flat (that is, skinned) side down, on each platform. Place the two orange halves cut side down on the grill grate.

4. Cover the grill and cook until the fish is firm but opaque, cooked through without being flaky, about 10 minutes.

5. Use a large spatula to transfer each fillet and its platform to a serving plate. Remove the orange halves and wait a minute to let them cool down. Squeeze the juice from the halves over the salmon fillets. Drizzle about ½ tablespoon olive oil over each serving, sprinkle each with ½ tablespoon pine nuts, and serve.

Test Kitchen Notes

- Salmon skin will never get crisp and delicious with this technique, so make sure the salmon fillets are skinned.

- For heat, sprinkle on a few red pepper flakes with the basil.

Smoky White Fish with Charred Lime Salsa

Makes 4 servings

Test Kitchen Notes

- The lime slices must be even to create a flat bed for the fish.

- Use juicy limes. They should be thin-skinned and heavy to the hand, not hard but with some give in the skin.

Here, lime slices create a large bed to hold snapper, scrod, or sea bass fillets. Those limes are then chopped up and turned into a salsa with chiles, scallions, and a splash of rum. In this case, you *do* have to grease the grate with nonstick spray, since you'll baste the fish with melted butter. (Milk solids in the butter can get between the lime slices, burn, and cause them to stick. Spraying the citrus rounds themselves may leave small, ungreased sections—which can be a problem. Also, lime slices are small by nature and a pain to spray one by one.) Serve the fish and salsa with rice and beans on the side.

Nonstick spray

4 tablespoons (½ stick) unsalted butter, melted

1 teaspoon dried thyme

½ teaspoon mild smoked paprika

½ teaspoon table salt

¼ teaspoon ground black pepper

5 large limes, thinly sliced

Four 6-ounce thick-fleshed white fish fillets, such as snapper, scrod, or sea bass

2 medium scallions, trimmed and thinly sliced

1 small fresh jalapeño, stemmed, seeded, and minced

1 tablespoon aged rum

1. Brush the grill grate clean, then generously coat it with nonstick spray. Prepare the grill for direct, medium-heat cooking.

2. Mix the butter, thyme, smoked paprika, salt, and pepper in a small bowl.

3. Set the lime slices on the prepared grate directly over the heat, creating a large bed for the fish. Place the fillets on this bed. Brush the butter mixture evenly over the fillets.

4. Cover and grill until the lime slices are charred and the fish is firm but opaque, 10 to 12 minutes.

5. Use a wide, metal spatula to transfer the fillets to serving plates or a serving platter.

6. Transfer the lime slices to a cutting board. Chop up enough of them (rind and all) to make 1 cup of fine bits. Mix these in a bowl with the scallions, jalapeño, and rum. Spoon over the fillets and serve.

SIDES

These days, side dishes are afterthoughts. First off, they're the easiest thing to buy at the prepared food counter. And secondly, unless you're something of a pro, they often muck up the timing of the main course.

That said, here are a set of side dishes that are for the times when the effort counts, when you're ready to step up and do a little more. Microwaving green beans or mixing bagged slaw mix with dressing is a simple shortcut—but you already know that. These recipes go beyond the semi-homemade. Some, like the speedy ways to make tasty risotto, may well be dinner in and of themselves on a weeknight.

Whether you're preparing or even buying side dishes, embrace convenience *but examine it*. Take your glasses to the supermarket. Check those labels. Know what you're buying. Don't fall in love at first sight. Don't pay attention to label bursts. Look among the cans of, say, bean dip, or the jars of mustard, or the packages of bread dough mix. In most cases, the right one has only the ingredients you would put in the food if you were making it from scratch.

In the end, the best convenience products in the supermarket may well be frozen vegetables and fruits. Given many of the recipes in this book, you now know they don't need to be thawed before they can be used.

But there's another reason to pick all that frozen fare. Frozen berries, corn, bell pepper strips, broccoli florets, cauliflower florets—and more—have often been picked closer to ripeness than the same produce headed for the fresh produce bins. Producers depend on transport time to "ripen" much of the bounty; in fact, underripe fruits and vegetables withstand long-haul trucking better. But the parts of the crop meant to be frozen have no such built-in time lag. They must be picked closer to perfection and are often flash-frozen right in the field—which means frozen fruits and vegetables may be better stocked with vitamins and nutrients.

And a final word about convenience: If you buy in bulk, don't store in bulk. Separate that 5-pound box of broccoli into 2-cup bags for the fridge. Same with the 10-pound bag of potatoes. Or that 20-pound bag of carrots. (By the way, how many carrots do you intend to eat?)

And remember: An organized kitchen is already a shortcut-ready kitchen. No, you don't need to alphabetize the spice drawer or arrange the boxed breakfast cereals by increasing sugar content. Just put like with like so you can better find it in a hurry.

The Only Mashed Potatoes You'll Ever Make

Makes 4 servings

Test Kitchen Notes

- This technique only works with yellow-fleshed potatoes like Yukon Golds.

- Pick out your potatoes from the bulk bin. Start with 16 small ones and weigh them, then add more as necessary to make 1½ pounds.

- Use only microwave-safe cookware and plastic wrap.

- Adding the butter before the other ingredients produces more buttery-tasting mashed potatoes. It's a complex, chemical issue of how the fat is absorbed and held by the starches. But it works.

- For a richer flavor, instead of butter, try cream cheese.

Voilà! Make baked potatoes in a slow cooker: Use 12-ounce russet potatoes, as many as will fit in your cooker with each one touching the bottom. (The potatoes can stand up on their ends like silent soldiers.) Rub each potato with a little olive oil and sprinkle with kosher salt, then wrap each in aluminum foil. Snuggle in the slow cooker, cover, and cook on high for 5 hours or low for 9 hours.

Believe it or not, the microwave makes the creamiest mashed potatoes. The secret is not to poke or prod the potatoes before or even as they cook. The skin will seal in all the moisture—which will super-heat and cook the potatoes to perfection from the inside. Sure, there'll be skins in the mash, but they just add to the texture in the dish.

1½ pounds small yellow-fleshed potatoes (probably 16), such as Yukon Golds

2 to 3 tablespoons unsalted butter

½ cup whole, low-fat, or fat-free milk

⅓ cup regular or low-fat sour cream

2 tablespoons minced chives or the green part of a scallion

Up to 1 teaspoon table salt

½ teaspoon ground black pepper

1. Wash the potatoes of any surface dirt, then place them, still damp, in a large, deep, microwave-safe bowl with a lid. Tightly cover the bowl with its lid and open the vent slit. Or tightly cover the top of the bowl with microwave-safe plastic wrap and make one 3-inch slit in the wrap.

2. Microwave on high for 8 minutes. Set aside, still covered, for 2 minutes.

3. Unseal the bowl, add the butter, and use a potato masher or electric mixer to mash it into the potatoes.

4. Add the milk, sour cream, chives, salt, and pepper. Continue mashing until either somewhat creamy with a little chunky texture or very smooth and creamy, depending on your taste.

Potato-Bacon Rosettes

TASTIER

GLUTEN-FREE

Makes 6 servings (2 rosettes each)

Muffin tins aren't just for muffins. They're for bacon! Roll strips of bacon and thin slices of potato together to create small rosettes, then bake them in a muffin tin for an elegant side dish to go alongside just about anything roasted or grilled—or to offer on their own with drinks this weekend. If desired, smear each slice of bacon with a little Dijon mustard, or sprinkle them with a dried spice blend, like Italian seasoning or just chile powder.

Nonstick spray

2 large, fairly long russet potatoes (about 15 ounces each)

12 thin bacon slices (about a 1-pound package)

1. Position the rack in the center of the oven; heat the oven to 375°F. Lightly coat the 12 cups of a standard muffin tin (or the 12 cups of two 6-muffin tins) with nonstick spray.

2. Do not peel the potatoes but slice a thin strip off one long side of each potato so it will more easily glide over the blade. Using a mandoline at the ⅛-inch setting and the safety guard that comes with this kitchen tool, slice the potatoes lengthwise into thin strips. Discard the parts that can no longer be held by the safety guard as well as any imperfect strips. Cut the remaining potato strips in half lengthwise.

3. Lay a strip of bacon on a clean, dry work surface. Overlap three potato strips end to end to make a long strip that covers the slice of bacon. Roll loosely from one end, then set in a cup of the prepared muffin tin, standing it up on its side to make a small rosette.

4. Repeat step 3 to make 12 rosettes.

5. Bake until the potatoes are tender with crispy edges, 45 to 50 minutes. Cool in the muffin tin for 5 minutes before transferring to a serving platter or individual plates to serve warm.

Test Kitchen Notes

- Don't attempt this with any other type of potato than russets. None has the right starch content.

- Do not use thick-cut bacon.

- Almost all bacon is gluten-free, but check the package label to be sure.

- A mandoline is an exquisitely precise kitchen tool—and a dangerous one, to boot. Grasp the potato with the safety guide that's included with all home mandolines before running the vegetable over the blade, thereby keeping your fingers as far away from the sharp edge as possible.

- Don't have a mandoline? Cut each potato in quarters lengthwise, then use a large vegetable peeler to make long strips from one of the cut sides of each quarter, pressing down as much as you can to create the thickest strips.

Creamy Potato Gratin in Half the Time

Makes 4 to 6 servings

Test Kitchen Notes

- You can use a food processor fitted with the slicing blade to cut the potatoes. However, that blade does tend to "juice" the spuds, rendering the gratin a little drier.

- Don't substitute other potatoes for the russets—only they have the necessary starch content to thicken the liquid.

- If you'd like, substitute 1½ tablespoons dried chives for the fresh.

Voilà! The best way to keep mashed potatoes and other side dishes warm before serving is to set their pot over a heat diffuser and turn the heat to very low. Don't have a heat diffuser? Set a skillet over very low heat, then set the saucepan in the skillet.

By simmering potato slices in a cream mixture on the stovetop, you're basically "power cooking" them, giving them a long head start to their time in the oven. So here's a shortcut, a one-skillet answer to a traditional gratin. It takes about half the time, if not less. Use the time that the gratin cooks to roast or grill a main course to serve alongside.

2 pounds russet potatoes, peeled

1½ cups vegetable broth

½ cup heavy cream

2 tablespoons minced chives or the green part of a scallion

2 teaspoons Dijon mustard

½ teaspoon table salt

½ teaspoon ground black pepper

1 cup grated Cheddar, Swiss, or Emmentaler cheese (about 4 ounces)

1. Position the rack in the center of the oven; heat the oven to 400°F.

2. Cut the peeled potatoes into ¼-inch-thick disks, starting at one of the small ends of each spud.

3. Arrange the potato slices so that they all go in one direction and form as compact an arrangement as possible in a 10-inch skillet, preferably cast-iron.

4. Whisk the broth, cream, chives, mustard, salt, and pepper in a medium bowl until uniform. Pour over the potato slices.

5. Set the skillet over medium heat and bring to a simmer. Cover and simmer for 15 minutes.

6. Uncover the skillet and sprinkle the cheese over the gratin. Transfer the skillet to the oven and bake until the cheese has melted and even browned a bit, about 12 minutes. Cool at room temperature for at least 10 minutes before serving.

Even Faster Oven-Fried Veggies

Makes 4 to 6 servings

Cut down the time of oven-fried vegetables by using frozen ones. We know: It sounds wrong. They'll be mushy, right? But freezing, then thawing the vegetables breaks down some of their natural fibers so they get crisper faster in the oven. And who doesn't want to see a big baking sheet of oven-fried veggies get to the table faster? Besides being a great side dish to just about anything roasted or grilled, these oven-fried veggies are terrific alongside a glass of iced tea with the game on TV.

Test Kitchen Notes

- Check if the seasoning blend you use includes salt. If not, salt the vegetables *after* baking.

- When you put the thawed vegetables in the bowl in step 2, there should be no additional liquid before adding the buttermilk. If there's some left over from thawing, blot the vegetables dry with paper towels.

- For super-crunchy vegetables, coat them heavily with nonstick spray. Also, use the convection fan, if your oven has one. Or turn a standard oven up to 475°F to heat, then back down to 400°F once the vegetables go in.

Nonstick spray

1 pound frozen broccoli florets, cauliflower florets, sliced okra, sliced zucchini, and/ or artichoke heart quarters, thawed

¼ cup buttermilk

1 cup plain dried breadcrumbs

½ cup all-purpose flour

Up to 1 tablespoon your seasoning mixture of choice, such as Cajun seasoning, crab boil seasoning, herbs de Provence, Italian blend dried seasoning mix, jerk seasoning, dried oregano, dried sage, or your favorite dried herbs and spices, to taste

1. Position the rack in the center of the oven; heat the oven to 400°F. Lightly coat a large lipped baking sheet with nonstick spray.

2. Put the vegetables in a large bowl and add the buttermilk. Stir gently until thoroughly and evenly coated.

3. Combine the breadcrumbs, flour, and seasoning in a paper bag. Use tongs to transfer the vegetables to the bag. Seal and shake to coat.

4. Remove the vegetables from the bag, leaving any excess dry mixture behind and arranging the pieces in one layer on the baking sheet. Generously coat the vegetables with nonstick spray.

5. Bake until golden and crisp, about 18 minutes. Cool a minute or two on a wire rack, then serve hot.

Atomic Ratatouille

Makes 4 to 6 servings

FASTER

VEGETARIAN

GLUTEN-FREE

Don't want to spend all Tuesday night stirring to make a side dish to go with steaks or chops off the grill? Make this simple ratatouille spiked with caponata, a Sicilian eggplant spread you can find at your local grocery store. The side dish is done in minutes in the microwave with very little fuss.

2 medium zucchini, thinly sliced

1 large green bell pepper, stemmed, cored, and cut into strips

1 medium yellow onion, thinly sliced

One 14-ounce can diced tomatoes, drained

One 8-ounce jar caponata

1 cup finely grated Parmigiano-Reggiano (about 2 ounces)

1. Combine the zucchini, bell pepper, onion, tomatoes, and caponata in a large microwave-safe bowl.

2. Cover with microwave-safe plastic wrap or a lid with the vent closed. Microwave on high, stirring after 7 minutes, for 14 minutes. Sprinkle with the cheese before serving.

Voilà! To clean up dried, splattered food in a microwave, mix 1 cup water and ¼ cup distilled white vinegar in a microwave-safe bowl, then microwave on high until boiling, 3 to 4 minutes for most ovens. Leave the steaming bowl in the closed oven for 5 minutes. The steam will loosen food bits and deodorize the oven. Just wipe clean.

Test Kitchen Notes

- The thinner you slice the zucchini, the more the rounds will melt into the classic consistency. Consider ⅛ inch to be the right thickness. If you find that the ratatouille is a bit too soft for your taste, increase the slices to just shy of ¼ inch thick on the next go-round.

- To thinly slice an onion into strips, slice off the root end, cut in half through the stem (i.e., not through the equator), and set it cut side down on the cutting board, stem pointing away from you. Make thin slices across the onion, thereby producing thin strips instead of rings.

- The canned tomatoes must be drained. Use a fine-mesh colander or line a standard colander with paper towels.

- If you're concerned about plastic wrap touching hot food, cover the bowl with a plate instead.

- Some store-bought caponata is thickened with wheat-based additives. If gluten is an issue, check the label to be sure.

Overnight Pickles

Makes about 1 gallon

EASIER

VEGETARIAN

GLUTEN-FREE

It doesn't take a barrel and weeks to make good pickles. It takes a big bowl and overnight in the fridge. And why stand on ceremony with cucumbers, when you can pickle cauliflower, carrots, and green beans instead? The secret here is par-cooking the vegetables, which gives them just a little time in the heat to begin to break down their fibers and let the vinegar do its job more quickly *and* more efficiently. Try the pickles on a turkey club. Or use the cauliflower florets in martinis instead of olives.

4½ cups water

10 medium carrots, peeled and cut into ½-inch-thick slices

1 medium cauliflower head, cored, any leaves removed, and broken into 1-inch florets

1 pound green beans, trimmed

4 cups (1 quart) white vinegar

½ cup granulated white sugar

¼ cup packed whole dill fronds

3 tablespoons kosher salt

4 large garlic cloves, peeled

3 bay leaves

1. Bring the water to a boil in a large pot set over medium heat.

2. Add the carrots and cook for 1 minute from the time they hit the water.

3. Add the cauliflower florets and cook for 1 minute from the time they hit the water.

4. Add the green beans and cook for an additional 30 seconds. The water may never come back to a full boil.

5. Using a slotted spoon, transfer the vegetables to a very large colander (or two) set in the sink. Rinse under cool tap water until room temperature, then drain well, shaking the colander a few times. Transfer the vegetables to a very large bowl or 1-gallon heat-safe glass jar.

6. Stir the vinegar, sugar, dill fronds, salt, garlic, and bay leaves into the water remaining in the pot. Bring back to a boil over high heat, then pour over the vegetables in the bowl.

7. Cover tightly and refrigerate for at least 12 hours or up to 1 week.

Test Kitchen Notes

- The dill fronds will get slimy over time if you store them with the pickles. Remove them from the brine after a day or two.

Voilà! The best tool for trimming green beans and scallions are kitchen scissors. Hold a handful of green beans (or a few scallions) together in your fist, then snip off the tips or roots.

FASTER VEGETABLES

Though we've tried to come up with techniques that make cooking almost anything faster, some vegetables just take longer than others. To make quick cooking on the fly easier, think about dividing the produce section of your supermarket into what's fast to cook and what's not. Like this:

QUICKER		SLOWER	
Asparagus	Green beans	Beets	Rutabaga
Bean sprouts	Mushrooms	Broccoli stems	Sweet potatoes
Bell peppers	Onions	Carrots	Turnips
Broccoli florets	Radishes	Celeriac	Winter squash, like butternut or acorn squash
Brussels sprouts	Shelled peas	Parsnips	
Cauliflower florets	Sugar snap peas	Potatoes	Yucca
Corn	Summer (or yellow) squash		
Eggplant	Tomatoes		
Fennel	Zucchini		

However, here are three qualifications:

1. Most quick-cooking vegetables can also be eaten raw—the fastest cooking method of all!

2. Some quick-cooking vegetables, like mushrooms, tomatoes, and fennel, can also benefit from prolonged cooking to become sweeter and more flavorful.

3. Most long-cooking vegetables can cook quickly if they are cut into *very* small pieces. For example, carrots, sliced into paper-thin coins or shredded through the large holes of a box grater, can be added to many a quick sauté.

The World's Easiest Polenta

EASIER

VEGETARIAN

GLUTEN-FREE

Makes 6 servings

The slow cooker makes the most amazing polenta. The moist environment softens the dried corn into something absurdly luxurious, and you only need to stir the whole thing once. This is a very plain polenta, meant to be served under a hearty stew or topped with a couple of fried eggs. You may think we've gone mad here; but to tell the truth, this is the only way we make polenta anymore, even for the fanciest dinner parties.

4 cups (1 quart) vegetable broth

1 cup coarse-grain polenta (do not use instant polenta)

½ teaspoon table salt

½ teaspoon ground black pepper

½ cup finely grated Parmigiano-Reggiano (about 1 ounce)

1. Stir the broth, polenta, salt, and pepper in a 4- to 6-quart slow cooker.

2. Cover and cook on high for 45 minutes.

3. Stir well. Cover again and cook on high until the polenta is creamy and all the broth has been absorbed, about 45 minutes longer. Stir in the cheese just before serving.

Test Kitchen Notes

- Although this is a vegetarian polenta, it is undoubtedly richer if you substitute chicken broth.

- For an even richer polenta, use just 3½ cups broth (vegetable or chicken) and add ½ cup heavy cream.

- If desired, add up to 1 tablespoon minced fresh herbs with the table salt and pepper.

- Don't have perfect timing? If the polenta is done before the rest of dinner, you can turn off the slow cooker and set it aside, covered, for up to 30 minutes before you stir the cheese into the polenta.

Voilà! Stock up on quick-cooking grains for other fast side dishes: buckwheat, quick-cooking bulgur (sometimes called "instant bulgur"), and quinoa.

TWENTY-MINUTE ROASTED ROOTS, POTATOES, AND MORE

Sure, you can cook root vegetables in a microwave oven. But you end up with mushy vegetables and miss out on the crunchy bits, the best parts from roasting. So reach a compromise: Give the roots a head start in the microwave, then transfer them to the oven to crisp up, putting irresistibly crunchy vegetables within reach on an average weeknight.

Test Kitchen Notes

- To work in advance, microwave the roots, toss them with the remaining ingredients, and set aside, loosely covered with a kitchen towel, for up to 4 hours.

- For the best results, use an 11 x 17-inch or 13 x 18-inch baking sheet so that everything can fit in one layer to make good contact with the hot surface.

Roasted Carrots, Sweet Potatoes, and Butternut Squash

Makes 6 servings

The only trick here is to make sure the vegetables are cut into evenly sized pieces. If you buy cut-up butternut squash chunks from the produce section (and you should, to save time), you may need to cut them down into smaller 1-inch chunks for this technique.

3 medium carrots, peeled and cut into 1-inch pieces

1 large sweet potato, peeled and cut into 1-inch cubes

1 pound butternut squash, peeled, seeded, and cut into 1-inch pieces

2 tablespoons olive oil

1 tablespoon unsalted butter

½ teaspoon table salt

½ teaspoon ground cinnamon

¼ teaspoon cayenne, optional

1. Position the rack in the center of the oven. Set a large lipped baking sheet in the oven and heat the oven to 375°F.

2. Place the carrots, sweet potatoes, and squash in a large, microwave-safe bowl. Add enough water so that the vegetables are barely covered.

3. In a 950-watt oven, microwave the vegetables on high for 5 minutes; in a 1200-watt oven, microwave on high for 4 minutes.

4. Drain the roots in a colander set in the sink. Return them to the bowl. Add the oil, butter, salt, cinnamon, and cayenne, if using. Toss until the butter has melted and coated the roots.

5. Pour the vegetables onto the hot baking sheet, spreading them into one layer. Bake, tossing a few times, until crisp at the edges yet tender at the centers, about 20 minutes.

FASTER

VEGETARIAN

GLUTEN-FREE

Roasted Parsnips, Brussels Sprouts, and Shallots

Makes 6 servings

There's something incredible about the combo of parsnips and Brussels sprouts: earthy but sweet, bitter but savory. This tray of roasted vegetables goes best with roast chicken—or even a rotisserie chicken from the supermarket.

2 pounds medium parsnips, peeled and cut into 1-inch sections

12 ounces large Brussels sprouts, quartered

6 medium shallots, peeled and quartered

3 tablespoons canola or vegetable oil

1 teaspoon caraway seeds

1 teaspoon table salt

½ teaspoon granulated white sugar

Up to 1 tablespoon minced fresh dill fronds

1. Position the rack in the center of the oven. Place a large lipped baking sheet in the oven and heat the oven to 375°F.

2. Place the parsnips in a medium, microwave-safe bowl and add enough water to barely cover them.

3. In a 950-watt oven, microwave the parsnips on high for 5 minutes; in a 1200-watt oven, microwave on high for 4 minutes.

4. Drain in a colander set in the sink. Return the parsnips to the bowl; add the Brussels sprouts, shallots, oil, caraway seeds, salt, and sugar. Toss well to coat.

5. Scrape the vegetables and every speck of the oil mixture onto the hot baking sheet. Arrange the vegetables in a single layer. Roast, tossing a couple of times, until the shallots are soft and the parsnips have browned but are still tender, not mushy, about 20 minutes. Add the dill while still hot and toss well before serving.

Orange-Scented Roasted Beets and Walnuts

FASTER
VEGETARIAN
GLUTEN-FREE

Makes 6 servings

Why don't more people love beets? They're sweet and earthy, nutritious and tasty. And they're much better roasted than steamed! The one problem is the way they can stain your hands (and counter and clothes). For your hands, wear rubber gloves if you're worried. Or use a pumice soap to clean up. Or substitute so-called candy-stripe beets for the purple ones. For your counters, a good surface cleaner can take up the mess (except for wood, which will have to wear away). As for your clothes, you're on your own.

3 pounds purple beets, peeled and cut into 1-inch cubes

2 tablespoons olive oil

½ cup chopped walnuts

2 tablespoons chopped fresh rosemary

2 tablespoons red wine vinegar

1 tablespoon finely grated orange zest

1 tablespoon honey

½ teaspoon table salt

1. Position the rack in the center of the oven. Place a large lipped baking sheet in the oven and heat the oven to 375°F.

2. Put the beets in a medium, microwave-safe bowl. Add enough water to barely cover them.

3. In a 950-watt oven, microwave the beets on high for 7 minutes; in a 1200-watt oven, microwave on high for 6 minutes.

4. Drain in a colander set in the sink. Return the beets to the bowl and add the oil. Toss well to coat.

5. Scrape the beets and any oil onto the hot baking sheet. Arrange the beets in one layer. Roast for 15 minutes, tossing once.

6. Add the walnuts, rosemary, vinegar, orange zest, honey, and salt. Toss well, then continue roasting until the beets are tender, about 5 minutes.

Voilà! It's easy to make whole grains like wheat berries, rye berries, and triticale as a side dish in a slow cooker—with no soaking beforehand. Mix the grains with plenty of water (figure on a ratio of about 1 cup grain to 2 cups water). Cover and cook on low for 7 to 9 hours, depending on the grains' moisture content before cooking. Serve them with butter, table salt, and pepper—or go further with a smooth red hot sauce like Sriracha, grated nutmeg, and walnut oil; or finely grated Parmigiano-Reggiano, minced fresh oregano, and Worcestershire sauce.

FASTER

GLUTEN-FREE

Garlic- and Herb-Roasted Potatoes with Bacon

Makes 6 servings

Voilà! An apple placed in a bag of potatoes will slow down their sprouting.

Roasted potatoes are one of life's true pleasures. So why not have them more often, given this shortcut technique? However, there's one caveat: The microwaved potatoes can stick to the sheet as they roast. Toss them on the pan more often than you might think, maybe three times during the first 10 minutes in the oven.

3 pounds golf ball–size yellow-fleshed potatoes, such as Yukon Golds, halved

4 ounces bacon (preferably thick-cut, and gluten-free if that's a concern), diced

2 tablespoons olive oil

Up to 1 tablespoon minced garlic

6 fresh thyme sprigs

½ teaspoon ground black pepper

1. Position the rack in the center of the oven. Place a large lipped baking sheet in the oven and heat the oven to 400°F.

2. Place the potatoes in a large, microwave-safe bowl. Add enough water so they're barely covered.

3. In a 950-watt oven, microwave the potatoes on high for 7 minutes; in a 1200-watt oven, microwave on high for 6 minutes.

4. Drain in a colander set in the sink. Return the potatoes to the bowl and toss with the bacon pieces, olive oil, garlic, thyme, and pepper.

5. Scrape the potatoes and every speck of seasoning and oil from the bowl onto the hot baking sheet. Arrange the ingredients in one layer. Roast, stirring many times, until browned yet tender, about 20 minutes.

THICK-CUT VEGGIE FRIES

The best way to make fast, easy, thick-cut steak fries out of almost any vegetable is to use an apple slicer. Slice a small bit off of the bottom of the vegetable so it can stand upright on a cutting board. Then press the slicer down and through the vegetable, creating thick steak fries. And don't throw out the core. Roast it, too!

Test Kitchen Notes

- Like knives, apple slicers go dull over time. Consider replacing an aging tool.

- For this to work, the vegetables can be no wider (at any point) than the diameter of your apple slicer. Standard models are 3½ inches in diameter. Measure yours before you shop, just to make sure.

- These recipes are made in a medium roasting pan. You can also use your oven's broiler pan (if the oven is old enough to have come with one). Or you can use a medium lipped sheet pan, although the lower sides may cause the tops of the vegetables to darken more quickly—at which point you'll need to stir and rearrange them more frequently in the pan. Do not use a nonstick baking sheet (too easily nicked) or an insulated one (too much heat diffusion so the vegetables won't get brown and crunchy).

Garlic- and Parsley-Coated Steak Fries

Makes 4 to 6 servings

There's no need to turn these potatoes as they roast. The more contact one side of each fry has with the hot metal, the crunchier they will get. That said, you do need to loosen the potatoes from the roasting pan to make sure they don't stick. As they bake, periodically run a metal spatula under them to make sure they're not sticking to the hot surface. Or shake the pan repeatedly during the first half hour.

4 large russet potatoes (about 3 pounds), peeled

3 tablespoons olive oil

3 tablespoons minced garlic

1 teaspoon table salt

1 teaspoon ground black pepper

¼ cup minced fresh parsley leaves

1. Position the rack in the center of the oven; heat the oven to 400°F.

2. Cut a small slice off one end of each potato so it will sit flat and stand up tall on your cutting board or work surface. Use an apple slicer to press down through each potato, slicing it into wedges.

3. Place the wedges in a medium roasting or broiler pan. Add the oil, garlic, salt, and pepper. Toss well to coat evenly.

4. Roast until the potatoes are crisp and golden brown, about 50 minutes, loosening them from the pan about halfway through the baking.

5. Remove from the oven and sprinkle the parsley all over the wedges. Set aside for a couple of minutes to cool before serving.

Voilà! If you're not going to buy minced garlic in jars, you can quickly make a fine garlic paste by putting a small handful of peeled cloves in a plastic bag, squeezing out the air, sealing it closed, and bashing it with a rolling pin. The flavor of the paste will be more concentrated, so use about 25 percent less than jarred minced garlic. Store the remainder right in that sealed bag in the fridge for a couple of weeks.

More! The garlic will turn quite brown, not to everyone's taste. If you're in that camp, add the garlic to the sheet pan after it has been in the oven for 30 minutes.

Spicy Sweet Potato Fries

Makes 4 to 6 servings

The problem with sweet potato fries is their inherent mushiness. To get more crunch per fry, you must treat the sweet potato as an entirely different vegetable than the potato. After all, sweet potatoes are not actually tubers, but rather rhizomes, related to ginger. Because of the extra sugar and moisture content in sweet potatoes, you need to turn these fries quite a few times, making sure all sides come in contact with the hot baking sheet. For even crunchier fries, set the baking sheet in the oven as it heats to get a good sear on one side of each fry.

4 medium sweet potatoes (about 3 pounds), peeled

3 tablespoons peanut or vegetable oil

1 teaspoon ground cumin

1 teaspoon garlic powder

1 teaspoon light brown sugar

1 teaspoon table salt

Up to 1 teaspoon ground black pepper

1. Position the rack in the center of the oven; heat the oven to 400°F.

2. Cut a small slice off one end of each sweet potato so it will stand up tall on your cutting board or work surface. Cut each sweet potato in half widthwise. Set them with the large cut side down on a cutting board. Use an apple slicer to press down through each sweet potato, slicing it into wedges.

3. Place the wedges in a medium roasting or broiler pan. Add the oil, cumin, garlic powder, brown sugar, salt, and pepper. Toss well to coat evenly.

4. Roast, turning several times, until the wedges are lightly browned and crisp at the edges but tender at their centers, about 45 minutes. Cool a couple of minutes before serving.

Cheese-Covered Turnip Fries

Makes 4 to 6 servings

Okay, this one's a little far afield. Turnips? As fries? Why not! Turnips are a little bitter but have a sweet, earthy flavor. By tossing them with plenty of grated cheese, they may even appeal to picky eaters. No promises. And if not, there's more for you.

6 medium-large turnips (about 3 pounds), peeled

3 tablespoons olive oil

1 teaspoon table salt

½ teaspoon grated nutmeg

¼ teaspoon cayenne

½ cup finely grated Parmigiano-Reggiano (about 1 ounce)

1. Position the rack in the center of the oven; heat the oven to 400°F.

2. Slice a small piece off one end of each turnip so they'll sit firm on your cutting board. Use an apple slicer to push down through each, slicing it into wedges.

3. Place the wedges in a medium roasting or broiler pan. Add the oil, salt, nutmeg, and cayenne. Toss well to coat evenly.

4. Roast, turning the wedges once, until lightly browned and crisp at the edges but tender at the centers, about 35 minutes.

5. Sprinkle the wedges with the grated cheese. Set aside for a couple minutes as the cheese melts, then serve.

SUPERFAST RISOTTO

Risotto, that vaunted rice dish, is always a nightmare of stirring. So much time at the stove! But here are two techniques that cut down on the stirring and the grief.

The first uses a pressure cooker. To complete the task successfully, you'll need to know the amount of pressure your pot uses for its high setting. And you'll need to ignore the presets on an electric machine to cook the risotto on high for the timings given.

If you don't have a pressure cooker, try the second technique: It uses the microwave and is a little more intense, though not much more. The recipes are calibrated for a 950-watt microwave oven. A 1200-watt oven will get the job done in about 10 minutes.

These recipes are presented somewhat like quirky road maps—meaning the ingredient lists come first, then there are the techniques: You'll start with a fat like butter or olive oil, then add aromatics like onions or shallots. After that, you'll add rice, a booster liquid of some sort (wine, juice), and then broth, a vegetable (or two), and seasonings. At that point, you're minutes away from risotto.

The hope is that you'll treat these as templates and create your own signature version. Just treat the rice and total liquid amounts as sacred.

Superfast Risotto

Makes 6 side-course servings or 4 main-course servings

Test Kitchen Notes

- Use *white* arborio rice (not brown arborio), or substitute white Valencia rice.

- Do not use frozen chopped onions in these recipes. They don't provide enough flavor.

- Some of these recipes call for vegetarian broth; others, chicken. Honestly, you could use either in any case. Chicken broth will always give the dish more heft.

- A low-sodium broth is the best option for the pressure-cooker versions. Pressure cookers seem to concentrate the saltiness of the broth. Better to add your own at the table.

First, here are the ingredient lists for five kinds of risotto!

Vegetarian Butternut Squash and Mushroom Risotto

Fat: **2 tablespoons unsalted butter**

Aromatic: **1 large leek, white and pale green parts only, halved lengthwise, washed for sand, and sliced into thin half-moons**

Cured meat: **None**

Rice: **1½ cups white arborio rice**

Booster liquid: **¼ cup dry vermouth, dry white wine, or water**

Broth: **4 cups (1 quart) vegetable broth**

Vegetable: **2 cups diced peeled seeded butternut squash**

Seasonings: **½ ounce crumbled dried porcini mushrooms; 1 tablespoon minced fresh sage leaves; ½ teaspoon table salt; ½ teaspoon ground black pepper; and ⅛ teaspoon saffron**

Cheese: **1 cup finely grated Parmigiano-Reggiano (about 2 ounces)**

Pea and Pancetta Risotto

Fat: **2 tablespoons unsalted butter**

Aromatic: **2 medium shallots, finely chopped**

Cured meat: **2 ounces pancetta, diced**

Rice: **1½ cups white arborio rice**

Booster liquid: **¼ cup rosé wine or unsweetened apple juice**

Broth: **4 cups (1 quart) chicken broth**

Vegetable: **1 cup fresh peas or thawed frozen peas**

Seasonings: **2 tablespoons minced fresh tarragon leaves; ½ teaspoon table salt; and ½ teaspoon ground black pepper**

Cheese: **1 cup finely grated aged Asiago (about 2 ounces)**

Vegetarian Artichoke and Lemon Risotto

Fat: **2 tablespoons olive oil**

Aromatic: **1 medium yellow onion, finely chopped**

Cured meat: **None**

Rice: **1½ cups white arborio rice**

Booster liquid: **¼ cup dry vermouth or water**

Broth: **4 cups (1 quart) vegetable broth**

Vegetable: **one 9-ounce box frozen artichoke heart quarters, thawed**

Seasonings: **2 teaspoons fresh thyme leaves; up to 2 teaspoons finely grated lemon zest; ½ teaspoon table salt; and ½ teaspoon ground black pepper**

Cheese: **about ½ cup crumbled soft fresh goat cheese (about 2 ounces); or ½ cup diced, rind-removed Brie (about 2½ ounces)**

Chard and Sun-Dried Tomato Risotto

Fat: 2 tablespoons olive oil

Aromatics: 1 medium yellow onion, chopped; 1 teaspoon minced garlic

Cured meat: None

Rice: 1½ cups white arborio rice

Booster liquid: ¼ cup red vermouth, cranberry juice, or water

Broth: 4 cups (1 quart) chicken broth

Vegetables: 1½ cups packed chopped stemmed Swiss chard leaves and ¼ cup chopped sun-dried tomatoes

Seasonings: 1 tablespoon minced fresh oregano leaves; ½ teaspoon table salt; and ½ teaspoon ground black pepper

Cheese: 1 cup finely grated Pecorino (about 2 ounces)

Vegetarian Curried Cauliflower Risotto

Fat: 2 tablespoons unsalted butter

Aromatics: 1 medium yellow onion, chopped; 1 tablespoon minced peeled fresh ginger; and 1 teaspoon minced garlic

Cured meat: None

Rice: 1½ cups white arborio rice

Booster liquid: ¼ cup sweet white wine, unsweetened apple cider, or water

Broth: 4 cups (1 quart) vegetable broth

Vegetable: 2 cups small cauliflower florets

Seasonings: 2 teaspoons yellow curry powder; ½ teaspoon table salt; and ¼ teaspoon cayenne

Cheese: None—or ½ cup plain Greek yogurt if desired

Pressure-Cooker Risotto

1. Heat the fat in the pot of the pressure cooker, either setting a stovetop pot over medium heat or turning an electric cooker to its browning or sautéing setting. Add the aromatic(s) as well as cured meat (if using). Cook until the aromatics soften a bit, usually just a couple of minutes.

2. Add the rice and stir until the grains are translucent at their outer edges, about 3 minutes.

3. Add the booster liquid and stir until almost all has been absorbed by the rice.

4. Pour in the broth, then add the vegetable(s) and seasonings.

5. Lock on the lid, cover, and bring the pot to high pressure. Cook at high pressure for 7 minutes in a stovetop pressure cooker (15 psi), or for 10 minutes in an electric pressure cooker (9 to 11 psi).

6. Use the quick-release method to open the pot.

7. Stir in the cheese, cover (without engaging any pressure mechanism), and set aside for 2 minutes to help the risotto firm up and to blend the flavors. Stir again before serving.

Microwave Risotto

1. Place the fat, aromatic(s), and cured meat (if using) in a round, high-sided 2-quart microwave-safe baking or soufflé dish.

2. Cook in the microwave on high for 1 minute. Stir well.

3. Add the rice and stir well to coat.

4. Add the booster liquid and half the broth. Stir well. Cook on high for 10 minutes.

5. Add the remainder of the broth, as well as the vegetable(s) and seasonings. Cook on high for 12 minutes, stirring in 2-minute increments, until the rice is tender but still has a little chew inside each grain.

6. Stir in the cheese. Set aside for 2 minutes to help the risotto tighten up and to blend the flavors.

8

DESSERTS
AND
SWEET ENDINGS

If you're looking for kitchen shortcuts, you're probably looking for ways to get dinner on the table more quickly—or at least more efficiently. You may not be looking for a quick dessert. Is there even such a thing as a decent 5-minute treat?

Indeed, yes. You haven't yet tried the most decadent chocolate pudding imaginable. (It's made—spoiler alert!—with tofu.) Or crisp little ginger cookies that don't require a rolling pin. (Just a package of wonton wrappers.) Or an orange sheet cake that never dirties a bowl or a whisk. (It's made in a food processor, right down to grinding the orange into the batter.)

Cooking is physics, all heat and sizzle. But baking is chemistry, a complex set of ratios. In these recipes, pay close attention to the ingredient amounts. Don't go varying them (or the ingredients themselves) unless you know what you're doing. There is no shortcut out of a bad cake.

Some of these recipes call for *baking spray,* not nonstick spray. Baking spray is a combination of flour and oil. Naturally, it's a great time-saver for a busy cook. But note that there's no need to spray a pan so that it's thickly coated in white foam. Instead, give it a light but thorough coating, with no holes or gaps visible, paying careful attention to the crevices where the sides of the pan meet its bottom.

If you want to skip the canned spray and go old-school, use softened butter and all-purpose flour. (Or canola oil on a paper towel, if there's no butter in the recipe.) The easiest way to butter a pan is to let the required butter soften to room temperature in its wrapper. When you unwrap it, some butter will inevitably stick to the wrapper. Run the buttered side of this wrapper all over the inside of the pan. Dust the pan with flour by adding only a tablespoon or two, then shifting the pan this way and that, tipping it on its sides, all to move the flour around to all the available interior surface. You'll also be able to spot any sections you missed with the butter or oil. Fix these before going on. And tap out any excess flour into the garbage can.

Finally, just before dessert, one more piece of advice, maybe not strictly culinary, just run-of-the-mill friendly: Use your time wisely. Not your time in the kitchen. Well, yes, that, as this book illustrates again and again—but mostly your time elsewhere. If you're saving it, you're doing so for a reason, right? To have more of it? Then take the pleasure of it. Don't feel you must be productive every found second. Instead, treat that extra time as a gift. In the same way that it's (rarely) fun to get a rake or a feather duster for your birthday, consider the gift of extra time to be a modern luxury, not a hard-fought necessity. If the point of saving time is to have it, then the point of having it should be to enjoy it.

TASTIER

VEGETARIAN

No-Fail Box-Grater Shortbread

Makes 18 bar cookies

Test Kitchen Notes

- Freeze the dough for exactly 1 hour. It must not be rock hard.

- Use a metal or ceramic baking pan. Glass will overheat the dough and burn the edges.

- Once baked, the cookies can be stored in the freezer in a sealed bag for up to 3 months.

Voilà! Want more easy baking with a box grater? Instead of cutting butter into flour for a pie crust, grate very cold butter into the flour using the large holes of a box grater. Continue on with the recipe as stated, simply stirring it together with cold water.

Shortbread dough can be a pain to roll out. And while rolling it out, it can take on too much flour, rendering the cookies tough. This shortcut lets you skip the rolling by grating cold dough directly into the baking pan. The shreds will melt to the right consistency and morph into irresistible cookies.

4 cups all-purpose flour

2 teaspoons baking powder

½ teaspoon table salt

2 cups (4 sticks or 1 pound) unsalted butter, at room temperature, plus more for the baking dish

2 cups granulated white sugar

4 large egg yolks, at room temperature

Confectioners' sugar, for garnishing

1. Whisk the flour, baking powder, and salt in a large bowl until uniform.

2. Using a stand mixer with the paddle attachment or a handheld mixer, cream the butter and granulated sugar in a second large bowl at medium speed until light and fluffy, about 4 minutes. Beat in the egg yolks one at a time, then turn off the machine. Scrape down the inside of the bowl, then continue beating until smooth.

3. Scrape down and remove the beaters. Using a wooden spoon, stir in the flour mixture until a dough forms. Gather the dough into a ball, seal in plastic wrap, and freeze for 1 hour.

4. Meanwhile, position the rack in the center of the oven; heat the oven to 350°F. Lightly butter the inside of a metal or ceramic 9 x 13-inch baking pan.

5. Grate the semi-frozen ball of dough into the pan through the large holes of a box grater. Gently pat the shreds down so they evenly fill the pan without compacting or compressing them.

6. Bake until brown and set to the touch, about 40 minutes. Cool in the pan on a wire rack to room temperature, about 1 hour. Cut into small squares and dust these with confectioners' sugar to serve.

Instant Ginger-Sugar Crisps

Makes 32 crisps

These aren't traditional gingersnaps, but they pack a wallop of ginger flavor and a satisfying crunch. Why roll out cookie dough when you can make delicate, light crisps with wonton wrappers? The wrappers are not sweetened, so feel free to add lots of spiced sugar to the tops before they bake. Since these cookies are so tender and light, eat them up the day you make them.

¼ cup granulated white sugar

1 tablespoon ground ginger

¼ teaspoon table salt

32 wonton wrappers

4 tablespoons (½ stick) unsalted butter, melted

1. Position the rack in the center of the oven; heat the oven to 400°F.

2. Use a fork to mix the sugar, ginger, and salt in a small bowl until uniform.

3. Arrange the wrappers on several baking sheets. Brush each wrapper with melted butter, then sprinkle each with a scant ½ teaspoon of the sugar mixture.

4. Bake one batch at a time until crisp, about 5 minutes, then continue baking more sheets. Cool the crisps on a large wire rack for at least 10 minutes.

Test Kitchen Notes

- Look for wonton wrappers in the refrigerator case of the produce section, sometimes near the tofu. When you see them, snap them up, then store in the freezer.

- And freeze leftover wrappers for the next time you want these crisps.

- Use a pastry brush to get the butter onto the wrappers.

- Feel free to vary the spices mixed into the sugar. Because other dried spices pack a bigger punch than ground ginger, substitute only 2 teaspoons ground cinnamon, ground cloves, and/or ground cardamom. Or use 1½ teaspoons grated nutmeg.

EASIER

VEGETARIAN

Freezer Cupcakes with Freezer Chocolate Frosting

Makes 12 cupcakes

Test Kitchen Notes

- You must use whole milk. Low-fat, fat-free—even nut or soy—milks have too much excess water to work in this technique.

- There is really no such thing as a "standard" muffin tin. The size of the indentations can vary widely. We used tins during testing with cups that held between ½ cup and ⅔ cup of water when filled. We do not recommend using this technique for mini muffins.

- Once the batter freezes in the cups, you can remove the filled papers from the tin and store them flat in a sealed plastic bag. You can then set a few of the cups with their frozen batter in a muffin tin and bake as many as you want at any given time.

These yellow cupcakes won't puff tall like muffins, partly because they're baked straight from frozen. That seems a small price to pay for cupcakes that are so light, almost ephemeral—and that can be made so far in advance! The frosting is a buttercream that also holds up to storage in the freezer. In fact, make an extra batch and stock it away. You never know when you might need chocolate frosting!

For the Cupcakes

1½ cups cake flour

1 tablespoon baking powder

½ teaspoon table salt

1 cup granulated white sugar

½ cup (1 stick) cool unsalted butter, cut into cubes

2 large eggs

½ cup whole milk

1 teaspoon vanilla extract

For the Frosting

1¾ cup confectioners' sugar

½ cup (1 stick) unsalted butter, at room temperature

¼ cup unsweetened cocoa powder

¼ teaspoon table salt

2 teaspoons vanilla extract

Up to 3 tablespoons heavy cream

To Make the Cupcakes

1. Line a standard 12-cup muffin tin with paper cupcake liners.

2. Whisk the flour, baking powder, and salt in a small bowl until uniform.

3. With an electric mixer at medium speed, beat the granulated sugar and butter in a large bowl until creamy and light, about 4 minutes. Beat in the eggs one at a time.

4. Turn off the beaters and scrape down the inside of the bowl. Pour the flour mixture evenly over the top. Then beat at medium speed while slowly pouring in the milk until all the flour has been moistened. Beat in the vanilla.

5. Divide the batter among the lined cups. Cover the tin tightly with plastic wrap and freeze for up to 4 months.

To Make the Frosting

6. Process the confectioners' sugar, butter, cocoa powder, salt, and vanilla in a food processor until smooth.

7. Add the cream in dribs and drabs through the feed tube with the machine running to form a thick but spreadable and certainly not runny frosting.

8. Scrape the frosting into a plastic freezer bag, squeeze out the excess air, seal, and freeze for up to 4 months.

To Bake and Frost the Cupcakes

9. Set the bag of frosting out on the counter to defrost. Either unwrap the muffin tin with its cupcakes from the freezer and set it on the counter—or set out as many cupcakes as you'd like to bake and place in a separate tin.

10. Position the rack in the center of the oven and heat the oven to 350°F.

11. Bake the cupcakes until set and a toothpick inserted into the center of a couple of them comes out clean, 21 to 24 minutes.

12. Cool in the tin on a wire rack for 10 minutes, then turn the muffins out onto the rack and continue cooling to room temperature, about 1½ hours.

13. Once cooled, cut a corner off the bottom of the frosting bag. Frost the cupcakes by squeezing the frosting in decorative circles all around their tops.

Voilà! If you don't have giant ice cube molds for hip drinks, make big cubes in a muffin tin. Run warm tap water over the back of the pan to loosen them.

FASTER

VEGETARIAN

Pressure-Cooker Vanilla-Almond Cheesecake with Blueberry Sauce

Makes 8 servings

The best cheesecakes come out of a pressure cooker. The humid environment means that the cake has almost no chance of drying out and cracking. And believe it or not, heavy cream lightens this cheesecake, making it less dense and chewy. Your pressure cooker must be able to fit a 7-inch springform pan—which means it must be a standard 6- or 8-quart model. You might even be able to make this cheesecake in a big 10-quart model, but you certainly can't in the new smaller 3-quart cookers. In any event, the results are perfect for a casual evening on the deck or at your holiday table.

Test Kitchen Notes

- Look for a 7-inch springform pan in high-end cookware stores or order from a variety of online outlets. (A Google search will yield dozens of choices.)

- You'll need a rack for the pressure cooker. Because of varying diameters among pressure cookers, as well as a variety of surfaces (nonstick, stainless steel, ceramic), you need to use a rack made specifically for your model—but almost all pressure cookers sold these days come with a rack. If not, all manufacturers sell racks for their models separately. You'll find what you need with a quick online search.

- Grind 20 vanilla wafer cookies in the food processor, then measure the crumbs to make sure you have ¾ cup.

- Check the manufacturer's instructions for bringing a stovetop cooker to low pressure.

- In electric cookers, override all presets to cook at high pressure. However, some electric pressure cookers work at a higher pressure (around 12 psi). For these, use the stovetop timings for this recipe.

For the Cheesecake

¾ cup vanilla wafer crumbs (from about 20 cookies)

¼ cup sliced almonds

2 tablespoons unsalted butter, cut into small bits, plus more for greasing the baking pan

5 tablespoons granulated white sugar

1 pound cream cheese

⅓ cup packed light brown sugar

2 large eggs, at room temperature

2 tablespoons heavy cream

2 tablespoons almond flavored liqueur, such as Amaretto

2 tablespoons all-purpose flour

For the Blueberry Sauce

2 cups blueberries

¼ cup granulated white sugar

½ teaspoon ground cinnamon

¼ teaspoon table salt

2 teaspoons cornstarch

RECIPE CONTINUES ➤➤

To Make the Cheesecake

1. Place rack inside a 6- to 8-quart stovetop or electric pressure cooker; pour in 2 cups water.

2. Put the wafer crumbs, almonds, butter, and 2 tablespoons of the granulated sugar in a food processor fitted with the chopping blade; cover and process until finely ground, about like coarse sand.

3. Lightly butter the inside of a 7-inch springform pan; pour in the crumb mixture and press into an even crust on the bottom and halfway up the sides.

4. Wipe out the food processor. Add the cream cheese, brown sugar, and 3 tablespoons granulated sugar; cover and process until smooth, scraping down the inside of the bowl a couple of times.

5. With the machine running, add the eggs one at a time through the feed tube. Scrape down the bowl, then add the cream and liqueur, followed by the flour, processing each until smooth.

6. Scrape down the bowl one more time and process until creamy, almost velvety. Pour the batter into the prepared pan. Do not cover.

7. Make an aluminum foil sling (see **More!**), set the pan on it, and use the sling to lower the pan onto the rack in the cooker. Fold down the ends of the sling so they fit inside the cooker, and lock the lid onto the pot.

8. To cook the cheesecake in a stovetop pressure cooker: Set the pot over high heat and bring it to low pressure (8 psi). Once this pressure has been reached, reduce the heat as much as possible while maintaining this pressure. Cook at low pressure for 35 minutes.

To cook the cheesecake in an electric pressure cooker: Set the machine to cook at high pressure (9 to 11 psi). Cook at high pressure for 25 minutes.

9. Set the stovetop cooker off the heat or unplug the electric pot; let the pressure come back to normal naturally, about 15 minutes.

10. Unlock and remove the lid. Use the sling to transfer the pan to a wire cooling rack. Cool for 1 hour.

11. Unfasten, loosen, and remove the pan's collar. Refrigerate for at least 6 hours before slicing.

To Make the Blueberry Sauce

12. As the cheesecake cools, make the blueberry sauce by combining the blueberries, sugar, cinnamon, and salt in a small saucepan. Bring to a simmer over medium heat, stirring occasionally, until the blueberries begin to pop and break down, about 5 minutes. Stir in the cornstarch and cook until thickened, less than a minute, stirring constantly. Cool off the heat to room temperature.

13. Scrape the sauce into a bowl, cover with plastic wrap, and refrigerate until the cheesecake is ready to serve.

14. Spread the blueberry sauce over the top of the cake to run down its sides before slicing.

 An aluminum foil sling helps get bakeware out
More! of a hot pressure cooker. Fold a 2-foot-long sheet of foil in half lengthwise, then again in half lengthwise. Set the baking pan in the center, lift up the ends, and hoist the pan into the cooker. Fold these ends down a bit before you lock on the lid. When the pressure is back to normal, unfold them and use them to lift the pan out of the cooker.

Rich and Creamy Frozen Berry Yogurt Without an Ice Cream Machine

FASTER

VEGETARIAN

GLUTEN-FREE

Makes about 1 quart

No, you don't need an ice cream machine to make frozen yogurt. But you do need a food processor. By whirring frozen berries, then adding Greek yogurt, you can make a frozen treat in minutes. It's scoopable but not cone-able, so better for a bowl (at least at first). For firmer froyo, pack it into a 1-quart container, cover, and freeze for up to 3 months. Set it out on the counter for 10 to 15 minutes before scooping into balls.

1 pound frozen berries, such as strawberries, raspberries, and/ or blackberries (do not thaw)

¼ cup granulated white sugar

¾ cup full-fat Greek yogurt

⅓ cup jam of the same flavor as the frozen berries (or the dominant one in a mix of berries)

2 tablespoons heavy cream

½ teaspoon vanilla extract

¼ teaspoon table salt, optional

1. Put the frozen berries and sugar in a food processor. Cover and process until any large pieces are chopped up, stopping the machine and rearranging them once if necessary. The mixture should be quite thick and still slushy-frozen.

2. Add the yogurt, jam, cream, vanilla, and salt, if using. Cover and process until thick and rich, not too long, just until creamy and smooth. Dish up into bowls with an ice-cream scoop at once.

Test Kitchen Notes

- Don't use low-fat or fat-free yogurt. They're too watery.

- The frozen yogurt gets even richer with double-cream Greek yogurt.

- The jam is a large part of the flavor here. Use the best you can.

Voilà! Here's how to make perfect ice cream sandwiches: Buy large cookies and pints of premium ice cream. Place a pint on its side and use a serrated knife to cut through the container to make 1-inch-thick slices. Peel off the container and sandwich the ice cream disk between two cookies.

Five-Minute Lemon Curd

Makes about 2¼ cups

Test Kitchen Notes

- Only fresh lemon juice has enough acidity to set the curd in this recipe. Skip the bottled stuff.

- Use a rasp or a Microplane to remove the zest from the lemons. The filaments should be as tiny as possible.

- To see what's going on with the curd while it's in the microwave, use a large microwave-safe Pyrex or glass measuring cup as the vessel.

- This recipe is calibrated for a 950-watt microwave oven. If you've got a 1200-watt machine, you'll need to reduce the timings by about a third and stir more frequently in step 2, about every 15 seconds. However, pay more attention to visual cues throughout than the adjusted timings.

Put away the double boiler! Stop stirring, too! Lemon curd is within reach at 9:30 on a Tuesday night. (Or at 7:00 in the morning for breakfast.) And nothing beats fresh lemon curd. The commercial brands are too sweet, not sour enough, not lemony enough. Make your own. You can in 5 minutes.

6 tablespoons (¾ stick) unsalted butter

⅔ cup granulated white sugar

2 large eggs, at room temperature

Finely grated zest of 2 medium lemons

⅔ cup fresh lemon juice

1. In a 950-watt microwave oven, begin to melt the butter in a medium, microwave-safe bowl on high in 10-second increments until about two-thirds liquid, about 30 seconds in all. Remove from the microwave and whisk until smooth.

2. Whisk the sugar into the butter until creamy, then whisk in the eggs and lemon zest and juice. Cook in the microwave on high in 30-second bursts, whisking well after each, until the mixture is thick enough to coat the back of a wooden spoon, about 3 minutes. Be careful as it thickens; the curd can overflow. Stop the microwave as soon as the mixture begins to boil and whisk until it cools enough to continue.

3. Refrigerate until thickened, about 1 hour. Cover with plastic wrap and store in the fridge for up to 4 days.

HALF A DOZEN THINGS TO DO WITH LEMON CURD

1. For the best lemon ice cream, whisk 2 cups heavy cream into all the lemon curd made in this recipe and freeze in an ice cream machine according to the manufacturer's instructions.

2. Bake store-bought puff pastry shells, then fill with lemon curd and top with either whipped cream or a drizzle of melted chocolate.

3. Spoon the lemon curd into plain Greek yogurt for a dessert treat.

4. Or stir it into your morning oatmeal.

5. Use it instead of chocolate in s'mores.

6. Drizzle a little on a triple-crème cheese like Saint André or Cambozola to serve with crackers.

No-Churn Butter Pecan Ice Cream

EASIER

VEGETARIAN

GLUTEN-FREE

Makes about 1 quart

You can forego not only a machine for this ice cream but also all that stirring of a custard base over the heat. The resulting frozen dessert is ridiculously velvety, although it does not freeze hard. Eat it quickly from a cone. Or savor it slowly from a bowl. It probably needs shortbread cookies (page 292).

3 tablespoons unsalted butter

2 cups heavy cream

One 14-ounce can sweetened condensed milk

¾ cup finely chopped pecans

1 teaspoon vanilla extract

1. Melt the butter in a small skillet or saucepan over medium-low heat until it begins to brown. Remove from the heat and pour into a heat-safe ramekin. Cool to room temperature, about 10 minutes.

2. Meanwhile, use a handheld electric mixer or a stand mixer with the whisk attachment to beat the cream at high speed until soft peaks can be formed off a silicone spatula, about 2 minutes.

3. Whisk the browned butter, condensed milk, pecans, and vanilla in a small bowl until uniform. Gently fold this mixture into the beaten cream until almost (if not quite) uniform.

4. Scrape this mixture into a 1-quart round baking dish or other 1-quart freezer-safe serving dish such as a round high-sided soufflé dish. Cover with plastic wrap and freeze for at least 8 hours or up to 1 week. Serve at will.

Test Kitchen Notes

- Gently fold the condensed milk mixture into the whipped cream using long, slow, steady arcs with a silicone spatula, so as not to deflate the cream too much.

- Switch out the pecans for the nuts of your choosing.

- If you like, omit the butter and substitute ¾ cup mini chocolate chips for the nuts.

- For a caramel base, omit the butter and vanilla and fold ¼ cup store-bought caramel sauce into the condensed milk before adding to the whipped cream.

- Do not use low-fat or fat-free sweetened condensed milk.

 Voilà! If you've got a turbo blender like a Vitamix or Blendtec, you can make hot fudge sauce in minutes because the blender is powerful enough to actually heat ingredients. (This trick won't work in a more standard blender.) Combine 1 cup half-and-half, ¼ cup granulated white sugar, and ¼ cup light corn syrup in a turbo blender. Cover and blend at the highest speed until steaming, about 4 minutes, stopping the machine once to scrape down the inside of the canister. Add 8 ounces semisweet chocolate chips, 4 tablespoons (½ stick) unsalted butter, and 1 teaspoon vanilla extract. Cover and blend until hot and thick, about 2 minutes. Cool for a bit before using—or once cooled, store in a covered container in the fridge for up to 2 weeks.

Superfast Lemony Semifreddo

Makes about 8 servings

Making a true semifreddo (not just softened ice cream in a loaf pan) is a labor of love: zabaglione + Swiss meringue + whipped cream, all folded together and frozen. Here's the good news: You can fake it with whipped cream, lemon curd, and marshmallow creme for astounding results. Yes, you'll have to dirty two bowls. But you don't have to turn on the stove. And you'll actually make a cake (more like a bombe) that you can cut into wedges and serve with blueberry sauce (pages 296–98) or Instant Ginger-Sugar Crisps (page 293).

2 cups heavy cream

One 7½-ounce jar marshmallow creme

½ cup lemon curd, store-bought or homemade (page 300)

2 teaspoons vanilla extract

1. Line a round high-sided 1-quart baking dish (such as a soufflé dish) with 2 pieces of plastic wrap, leaving enough plastic wrap hanging over the edges to be able to later cover the top. Set the dish in the freezer as you continue with the recipe.

2. Beat the cream in a large bowl with an electric mixer at high speed until the cream has doubled in volume and holds soft peaks when the beaters are stopped and pulled up, about 3 minutes. Set aside.

3. In a second large bowl, fold together the marshmallow creme, lemon curd, and vanilla until smooth.

4. Gently fold the whipped cream into the marshmallow creme mixture so as not to deflate the whipped cream.

5. Scrape and smooth this mixture into the prepared baking dish. Fold the excess plastic wrap over the top to cover. Freeze until cold and set but still soft, about 8 hours.

6. To serve, peel the excess plastic wrap off the surface of the semifreddo. Turn the baking dish upside down on a cutting board or serving platter. Gently wriggle it around, holding onto the plastic wrap, until the semifreddo comes loose and pops out. Remove the dish and any plastic wrap; slice the cake into wedges. You can rewrap any leftovers, set them back in the baking dish, and freeze them again for another time.

Test Kitchen Notes

- Heavy cream whips better when it's cold, right out of the refrigerator. In fact, it whips best if the bowl and beaters are cold from the fridge, too.

- Believe it or not, there's no gelatin in Marshmallow Fluff, making the popular marshmallow creme a vegetarian delight!

- One piece of plastic wrap won't do it for the baking dish. You'll need to use two—and work to make sure there are no bare spots.

Pie-Crust Pinwheel Cookies

Makes about 20 cookies

Although a store-bought pie crust is rather lackluster under a pie, it's a terrific dough for cookies. Here are the best ways to turn that dough into pinwheel cookies, spirals of jam and fruit wrapped into tender pastry. Yes, you have to roll the dough a little thinner to make sure the cookies are crisp. But there's little else to do for such an old-school treat.

Walnut-Cranberry-Ginger Pinwheel Cookies

One 14.1-ounce box pie shells (2 unbaked crusts)

1½ cups walnut pieces

1 cup packed dried cranberries

¼ cup ginger jam

¼ cup light brown sugar

2 tablespoons unsalted butter, melted and cooled

1 teaspoon ground dried ginger

1 large egg

2 tablespoons water

About 7 tablespoons honey or maple syrup, optional

Pistachio-Apricot Pinwheel Cookies

One 14.1-ounce box pie shells (2 unbaked crusts)

1½ cups unsalted shelled pistachios

1 cup dried apricots, chopped

¼ cup orange marmalade

¼ cup granulated white sugar

2 tablespoons unsalted butter, melted and cooled

1 teaspoon finely grated lemon zest

1 large egg

2 tablespoons water

About 7 tablespoons honey or maple syrup, optional

Good Ol' Cherry Pie Pinwheel Cookies

One 14.1-ounce box pie shells (2 unbaked crusts)

1½ cups blanched almonds

1 cup packed dried cherries

¼ cup cherry jam

¼ cup light brown sugar

2 tablespoons unsalted butter, melted and cooled

¼ teaspoon grated nutmeg

1 large egg

2 tablespoons water

About 7 tablespoons honey or maple syrup, optional

Test Kitchen Notes

- We're offering up five pinwheel cookies; take your pick from the different ingredient lists.

- Don't use the store-bought pie shells that are already pressed into pie plates. Rather, buy the boxed rounds that are *meant* to be pressed into those plates (but here will be used to create cookies).

- Read the package instructions for the proper way to thaw and unwrap store-bought pie shells. In general, the dough won't unroll well straight out of the refrigerator.

- Use jam, not jelly, in the filling. Its thicker texture won't be as watery.

- Chop larger pieces of dried fruit into small bits that are no larger than raisins.

- Do *not* pack the brown sugar into the measuring cup. Scoop it up and level it off.

- All 20 cookies will fit on a large 13 x 18-inch baking sheet. If you have a smaller sheet, you may need to bake the cookies in two batches. Make sure the baking sheet has cooled to room temperature before adding the second batch of unbaked pinwheels. (In New England, we set it outside on the deck for 5 minutes.)

RECIPE CONTINUES ▶▶

PB&J Pinwheel Cookies

One 14.1-ounce box pie shells (2 unbaked crusts)

1½ cups roasted unsalted peanuts

1 cup golden raisins

¼ cup grape jam

¼ cup granulated white sugar

2 tablespoons unsalted butter, melted and cooled

1 large egg

2 tablespoons water

About 7 tablespoons honey or maple syrup, optional

Tropical Pinwheel Cookies

One 14.1-ounce box pie shells (2 unbaked crusts)

1½ cups macadamia nuts

1 cup packed unsweetened flaked coconut

¼ cup pineapple jam

¼ cup light brown sugar

2 tablespoons unsalted butter, melted and cooled

1 teaspoon minced grated orange zest

1 large egg

2 tablespoons water

About 7 tablespoons honey or maple syrup, optional

1. Position the rack in the center of the oven; heat the oven. Lay a silicone baking mat or parchment paper in a large lipped baking sheet.

2. Separately unroll both shells. You'll need to turn these dough rounds into squares—but don't simply cut a square out of the "heart" of the round. Instead, cut small amounts off the "sides," giving them four straight edges, still with rounded corners. Use the cut-off dough to patch the rounded corners into truly square corners by tearing and molding the cut-off dough to fit. Seal the pieces together, then roll each piece into a 10-inch square.

3. Selecting from one of the ingredient lists, place the nuts, fruit, jam, sugar, melted butter, and spice or zest, if applicable, in a food processor. Cover and process just until finely chopped.

4. Top each square of dough with half of the filling. Tightly roll each square closed into a long, filled cigar and seal the edges.

5. Whisk the egg and water in a small bowl until uniform. Brush each log with this mixture. Cut each log into 10 sections, each about 1 inch thick. Lay cut side up on the baking sheet.

6. Bake until browned and set, 10 to 12 minutes. If desired, drizzle about 1 teaspoon honey or maple syrup on each pinwheel while still hot.

7. Cool on the baking sheet a minute or two, then transfer to a wire rack to continue cooling for at least 10 minutes or to room temperature, about 1 hour.

ONE-BOWL BAKING WITHOUT A MIXER

Eight zillion cookbook authors have tried to convince us that baking is a wonderfully meditative process, the antidote to a long afternoon. They're not wrong. Except that baking can be a pain when you don't have a long afternoon but still want a sweet treat. Here are three recipes that dirty only one bowl, don't use a mixer, and get the job done in no time with a whisk and a wooden spoon (and the oven, of course). For all of them, we altered the liquid/flour/fat ratios so there's no need to beat in lots of air. Yes, we all yearn for a long afternoon in the kitchen, but sometimes we need to get in and out in a few minutes.

Toasty Almond and White Chocolate No-Mixer Blondies

Makes 9 blondies

These are very sweet, buttery blondies, the best way to make your kitchen smell like a bakery. There's no leavening in the batter so the blondies retain that "bar cookie" feel. The batter gets too thick for a whisk when you stir in the flour in step 3. Pick up a wooden spoon.

1 cup sliced almonds

Baking spray

½ cup (1 stick) unsalted butter, melted and cooled, plus additional for greasing the pan

½ cup packed light brown sugar

¼ cup granulated white sugar

1 large egg, at room temperature

1 cup cake flour

½ teaspoon table salt

1 cup white chocolate chips

1. Scatter the almonds in a large skillet, then set it over medium-low heat and toast, stirring often, until the nuts are lightly browned and fragrant, about 4 minutes. Pour the nuts into a bowl and cool for at least 15 minutes.

2. Meanwhile, position the rack in the center of the oven and heat the oven to 350°F. Lightly coat the inside of an 8-inch square baking pan with baking spray.

3. Whisk the melted butter and both sugars in a large bowl until creamy, about 2 minutes. Whisk in the egg until uniform. Add the flour and salt; stir with a spoon just until a batter forms with no dry pockets. Stir in a scant two-thirds of the white chocolate chips and all of the toasted almonds.

4. Scrape and pour the batter into the prepared pan. Sprinkle the remaining white chocolate over the top. Bake until the blondies are golden and a toothpick or cake tester inserted into the center without hitting a chocolate chip comes out clean, about 40 minutes.

5. Cool in the pan on a wire rack for 20 minutes, then run a flatware knife around the sides of the pan and invert the slab onto a cutting board. Remove the pan and slice the slab into 9 squares, turning these right side up again.

Test Kitchen Notes

- The quality of white chocolate chips varies dramatically. Make sure yours are made with real white chocolate, not just flavored shortening.

- There's no vanilla extract in the mix because white chocolate has so many vanilla notes.

- Substitute milk chocolate chips, if desired. If so, add 1 teaspoon vanilla extract with the sugars.

Voilà! You can also toast nuts in a hot air popcorn popper until aromatic and lightly browned. (One warning: you can only toast ½ cup or so at a time.)

Deep, Dark, One-Bowl Chocolate Pound Cake

FASTER

VEGETARIAN

Makes one 9 x 5-inch cake

Admittedly, this intensely chocolate cake is more *like* pound cake than a true pound cake. In any case, it's dense and satisfying, if not buttery (we use nut oil), and a little chewier. It'll stay tender for days and is great toasted (on a baking sheet under the broiler) for breakfast some morning. Once baked and cooled, it freezes well, too—up to 4 months if tightly wrapped. Or just serve it warm from the oven with a scoop of vanilla ice cream.

Baking spray

⅓ cup unsweetened cocoa powder

1½ cups all-purpose flour

1 cup granulated white sugar

1 teaspoon baking soda

½ teaspoon table salt

1 cup regular or low-fat cultured buttermilk

¼ cup nut oil (walnut, almond, pecan, or hazelnut)

1 teaspoon vanilla extract

Raspberry or cherry jam, for serving

1. Position the rack in the center of the oven; heat the oven to 350°F. Lightly coat the inside of a 9 x 5-inch loaf pan with baking spray.

2. Sift the cocoa powder into a large bowl; whisk in the flour, sugar, baking soda, and salt until uniform.

3. Stir in the buttermilk, oil, and vanilla with a wooden spoon just until a slightly grainy batter forms. Make sure there are no pockets of dry flour at the bottom of the bowl.

4. Pour and scrape the batter into the prepared pan; smooth it to the corners.

5. Bake until puffed and firm and a toothpick inserted into the center of the cake comes out with a few moist crumbs attached, 60 to 70 minutes.

6. Cool in the pan on a wire rack for 10 minutes, then turn the cake out onto the rack, right it, and continue cooling the cake for at least 10 minutes or until room temperature. Slice into wedges and serve with a spoonful of jam on top of each.

Test Kitchen Notes

- Dutch process cocoa powder will dissolve more easily and make the cake darker in color—but will also give the cake a less pronounced chocolate flavor.

- Real buttermilk, the residue from making butter, is now available at many high-end supermarkets. It's actually fairly thin—and makes a noticeable difference in baking results for many recipes, leading sometimes to flattened cakes partly because of its extra water content but mostly because of its reduced acidity (and therefore, its less aggressive interaction with baking soda and baking powder). This recipe (and all others in this book) call for the more readily available *cultured* buttermilk, the kind found in all North American supermarkets (sometimes right next to the more artisanal stuff).

- The nut oil is for flavor. You can use canola oil, but the cake will be duller. Do not use peanut oil.

Salty Molasses-Spice No-Mixer Cookies

Makes about 30 cookies

Test Kitchen Notes

- The melted butter makes the cookies denser and a little chewier.

- Look for candied orange peel in the supermarket's baking aisle or near the dried fruit and nuts. Candied orange peel is familiar from your grandmother's holiday cookies and fruitcakes. At high-end supermarkets and kitchen stores, you may be able to find thin orangette strips, designed to be dipped into melted chocolate to make the classic French confection. If you use these, slice them into little bits about the size of dried currants.

- Kosher salt gives the cookies a great crunchy topping.

If you like gingerbread, you'll love these sophisticated little cookies, best with a cup of tea. They need to bake on parchment paper to keep them from getting too crisp before they set.

1¾ cups plus 1 tablespoon all-purpose flour

½ cup packed dark brown sugar

½ teaspoon baking soda

¾ teaspoon ground cinnamon

½ teaspoon ground dried ginger

¼ teaspoon grated nutmeg

⅛ teaspoon ground cloves

¼ cup (½ stick) unsalted butter, melted and cooled

¼ cup molasses

¼ cup whole or low-fat milk

1 large egg, at room temperature

3 tablespoons minced candied orange peel

2 tablespoons coarse sanding sugar

1 tablespoon kosher salt

1. Line two large baking sheets with parchment paper.

2. Whisk the flour, brown sugar, baking soda, cinnamon, ginger, nutmeg, and cloves in a large bowl until uniform.

3. Make a well in the middle of the dry ingredients. Add the melted butter, molasses, milk, egg, and orange peel. Use a wooden spoon to stir the mixture until a dough forms, with no dry bits of flour in the bowl.

4. Mix the sanding sugar and kosher salt in a small bowl. Roll about 1 tablespoon of the dough into a small ball, then roll in the sugar/salt mixture, getting a few grains all over the ball without going nuts. Repeat to roll and coat about 30 balls.

5. Line the balls up on the parchment-lined sheets, spacing them about 2 inches apart. Place the sheets in the refrigerator and chill for 15 minutes.

6. Meanwhile, position the rack in the center of the oven and heat the oven to 350°F.

7. Flatten the balls on one sheet with a sturdy drinking glass, just so they barely begin to crack at the edges. Transfer the sheet to the oven and bake the cookies until set, 10 to 12 minutes. Cool on the baking sheet for 5 minutes.

8. While the first batch cools, press out the remaining cookies and get them in the oven, repeating the baking and cooling procedure. Serve warm, or store in a sealed container at room temperature for up to 4 days.

Voilà! If you don't want to buy brown sugar for every recipe, keep a jar of molasses in your pantry. The ratio to make brown sugar is this: For every cup of granulated white sugar, add 1 tablespoon molasses for light brown sugar or 1½ tablespoons for dark. Whir in a food processor until evenly colored.

FOOD PROCESSOR
CAKES

Although you often have to beat the eggs, sugar, and butter to make a decent batter, you can also create tender if somewhat sturdier cakes in a food processor. They're well-structured with a dense crumb, more American-style (like a light pound cake), rather than the texture and crumb of genoise or sponge cakes. They're also made for lots of frosting. And you don't have to dirty bowls, mixer blades, spatulas, or whisks. Yes, there's that food processor. It has to be washed. But the overall load in the sink is certainly less. Besides, there are no cleanup-free cakes (except the ones you buy).

In all these recipes, it's imperative that the eggs be at room temperature to create an even batter. Leave them out on the counter (in their shells) for 20 to 30 minutes before beginning.

Espresso Date-Nut Quick Bread

FASTER

VEGETARIAN

Makes one 9 x 5-inch loaf cake

Move over, 1970s. This sweet quick bread is like the old recipes that mothers baked in coffee cans. Back in the day, those quick breads had the slight aroma of coffee, particularly if the can wasn't cleaned perfectly. This recipe puts the coffee right in the batter to make a weekend treat or a fast dessert for company. Do as they did back then: Serve the quick bread with cream cheese.

1 cup warm tap water

¾ cup packed dark brown sugar

1¾ cups all-purpose flour

4 tablespoons (½ stick) unsalted butter, at room temperature, plus additional for greasing the pan

1 large egg, at room temperature

1 tablespoon instant coffee or instant espresso powder

2 teaspoons vanilla extract

½ teaspoon baking powder

½ teaspoon baking soda

½ teaspoon table salt

2 cups packed whole soft pitted dates (about 8 ounces)

1 cup walnut pieces (about 4 ounces)

1. Position the rack in the middle of the oven; heat the oven to 350°F. Generously butter the inside of a 9 x 5-inch loaf pan, preferably a metal pan.

2. Put the water, brown sugar, flour, butter, egg, espresso powder, vanilla, baking powder, baking soda, and salt in that order in a food processor bowl, making sure the ingredients are evenly distributed and are not just dumped in piles.

3. Cover and process until smooth, stopping the machine once or twice to scrape down the inside of the bowl. Add the dates and nuts. Pulse several times to chop and combine.

4. Spread the thick batter into the prepared pan. Bake until puffed, cracked, and firm to the touch and a toothpick inserted into the center of the loaf without hitting a date comes out clean, 50 to 55 minutes.

5. Cool in the pan on a wire rack for 10 minutes, then turn the loaf onto the rack and continue cooling for at least 10 minutes longer or to room temperature before serving.

Test Kitchen Notes

- Look for soft, sweet, whole dates (not "baking dates" in little bits).

- Don't heat the water. Just use water that's as hot as bath water, not scalding.

EASIER

VEGETARIAN

Chocolate Malt Layer Cake with Brown Sugar–Cream Cheese Frosting

Makes one 8-inch layer cake

Test Kitchen Notes

- The butter must be softened to room temperature to allow for an even batter.

- The cake layers may mound a bit in the oven but they'll fall back as they cool.

- Do not use fat-free dairy.

- To unmold cake layers perfectly, don't let them get cold. The bottom should still be warm to the touch when tipping the layer out of the pan.

The hard part is gathering the ingredients. After that, this simple cake takes no time. It's somewhat less sweet than most chocolate cakes, partly to let the malt flavor shine. You'll want vanilla ice cream on the side.

For the Cake

1⅔ cups cake flour, plus additional for dusting the pans

6 tablespoons malted milk powder

⅔ cup granulated white sugar

1 tablespoon baking powder

½ teaspoon table salt

1 teaspoon vanilla extract

4 large eggs, at room temperature

10 tablespoons (1 stick plus 2 tablespoons) unsalted butter, at almost room temperature, cut into 1-tablespoon pieces, plus additional for greasing the pans

½ cup unsweetened cocoa powder

¾ cup plus 1 tablespoon whole or low-fat milk

For the Frosting

8 ounces regular or low-fat cream cheese, at room temperature

½ cup (1 stick) unsalted butter, at room temperature

½ cup packed dark brown sugar

¼ cup regular or low-fat sour cream

2 teaspoons vanilla extract

4 to 6 cups confectioners' sugar

To Make the Cake

1. Position the rack in the center of the oven; heat the oven to 350°F. Generously butter and lightly flour the inside of two 8-inch round cake pans.

2. Put the ingredients for the cake—in the order listed—in a food processor, making sure the ingredients (and especially the butter pieces) are distributed evenly throughout the bowl. Cover and process until smooth, stopping the machine once to scrape down the inside of the bowl.

3. Divide the batter between the prepared pans. Bake until springy but firm to the touch and a toothpick inserted into the center of one layer comes out clean, about 23 minutes.

4. Cool the cake layers in their pans on a wire rack for 15 minutes, then invert the layers, remove the pans, reinvert the cakes, and cool to room temperature, about 1 hour.

To Make the Frosting and Frost the Cake

5. Put the cream cheese, butter, brown sugar, sour cream, and vanilla in the clean food processor bowl. Cover and process until smooth, no more than a few seconds. Scrape down the inside of the bowl.

6. Add 4 cups confectioners' sugar. Cover and process until incorporated. Scrape down the bowl again, then continue adding confectioners' sugar in ½-cup increments, pulsing after each, until thick and spreadable.

7. Cover a cake stand or platter with several sheets of wax paper. Place one layer, top side up, on the wax paper (which will, of course, be removed later.) Spoon slightly less than a quarter of the frosting into the middle of the layer; use an offset spatula to spread into an even layer. Lay the second layer, top side down, over the frosting. Use frosting to fill in any gap between the layers. Dump the rest of the frosting on top, then use that offset spatula to smooth it out and fall down the sides of the cake, thereafter smoothing it against the sides as well to create an even frosting over the cake. Remove the wax paper to serve.

Voilà! After cutting out pieces from a layer cake, place white bread slices against both sides of the cut to keep the cake fresh and moist until the next day.

Orange Sheet Cake with Orange Buttercream

Makes one 9 x 13-inch cake

Here's an easy cake for picnics and deck parties. Even the oranges go right into the food processor to be ground into the batter. The zest (and the pith) offer a sophisticated hint of sour and bitter under all the sweet buttery goodness.

For the Cake

2 medium navel oranges

2 cups cake flour

2 teaspoons baking powder

1 teaspoon table salt

½ teaspoon ground cloves

1 cup plus 3 tablespoons granulated white sugar

1 cup (2 sticks) unsalted butter, at room temperature, cut into small pieces

4 large eggs, at room temperature

2 teaspoons vanilla extract

For the Buttercream

1 cup (2 sticks) unsalted butter, at room temperature

¼ cup heavy cream

2 tablespoons thawed frozen orange juice concentrate

1 teaspoon vanilla extract

½ teaspoon orange extract

¼ teaspoon table salt

4 to 6 cups confectioners' sugar

To Make the Cake

1. Position the rack in the center of the oven; heat the oven to 350°F. Generously butter and lightly flour the inside of a 9 x 13-inch baking pan (preferably not glass).

2. Cut the oranges into eighths; pick out and discard any seeds. Put the sections in a food processor; pulse several times to finely chop.

3. Add the remaining cake ingredients in the order stated, making sure the ingredients are evenly distributed throughout the bowl and are not dumped in piles. Cover and process until smooth, stopping the machine several times to scrape down the inside of the bowl.

4. Pour and scrape the batter into the prepared pan. Bake until the top of the cake is firm but spongy to the touch and a toothpick inserted into the cake comes out clean, about 27 minutes.

5. Cool the cake in its pan on a wire rack until room temperature, about 1 hour.

RECIPE CONTINUES ➡➡

Test Kitchen Notes

- Choose navel oranges with small "navels" and thin skins for the least amount of pith. Although they're food-safe, remove any labels from the oranges.

- For the best success, dot the butter all around the food processor bowl before processing.

- Some sheet cakes are made in large lipped baking sheets. (We know since we wrote a book on them.) This one, however, calls for a 9 x 13-inch baking dish.

- A metal baking dish works better for this cake, since the cake's edges will dry out against hot glass.

To Make the Buttercream and Frost the Cake

6. Put the butter, cream, orange juice concentrate, vanilla and orange extracts, and salt in the clean food processor bowl. Cover and process until smooth, just a few seconds. Scrape down the inside of the bowl.

7. Add 4 cups confectioners' sugar. Cover and process until smooth. Scrape down the bowl one more time, then continue adding confectioners' sugar in ½-cup increments, pulsing after each addition, until smooth and spreadable.

8. Spread the frosting all over the cooled cake. Set in the fridge to chill and set up, about 1 hour. However, set the cake out at room temperature for 15 minutes before serving to brighten the flavors.

Glazed Lemon Cake Muffins with Poppy Seeds

Makes 12 muffins

Because there's lemon zest *and* pith in these muffins, they have a surprisingly complex flavor, not just sweet, more like a sweet/ bitter/sour mash-up, probably not a favorite among the third-grade set. They've got a very light crumb, not dense like some muffins, partly from the way the food processor whirs the ingredients together.

1 medium lemon

¾ cup (1½ sticks) unsalted butter, at room temperature, plus additional for greasing

1 cup granulated white sugar

3 large eggs, at room temperature

½ cup whole or low-fat milk

2 cups all-purpose flour

1 teaspoon baking powder

½ teaspoon table salt

1½ cups confectioners' sugar, plus more if needed

3 tablespoons fresh lemon juice

Poppy seeds, for garnish

1. Position the rack in the center of the oven; heat the oven to 350°F. Lightly butter the 12 cups of a standard muffin pan.

2. Cut the lemon into 8 wedges and remove any seeds. Put the wedges in a food processor. Cover and process until mashed up, about 30 seconds.

3. Add the butter, granulated sugar, eggs, milk, flour, baking powder, and salt in that order, making sure the ingredients are evenly distributed and are not just dumped in piles. Cover and process until smooth, stopping the machine at least once, maybe twice, to scrape down the inside of the bowl.

4. Divide the batter into the prepared muffin pan cups. Bake until a toothpick inserted into the center of a couple of muffins comes out clean, about 18 minutes.

5. Set the pan on a wire rack and cool for 5 minutes, then turn the muffins out and continue cooling to room temperature.

6. To make the glaze, mix the confectioners' sugar and lemon juice in a medium bowl, adding more confectioners' sugar in 2-tablespoon increments, until a loose consistency that nonetheless holds its shape when drizzled. Drizzle onto the cooled muffins, then sprinkle the tops of each with some poppy seeds.

Test Kitchen Notes

- Lemons are sometimes waxed for storage. Scrub it well before using.

- Do not use an older lemon with a tough rind.

- Once again, the butter must be soft.

- Poppy seeds go rancid quickly. Store them in a sealed container in the freezer.

 More! With skim milk and heavy cream, you've always got low-fat or whole milk on hand. To make 1 cup, place the amount of cream indicated below in a glass liquid measuring vessel, then add enough skim milk to make 1 cup and stir well.

- 1 tablespoon heavy cream plus skim milk makes 1 cup 2% low-fat milk.

- 2 tablespoons heavy cream plus skim milk makes 1 cup whole milk.

- 5 tablespoons heavy cream plus skim milk makes 1 cup half-and-half.

MICROWAVE
MUG PUDDINGS

Microwave mug cakes were all the rage a while back—perhaps because no one realized how great microwave mug *pudding* is. No, the pudding isn't "instant." It must set up in the fridge. But it's a small price to pay for the ease of homemade pudding in under 2 minutes of active time.

Test Kitchen Notes

- The mug must be truly microwave safe. Some pottery can burst. Check manufacturer websites to be sure. If you've made tea in your mug in the microwave, you're probably good to go.

- Use only whole milk.

- The cornstarch must be completely dissolved, no little bits floating in the mix. A mini whisk will work better than a fork.

- Use a genuine pasteurized egg substitute, not pasteurized egg whites or separated egg whites from whole eggs. And not regular eggs, as they will curdle.

- Never take your eyes off that window in the microwave oven. Stop the microwave when the mixture boils to the rim of the mug, and stir it down before continuing.

- In each of these recipes, you microwave the pudding for a 30-second burst on high *or* until the mixture rises to the rim of the mug, then you soldier on with 10-second bursts. Unfortunately, the exact number of additional 10-second bursts can be tricky to determine. Various glazes on pottery retain more heat than others; the thickness of the walls of some pottery mugs insulates the pudding more effectively.

- These recipes make individual servings. You can double, triple, multiply them up as much as you want by using more and more microwave-safe mugs. However, microwave them one by one for the best set.

Chocolate Mug Pudding

Makes 1 serving

Cocoa powder gives this chocolate pudding a surprisingly deep flavor, a little less "candy-like" than melted chocolate would provide. Make sure the mixture has thickened before chilling.

⅔ cup whole milk

2 tablespoons granulated white sugar

1 tablespoon unsweetened cocoa powder

1 tablespoon pasteurized egg substitute

2½ teaspoons cornstarch

½ teaspoon vanilla extract

Pinch of table salt

1. Put the milk, sugar, cocoa powder, egg substitute, cornstarch, vanilla, and salt in a 10- to 12-ounce microwave-safe mug, stirring until the sugar and cornstarch are dissolved.

2. Cook on high in a 950-watt microwave oven for 1 minute.

3. Stir well. Cook on high for about 30 seconds, until the mixture bubbles up to the rim of the mug. Stop the oven immediately.

4. Stir well. Cook again on high for about 10 seconds, until the mixture bubbles up, then stop and stir. Repeat cooking in 10-second bursts, stopping and stirring the moment the mixture bubbles up, until the mixture is thick and rich, a total of perhaps three or five additional 10-second bursts.

5. Chill in the refrigerator, covering once cold, for at least 4 hours or up to 2 days.

Butterscotch Mug Pudding

Makes 1 serving

Creamy and smooth, this one's like old-fashioned butterscotch, made with that tasty combo of brown sugar and butter, rather than the caramel-like flavoring common in instant butterscotch pudding. The results will be soft, even after chilling. For a firmer set, increase the cornstarch to 2½ teaspoons.

⅔ cup whole milk

2 tablespoons pasteurized egg substitute

2 tablespoons dark brown sugar, plus additional for garnish

2 teaspoons cornstarch

¼ teaspoon vanilla extract

Pinch of table salt

1 tablespoon unsalted butter

1. Put the milk, egg substitute, brown sugar, cornstarch, vanilla, and salt in a 10- to 12-ounce microwave-safe mug, stirring until the brown sugar and cornstarch are dissolved.

2. Set the butter in the mixture. Cook on high in a 950-watt microwave oven for 1 minute.

3. Stir well. Cook on high for about 30 seconds, *or* until the mixture bubbles up to the rim of the mug. Stop the oven immediately.

4. Stir well. Cook again on high for about 10 seconds, until the mixture bubbles up, then stop and stir. Repeat cooking in 10-second bursts, stopping and stirring the moment the mixture bubbles up, until the mixture is thick and rich, a total of perhaps three or five additional 10-second bursts.

5. Chill in the refrigerator, covering once cold, for at least 4 hours or up to 2 days. Sprinkle a little brown sugar over the pudding as a garnish just before serving.

FASTER

VEGETARIAN

Four-Ingredient Maple Mug Pudding

Makes 1 serving

Voilà! Want whipped cream? Make it in a thoroughly cleaned French press: Pour in no more than 1½ cups *cold* heavy cream, then work the plunger over and over until you get a soft, creamy set. By the way, it would take a very long time to make the whipped cream firm with this technique. Plan on a more "saucy" consistency, more French restaurant than American.

Don't even think of using pancake syrup for this treat. Maple syrup can keep for up to a year in the fridge. If it ever develops any green-beige mold, slowly pour the syrup into a large bowl and skim the skin off. Then heat the remaining syrup to boiling, skim its surface, and repackage in a sealable container in the fridge. This pudding can actually roil more quickly than the others, mostly because the maple syrup is already liquefied sugar in the mix. Take extra care that the mug doesn't overflow. Stir the pudding down each time. For a note on the various grades of maple syrup, see page 48.

⅔ cup whole milk

2 tablespoons maple syrup, preferably Grade A Dark Color

1 tablespoon pasteurized egg substitute

2 teaspoons cornstarch

1. Stir the milk, maple syrup, egg substitute, and cornstarch in a 10- to 12-ounce microwave-safe mug.

2. Cook on high in a 950-watt microwave oven for 1 minute.

3. Stir well. Cook on high for 20 to 30 seconds, until the mixture bubbles up to the rim of the mug. Stop the oven immediately.

4. Stir well. Cook again on high for up to 10 seconds, until the mixture bubbles up, then stop and stir. Repeat cooking in 10-second bursts, stopping and stirring the moment the mixture bubbles up, until the mixture is thick and rich, a total of perhaps three or five additional 10-second bursts.

5. Chill in the refrigerator, covering once cold, for at least 2 hours or up to 2 days.

NO-COOK DESSERT
SUMMER ROLLS

Summer rolls are usually savory fare: rice paper wrappers surrounding carrot matchsticks, sprouts, shrimp, what have you. They're simple to make: no frying, no baking. And incredibly fresh tasting. So we decided to morph the classic into dessert rolls. They have less filling overall than their savory kin. You'll end up with more rice paper "layers" around the filling, reminiscent—in the spirit of dessert—of a puff pastry.

Test Kitchen Notes

- Rice paper wrappers are dried, thin, milky white (if still a bit translucent) sheets made from rice flour. They're available in the Asian aisle of large supermarkets or from suppliers online. Once purchased, the wrappers can be stored in a cool, dry pantry indefinitely.

- To make your life easier, look for square rice paper wrappers, which are easier to roll into filled tubes.

- Rice paper wrappers must be soaked before using. A shallow soup bowl works best. Don't soak more than one wrapper at a time. They get soft and tear in no time.

- Pull the wrappers out of the water like you might pull a shirt out of the wash, letting it hang and drip for a second before setting it down.

- Change the water often, after every five or six rolls, so it stays warm to soften each rice paper wrapper in about 20 seconds.

- You can make the rolls up to 2 hours in advance. Cover the platter with plastic wrap and store in the refrigerator.

EASIER

VEGETARIAN

Peach Pie Summer Rolls

Makes 16 rolls

These rolls are a simpler version of peach hand pies, although the fruit is fresh, not cooked. The quality of dessert stands on the freshness of the fruit. To tell if a peach will taste good, don't squeeze it. Smell it. It should smell sweet and fragrant. It's easier to work with freestone peaches than cling ones. Want to take it over the top? Substitute crumbled Amaretti cookies for the graham cracker crumbs.

3½ cups chopped pitted ripe peaches (about 6 large peaches)

½ cup graham cracker crumbs

2 tablespoons light brown sugar

½ teaspoon ground cinnamon

¼ teaspoon grated nutmeg

16 rice paper wrappers

1. Toss the peaches, crumbs, brown sugar, cinnamon, and nutmeg together in a medium bowl.

2. Fill a large soup plate or a 9-inch square baking pan with warm water. Soak one wrapper in the water until softened but not tearable, about 20 seconds.

3. Set the wrapper on a clean, dry work surface. Place ¼ cup of the peach filling at one end of the wrapper, making a fairly compact, 4- to 5-inch-long oval blob of filling. (The length of this blob will dictate the length of the summer roll.) Fold the sides over the filling and roll the wrapper closed.

4. Transfer the roll to a serving platter and continue making more rolls, changing the water occasionally so it stays warm and wiping your work surface as dry as you can to avoid sticking.

EASIER

VEGETARIAN

GLUTEN-FREE

Pineapple, Raspberry, and Thyme Summer Rolls

Makes 16 rolls

These rolls are a fork-and-knife affair, since each has a long, thin stick of pineapple in it. You can find peeled and cored pineapples in the refrigerator case of the produce section. These are easy to cut into the necessary 3 x ½-inch sticks. If the pineapple is very ripe, you won't need a knife at the table (although a fork will still be welcome).

1½ cups fresh raspberries

1 tablespoon agave nectar or honey

1 tablespoon fresh thyme leaves

16 rice paper wrappers

16 fresh pineapple sticks, about 3 x ½ inch (from about ½ a small pineapple)

1. Gently toss the raspberries, agave, and thyme in a small bowl until the agave evenly coats the berries.

2. Fill a large soup plate or a 9-inch square baking pan with warm water. Soak one wrapper in the water until softened but not tearable, about 20 seconds.

3. Set the wrapper on a clean, dry work surface. Place a pineapple stick at one end and spread a heaping tablespoon of the raspberry mixture along the pineapple. Fold the sides over the filling and roll the wrapper closed.

4. Transfer the roll to a serving platter and continue making more rolls, changing the water occasionally so it stays warm and wiping your work surface as dry as you can to avoid sticking.

Fig and Honey Summer Rolls

Makes 16 rolls

Here's a brilliant indulgence: fresh figs and honey-sweetened Greek yogurt. If you can find full-fat Greek yogurt (or even double-cream full-fat Greek yogurt), you'll be in for a real treat. For more flavor, add ¼ teaspoon rose or orange flower water to the yogurt. And try sprinkling chopped, unsalted, shelled pistachios over the filling before rolling the wrapper closed.

1¾ cups full-fat or low-fat plain Greek yogurt

¼ cup honey

1 teaspoon vanilla extract

16 rice paper wrappers

16 fresh figs, stemmed

1. Mix the yogurt, honey, and vanilla in a medium bowl until smooth.

2. Fill a large soup plate or a 9-inch square baking pan with warm water. Soak one wrapper in the water until softened but not tearable, about 20 seconds.

3. Set the wrapper on a clean, dry work surface. Spread 2 tablespoons of the yogurt mixture into a 4- to 5-inch-long oval at one end of the wrapper. Thinly slice a fig and overlap these slices on top of the yogurt. Fold the sides over the filling and roll the wrapper closed.

4. Transfer the roll to a serving platter and continue making more rolls, changing the water occasionally so it stays warm and wiping your work surface as dry as you can to avoid sticking.

More! Try this almond whipped cream as a dip for the rolls: Beat 1 cup cold heavy cream, 2 tablespoons confectioners' sugar, and ¼ teaspoon almond extract in a large bowl with an electric mixer at high speed until thick and luscious. Do not overwhip. The consistency should be more of a spread than mounded peaks.

BAKING WITH
MELTED ICE CREAM

The components of premium ice cream are exactly those necessary to make light cakes, custard pies, and bread pudding: eggs, sugar, cream. In fact, melted ice cream yields super-light and fluffy baked goods—which is surprising, given all the cream.

You must use full-fat premium ice cream. It has much less air whipped in, so it will melt to about the same volume as the container.

And believe it or not, what looks like a pint isn't always a pint. Some premium ice creams are now sold in pint-like containers while they in fact contain less (say, 14 ounces rather than 16). If the "pint" you have is indeed less than a pint, pour the melted ice cream into a liquid measuring container, then add enough whole milk, half-and-half, or heavy cream to bring the measure up to 1 pint (or 2 cups).

When the recipe says "melted," we mean it. Set the pint out on the counter for a good while—or leave it in the fridge overnight, then set it out on the counter while you gather the other ingredients and heat the oven. Microwaving the frozen ice cream won't work. You'll end up with spots that are too warm, which can then curdle the eggs right in the batter.

Unfortunately, these recipes will not work with coconut-, soy-, or nut-milk ice creams. They often have too many other stabilizers and thickeners to work here.

Chocolate Chocolate Chip Pound Cake

FASTER

VEGETARIAN

Makes one 9 x 5-inch loaf cake

This cake is dense yet tender, thanks to the cream in the ice cream. If you want to go over the top, serve each piece à la mode, preferably with the very same kind of ice cream used to make the cake. Or top the slices with macerated raspberries or strawberries. Or go old-school and thaw sliced, sweetened, frozen strawberries, a deliciously soupy mess that will force you to serve the cake in bowls.

Unsalted butter for greasing the pan

2 cups all-purpose flour

1 cup mini chocolate chips (about 6 ounces)

2 teaspoons baking powder

½ teaspoon table salt

1 pint chocolate premium ice cream, melted

1. Position the rack in the center of the oven and heat the oven to 350°F. Generously butter the inside of a 9 x 5-inch loaf pan, preferably a metal pan.

2. Stir the flour, chocolate chips, baking powder, and salt in a large bowl until uniform. Pour in the melted ice cream and stir to create a thick, sticky dough (thicker than a batter). Spread into the prepared loaf pan.

3. Bake until a toothpick inserted into the center of the cake comes out clean, about 30 minutes.

4. Cool in the pan on a wire rack for 10 minutes, then turn out and continue cooling the cake on the rack for 10 minutes longer, until room temperature.

Test Kitchen Notes

- Sub in your favorite flavor of the ice cream, but don't pick an ice cream with mix-ins (like nuts, chocolate chips, or fresh fruit). Those additions will alter the overall volume of liquid in the batter.

- When measuring, do not use a packed scoop of flour. Scoop the flour out of the bag without pressing it against the sides, and level the top of the measuring cup.

- If you use a glass loaf pan, reduce the oven's temperature to 325°F.

 More! Build an ice cream cake out of this pound cake: Cut it into ¼-inch-thick slices. Make a layer of cake in the bottom of a 9-inch round springform pan, cutting slices to fit and make a (mostly) even layer. Top with softened (not melted) ice cream. (Pistachio? Vanilla? Mint?) Then make another layer of cake, followed by another layer of ice cream, either the same flavor or a contrast. Finish it off with a layer of cake. Cover with plastic wrap and freeze for at least 6 hours or up to 1 week. To serve, unwrap, remove the springform ring, and slice into wedges.

Coconut Custard Pie

Makes one 9-inch pie

This supereasy pie uses two types of coconut: sweetened (often called "flaked") coconut and unsweetened (sometimes called "desiccated") coconut. The unsweetened coconut is sometimes powdery, sometimes in shreds or flakes. Any will work here, but pack the shreds into the measuring cup. The crust is a version of coconut macaroons, a lovely treat under the rich custard.

Nonstick spray

4 large eggs, at room temperature

3½ cups sweetened shredded coconut

⅔ cup sweetened condensed milk

1 teaspoon vanilla extract

1 pint vanilla premium ice cream, melted

1 cup unsweetened shredded coconut

1. Position the rack in the center of the oven and heat the oven to 350°F. Lightly coat a 9-inch pie plate with nonstick spray.

2. Separate one of the eggs, reserving the yolk. Mix the egg white, sweetened coconut, condensed milk, and vanilla in a large bowl until uniform.

3. Press this mixture into the prepared pie plate, forming an even crust across the bottom and up the sides of the plate. (Do not wash the bowl.) Bake for 12 minutes.

4. Meanwhile, separate a second egg. Place this egg yolk plus the reserved yolk and the 2 remaining whole eggs in the bowl you've already used. (Discard the remaining egg white or save for another use.) Add the melted ice cream and unsweetened coconut; whisk to combine well.

5. Pour this mixture into the crust. Continue baking until a flatware knife inserted into the set center of the pie comes out clean, about 20 minutes longer, maybe more.

6. Cool in the pie plate on a wire rack for at least 20 minutes before serving.

Strawberry Shortcake Pain Perdu

Makes about 8 servings

Pain perdu (or "lost bread") is the original French toast—and here a rich dessert, the way it would still be eaten abroad. In effect, you'll make jam sandwiches, then soak them overnight in a custard mixture. Consider serving more strawberry jam on the side. And maybe whipped cream.

Unsalted butter for greasing the baking dish

1 pint strawberry premium ice cream, melted

½ cup whole milk

4 large eggs, at room temperature

5 tablespoons strawberry jam

One 1-pound challah loaf, cut into 10 slices (between ½ to ¾ inch thick)

1. Lightly butter the inside of a 9 x 13-inch baking dish.

2. Whisk the melted ice cream, milk, and eggs in a large bowl until uniform.

3. Smear 1 tablespoon jam on five slices of bread. Set these jam side up in the prepared pan, squeezing and tearing them to create one layer. Place a second layer of bread on top, covering the slices below, again squeezing and tearing the pieces to fit.

4. Pour the melted ice cream mixture evenly over the bread. Use the back of a wooden spoon to press down lightly so the bread absorbs most of the liquid. Cover with plastic wrap and refrigerate for at least 12 hours or up to 24 hours.

5. Uncover the baking dish and set it on the counter while you position the rack in the center of the oven and heat the oven to 325°F.

6. Bake until puffed and set, about 30 minutes. Cool in the pan on a wire rack for at least 10 minutes before serving, either by dishing up large spoonfuls or cutting out squares.

Test Kitchen Notes

- The milk is necessary because the melted ice cream doesn't add quite enough liquid to the dish.

- Challah is a slightly sweet, dense egg bread. Look for it in the bakery department.

Butter Pecan Bread Pudding

Makes about 6 servings

Ice cream makes the perfect base for bread pudding. The brown sugar combines here with butter pecan ice cream to make a richer, sweeter dessert, more like a sticky toffee pudding than a standard American bread pudding. It's best warm, within an hour of coming out of the oven.

Unsalted butter for greasing the baking dish

1 pint butter pecan premium ice cream, melted

½ cup whole milk

½ cup packed light brown sugar

3 large eggs, at room temperature

12 ounces thinly sliced country-style white bread, cut into 1-inch squares (no need to remove the crusts)

1. Position the rack in the center of the oven and heat the oven to 350°F. Butter the inside of a round high-sided 2-quart baking dish, such as a soufflé dish.

2. Whisk the melted ice cream, milk, brown sugar, and eggs in a large bowl until smooth with no bits of egg white in the mix. Add the bread pieces and toss gently until almost all of the liquid has been absorbed. Pour this mixture into the prepared pan.

3. Bake until puffed and set, about 30 minutes. Cool in the pan on a wire rack for at least 15 minutes before serving.

Test Kitchen Notes

- Grease the dish very well, especially down into the crevice where the side meets the bottom.

- The eggs must be at room temperature so the pudding mixture sets quickly in the oven.

- The amount of cut-up bread comes out to about 6 cups.

- Tip the baking dish to the side to check whether it's done. There should be very little loose egg mixture.

ABSURDLY DECADENT NO-COOK TOFU (HUH?) DESSERTS

Silken firm tofu sets up like a custard when it's mixed with chocolate or other ingredients, sort of a marvel of no-bake baking. Look for silken tofu in the refrigerator case, packed in water in small containers. These must be drained: Poke the peel-off plastic lid with a paring knife and let the water drain out the hole. Or buy the shelf-stable aseptic-packaged silken firm tofu (packed sort of like juice boxes) which doesn't need to be drained. And you can keep it on hand in the pantry for months, just in case you want one of these desserts, some of the richest in the book.

Rich, Velvety, No-Cook Chocolate Pudding

Makes 8 servings

This velvety vegan pudding is high in protein, thanks to all that tofu. So make it for dessert or for someone's convalescence. The tofu will set up as the melted chocolate resolidifies in the fridge. Top the pudding with whipped cream—or for vegans, store-bought vegan whipped cream.

6 ounces bittersweet chocolate (about 60 percent cocoa solids), chopped

18 ounces silken firm tofu

6 tablespoons unsweetened cocoa powder

¾ cup granulated white sugar

1½ tablespoons vanilla extract

1. Put the chocolate in a microwave-safe bowl. Microwave on high in 15-second bursts, stirring after each, until the chocolate is about two-thirds melted. Remove from the microwave and continue stirring until smooth. Set aside to cool for 15 minutes.

2. Place the tofu, cocoa powder, sugar, and vanilla in a large food processor fitted with the chopping blade; scrape the melted chocolate into the bowl. Cover and process until smooth, scraping the inside of the bowl at least once.

3. Divide among eight ¾- to 1-cup ramekins or dessert dishes; chill in the fridge for at least 6 hours or up to 2 days before serving.

Test Kitchen Notes

- You cannot overprocess this mixture. Keep at it until it's completely smooth—not brown egg salad!

- Bittersweet chocolate gives more depth of flavor. Use semisweet chocolate for a sweeter dessert.

FASTER

VEGETARIAN

Peanut Butter and Chocolate Ice Box Pie

Makes 8 to 10 servings

Test Kitchen Notes

- Substitute a store-bought chocolate cookie crust for the graham cracker crust.

- When serving, dip the knife in hot water to make even slices.

This pie is like peanut butter fudge, chewy and rich. While it will be ready in a few hours, it will taste better if it chills for 24 hours in the refrigerator. For a super-decadent dessert, cover the top with whipped cream before adding the coffee beans.

8 ounces milk chocolate chips or chopped milk chocolate bars

1 pound (16 ounces) silken firm tofu

⅔ cup natural-style creamy peanut butter

¼ cup maple syrup

1 teaspoon vanilla extract

One 10-inch (9-ounce) store-bought graham cracker pie crust

Dark-roasted coffee beans or chocolate-covered coffee beans, for garnish

1. Put the chocolate in a microwave-safe bowl. Microwave on high in 15-second bursts, stirring after each, until the chocolate is about two-thirds melted. Remove from the microwave and continue stirring until smooth. Cool for 15 minutes.

2. Put the tofu, peanut butter, maple syrup, and vanilla in a food processor. Cover and process until smooth.

3. Scrape down the inside of the bowl, add the melted chocolate, cover, and process until smooth, again scraping down the inside of the bowl at least once.

4. Pour and scrape the mixture into the prepared pie crust. Refrigerate uncovered for at least 6 hours or up to 3 days, covering when cool.

5. Just before serving, place the coffee beans around the perimeter of the crust.

Five-Ingredient Lemon–White Chocolate Ice Box Pie

Makes 8 to 10 servings

Test Kitchen Notes

- If you like, substitute seedless blackberry or blueberry jam for the raspberry.

- For added sparkle, garnish the raspberry jam glaze with mint leaves.

- If you don't want to spread the jam over the pie, spoon it over each individual serving.

The filling is actually made with only three ingredients. There are no mix-ins for the filling, like raspberries or crumbled cookies. It's so wonderfully smooth, it stands on its own! Although store-bought lemon curd is easy, homemade is better. Our recipe on page 300 can be ready in a matter of minutes.

8 ounces white chocolate, chopped

1 pound silken firm tofu

One 10-ounce jar lemon curd, or 1 cup homemade lemon curd (page 300)

One 10-inch (9-ounce) store-bought graham cracker pie crust

⅓ cup seedless raspberry jam

1. Put the chocolate in a microwave-safe bowl. Microwave on high in 15-second bursts, stirring after each, until the chocolate is about two-thirds melted. Remove from the microwave and continue stirring until smooth. Set aside to cool for 15 minutes.

2. Put the tofu and lemon curd in a food processor. Cover and process until smooth.

3. Scrape down the inside of the bowl, add the melted white chocolate, cover, and process until smooth, again scraping down the inside of the bowl at least once.

4. Pour and scrape the mixture into the pie crust. Refrigerate uncovered for 6 hours or until firmly set.

5. To make the glaze, microwave the raspberry jam in a microwave-safe medium bowl for about 10 seconds or until you can stir it with a fork. The jam should not be warm. If so, cool to room temperature after stirring smooth.

6. Using an offset spatula, spread this glaze evenly over the set pie. Return the pie to the refrigerator and chill for 2 hours or up to 3 days.

ALL-EVENING
WINTER WARMERS

Back in the day, people kept hot punches on the sideboard at most holiday parties. But who has a sideboard with a warming tray anymore? Don't worry: You can still go retro and offer a hot punch at your next winter party, thanks to the slow cooker. It'll keep the punch perfect all evening, a great new use for an already useful kitchen tool. And don't forget: If you've got a multi-cooker that you're using for pressure-cooker recipes, it's got a slow-cooker setting and can certainly be used to prepare these tasty punches, so long as you don't engage the pressure valve.

Test Kitchen Notes

- If your slow cooker has a nonstick coating on its insert, use a plastic ladle, rather than a metal one, to keep from scratching the coating.

- Some slow cookers will only stay on a keep-warm setting for 4 hours. If so, unplug it and cover the cooker. Plug in again, set it on the low setting for 30 minutes, then let it again flip to its keep-warm setting.

- Have a couple of clean towels near the cooker if yours is a help-yourself affair.

Spiced Bourbon with Pear

Makes 16 servings

EASIER

VEGETARIAN

GLUTEN-FREE

Better than hot buttered rum, this spicy punch is sweet and comforting. And if you miss the butter, you can always float a pat in each mug. By the way, it's not always easy to stick cloves into an orange peel. If the cloves are old or if the peel is thick, the little stems will break. In such cases, use a toothpick to start the hole for the clove in the peel. (You can also use the tip of a paring knife but be careful not to make too large of a hole—in which case the clove will quickly fall out as the peel softens in the slow cooker.)

3 quarts pear cider or pear nectar

⅓ cup packed light brown sugar

¼ cup fresh lemon juice

1 small orange, halved

12 whole cloves

Two 4-inch cinnamon sticks

1 small pear, peeled, thinly sliced, and seeded

3 cups bourbon

1. Stir the pear cider, brown sugar, and lemon juice in a 4- to 6-quart slow cooker until the brown sugar dissolves.

2. Stud the peel of each half of the orange with the cloves, pushing them into the rind. Float these in the cider mixture and add the cinnamon sticks.

3. Cover and cook on high for 2 hours.

4. When the slow cooker flips to its keep-warm setting, remove and discard the orange halves, any loose cloves, and the cinnamon sticks. If desired, skim out any orange solids in the mix.

5. Add the pear slices and bourbon. Stir well, cover, and leave on the keep-warm setting for up to 6 hours.

EASIER

VEGETARIAN

GLUTEN-FREE

Warm Sangria Punch

Makes 16 servings

This libation is sort of a journey from Spain to Norway. Or maybe it's sangria meets *gløgg.* It's best in mugs, not wine glasses. And remember: No amount of spices can cover up the taste of cheap wine. There's no need to spend 20 bucks on a bottle, but certainly go for 10 or 12.

1 medium Granny Smith apple, halved

10 whole cloves

1 medium lemon, thinly sliced

1 medium orange, thinly sliced

One 4-inch cinnamon stick

1 star anise pod

Two 750-ml bottles dry red wine, preferably a Spanish red

1 quart cranberry juice

2 tablespoons honey

1 cup brandy

1. Stud the apple halves with the cloves. Put these, the lemon slices, orange slices, cinnamon stick, and star anise pod in a 4- to 6-quart slow cooker.

2. Pour in the wine and cranberry juice. Stir in the honey until dissolved.

3. Cover and cook on low for 2 hours.

4. Once the machine flips to its keep-warm setting, add the brandy, stir well, and serve. The sangria can stay on the keep-warm setting, covered, for up to 4 hours.

Mexican Coffee Punch

Makes 16 servings

Unfortunately, coffee pots don't make the number of cups they say they make. They make "cups," as in how many you'll drink, often in 3- to 4-ounce petite china cups, not the 8-ounce 1-cup measurements recipes require. So you'll have to make a lot of coffee to get 10 true cups, maybe two pots. Save the rest of the coffee in the fridge for iced coffee the next morning to wake you up after a night drinking this south-of-the-border take on Irish coffee.

10 cups strong coffee

1¾ cups vodka

1¾ cups coffee flavored liqueur, such as Kahlúa or Tia Maria

1½ cups heavy cream

⅓ cup packed light brown sugar

2 tablespoons unsweetened cocoa powder

One 4-inch cinnamon stick

1. Mix all the ingredients in a 4- to 6-quart slow cooker.

2. Cover and cook on low for 2 hours.

3. Remove and discard the cinnamon stick. The mixture can remain on the keep-warm setting for up to 4 hours.

Acknowledgments

A cookbook is like a great recipe: it's in process until dinner's served.

Thanks to **Michael Szczerban,** our editor, who worked with us through (yikes!) nine months of proposal rewrites to get this book to where it is. Mike, we saw you from afar and knew you were the editor for us. You made this book better at every turn.

Thanks, too, to our publisher, **Reagan Arthur,** for believing in us and in this book enough to get Little, Brown behind it in a challenging environment for books.

And thanks to **Nicky Guerreiro** for sloggin' away on the zillions of editorial changes in the manuscript. You and Mike worked so hard (and so gently) to make sure our voice came through, while bringing our words into greater focus.

We couldn't do this career without our agent, **Susan Ginsburg** at Writers House. Almost thirty books and counting? Not to mention the ghosted ones for celebs? And the knitting ones. And the memoir, almost finished. How is that possible? We make a great team. And you make a great osso buco.

Thanks, too, **Stacy Testa** at Writers House, who has never proved anything but extraordinary, even when we interrupt anything else (and probably everything else) you're doing.

We jumped for joy when we heard **Deri Reed** would be our copyeditor. We pray for the day when we can write your name into every contract we sign.

Laura Palese, the book designer—we had no idea how you were going to turn that absurdly complicated manuscript into something that worked on the page. You went beyond our imaginations. And we have prodigious imaginations.

Finally, at Little, Brown, we owe an unpayable debt to **Ben Allen,** our production editor, and to **Lisa Ferris,** our production manager, for so effortlessly (well, seemed like it) bringing this behemoth to heel (or to print, take your choice); to **Zea Moscone** for her PR work; to **Lauren Velasquez** for a marketing push; and to **Julianna Lee** for designing a cover so good, it may well start a trend.

Index

Use this index to find recipes for the ingredients you already have on hand. And if you need more help finding the recipe that's right for you, see the entries for EASIER, FASTER, TASTIER, VEGETARIAN, or GLUTEN-FREE recipes—as well as the category entries for BRAISES AND STEWS, BURGERS, CASSEROLES, PIES, and ROASTS. For a complete list of recipes in this book, see the table of contents starting on page 6.